D1475571

FORMATIVE JUDAISM
Seventh Series

SOUTH FLORIDA STUDIES IN THE HISTORY OF JUDAISM

Edited by
Jacob Neusner
William Scott Green, James Strange
Darrell J. Fasching, Sara Mandell

Number 94

Formative Judaism

by

Jacob Neusner

FORMATIVE JUDAISM
Religious, Historical, and Literary Studies

Seventh Series

The Formation of Judaism, Intentionality,
Feminization of Judaism,
and Other Current Results

by

Jacob Neusner

Scholars Press
Atlanta, Georgia

FORMATIVE JUDAISM

Seventh Series

The Formation of Judaism, Intentionality, Feminization of Judaism, and Other Current Results

Publication of this book was made possible by a grant from the Tisch Family Foundation, New York City. The University of South Florida acknowledges with thanks this important support for its scholarly projects.

Library of Congress Cataloging in Publication Data

Neusner, Jacob, 1932-
    Formative Judaism : religious, historical, and literary studies:
seventh series : the formation of Judaism, intentionality,
feminization of Judaism, and other current results / by Jacob
Neusner.
        p. cm. — (South Florida studies in the history of Judaism ;
no. 94)
    Includes index.
    ISBN 1-55540-928-8
    1. Judaism—History—Talmudic period, 10-425—Historiography.
2. Women in Judaism, 3. Rabbinical literature—History and
criticism. 4. Judaism—Doctrines. I. Title. II. Series.
BM177.N4726 1993
296'.09'01—dc20   93-40719
                                     CIP

Printed in the United States of America
on acid-free paper

Table of Contents

Preface

This is the seventh series of essays written for colleagues in fields other than the study of the history of religion or of Judaism in particular. A life's work of considerable volume, such as mine, proves accessible to colleagues only if I take the trouble to spell out in a succinct and economical way some of the more important results. Otherwise, the sheer quantity discourages those whose work may benefit from mine, but who cannot spend the time trying to find out precisely where and how my results intersect with their interests. To solve that perfectly natural problem, over the years I have published essays, sometimes first in journals, other times only in collections in books such as this one, to summarize large-scale results, deriving from protracted studies and appearing in their original form in many volumes of ongoing studies. The present collection carries forward that project, and, finding their way into libraries and onto the desks of co-workers in the study of the history of religion, these essays may provide a viewpoint or an idea that otherwise might not have registered.

My work over the years has followed a rhythm of concerns, moving easily back and forth from the presentation of results, to the consideration of method, and to reflection on matters of normative truth and human meaning. The results are collected in Part One. Papers on methodological issues as I frame them, and debates with colleagues about their methods and results, occupy Parts Two and Three, and some reflections on the religious meaning of these studies are spelled out, in an episodic way, in Part Four.

The first, second, and fourth papers present new ideas, the third reviews more familiar ones of mine. In Chapter One I lay out my overall field theory of the history of the formation of Judaism. In Chapter Two I turn to a question that has long occupied me, the matter of the feminine in Judaism (treated also in Chapter Seven in a methodological setting, a paper from long ago that I resurrect to stand behind my more current work on the feminization of the Judaism of the Dual Torah). Chapter

Three presents in a fresh way some more familiar ideas of mine. Chapter Four summarizes entirely new research, which seems to me of some modest interest. I have now completed my description of formative Judaism and the process of the formation of that Judaic system represented by rabbinic literature, and these represent some of the last results, as I proceed to entirely new problems of analysis, and, later on, description as well.

I review matters of method, presenting three fundamental points. First, I explain the methodological foundation of my history of the formation of Judaism, that is, the documentary history that I have now completed in a number of volumes. Second, I renew my interest in the matter of dating sayings, a problem that led me directly to invent the documentary method. And, finally, I recapitulate long-held views, which begin with my work on the Mishnah, on the requirement of systemic, as against thematic, description. These three points form the tripod upon which all else is built.

In Part Three I pursue episodic arguments, now with Professors Samuel Lachs, Lillian Sigal, Richard Kalmin, and E.P. Sanders. These seem to me productive, and in debate we are able to formulate our positions in response to the ideas of others. I have always found that an invigorating and productive exercise. Only when others explore alternatives to our methods and come up with different results from ours do we gain proper perspective on what we are doing and why.

Finally, as a practicing Jew, that is, a Judaist, I have taken an interest in formulating normative, and not only descriptive, statements. As usual, the trilogy of Israel, Torah, and God serves as my trope, though the issues here are occasional and the presentations merely episodic and even anecdotal. I am far from building a system of a theological character, though some of the descriptive and historical theology that I am undertaking may stimulate thought in that direction.

Colleagues may find of interest a simple statement of the work that I now contemplate, some of which is already under way. Having completed more than two decades of systematic descriptive work, I begin an analytical phase, and I hope that the results will prove of broad interest. My plan for the next decade or so is as follows:

The Religious-Historical Question

The Judaism behind the Texts. The Generative Premises of Rabbinic Literature.
   I. *The Mishnah.* A. *The Division of Agriculture* (Atlanta, 1993: Scholars Press for South Florida Studies in the History of Judaism).

The Judaism behind the Texts. The Generative Premises of Rabbinic Literature.
   I. *The Mishnah.* B. *The Divisions of Appointed Times, Women, and*

Damages (Atlanta, 1993: Scholars Press for South Florida Studies in the History of Judaism).

The Judaism behind the Texts. The Generative Premises of Rabbinic Literature. I. *The Mishnah.* C. *The Divisions of Holy Things and Purities* (Atlanta, 1993: Scholars Press for South Florida Studies in the History of Judaism).

The Judaism behind the Texts. The Generative Premises of Rabbinic Literature. II. *The Earlier Midrash Compilations: Sifré to Deuteronomy* (Atlanta, 1993: Scholars Press for South Florida Studies in the History of Judaism).

The Judaism behind the Texts. The Generative Premises of Rabbinic Literature. III. *The Intermediate Midrash Compilations: Genesis Rabbah, Leviticus Rabbah, and Pesiqta deRab Kahana* (Atlanta, 1993: Scholars Press for South Florida Studies in the History of Judaism).

The Judaism behind the Texts. The Generative Premises of Rabbinic Literature. IV. *The Talmud of Babylonia* (Atlanta, 1994: Scholars Press for South Florida Studies in the History of Judaism).

The Judaism behind the Texts. The Generative Premises of Rabbinic Literature. V. *The Later Midrash Compilations: Song of Songs Rabbah and Lamentations Rabbati* (Atlanta, 1994: Scholars Press for South Florida Studies in the History of Judaism).

Judaism from Before 70 to 600: The Judaism That Is Taken for Granted.

The Historical Question

From Text to Historical Context in Rabbinic Judaism: Historical Facts in Systemic Documents. I. *The Mishnah* (Atlanta, 1993: Scholars Press for South Florida Studies in the History of Judaism).

From Text to Historical Context in Rabbinic Judaism: Historical Facts in Systemic Documents. II. *Sifra and the Two Sifrés* (Atlanta, 1993: Scholars Press for South Florida Studies in the History of Judaism).

From Text to Historical Context in Rabbinic Judaism: Historical Facts in Systemic Documents. III. *The Later Midrash Compilations: Genesis Rabbah, Leviticus Rabbah, and Pesiqta deRab Kahana* (Atlanta, 1993: Scholars Press for South Florida Studies in the History of Judaism).

From Text to Historical Context in Rabbinic Judaism: Historical Facts in Systemic Documents. IV. *The Bavli* (Atlanta, 1994: Scholars Press for South Florida Studies in the History of Judaism).

From Text to Historical Context in Rabbinic Judaism: Historical Facts in Systemic Documents. V. *The Latest Midrash Compilations: Song of Songs*

Rabbah and Lamentations Rabbah (Atlanta, 1994: Scholars Press for South Florida Studies in the History of Judaism).

What the Canon of Rabbinic Judaism Tells Us about the History of the Jews in Late Antiquity (Atlanta, 1995: Scholars Press for South Florida Studies in the History of Judaism).

A Commentary to the Talmud of Babylonia: The Theological-Hermeneutical Issue in the Context of Specific Texts

Making Connections and Drawing Conclusions: A Redactional-Hermeneutical Commentary to the Talmud of Babylonia. Principles of Coherence in Large-Scale Compositions and Composites. I. *Selected Tractates in the Division of Appointed Times* (Atlanta, 1995: Scholars Press for South Florida Studies in the History of Judaism).

Making Connections and Drawing Conclusions: A Redactional-Hermeneutical Commentary to the Talmud of Babylonia. Principles of Coherence in Large-Scale Compositions and Composites. II. *Selected Tractates in the Division of Women* (Atlanta, 1996: Scholars Press for South Florida Studies in the History of Judaism).

Making Connections and Drawing Conclusions: A Redactional-Hermeneutical Commentary to the Talmud of Babylonia. Principles of Coherence in Large-Scale Compositions and Composites. III. *Selected Tractates in the Division of Damages* (Atlanta, 1997: Scholars Press for South Florida Studies in the History of Judaism).

Making Connections and Drawing Conclusions: A Redactional-Hermeneutical Commentary to the Talmud of Babylonia. Principles of Coherence in Large-Scale Compositions and Composites. IV. *Selected Tractates in the Division of Holy Things* (Atlanta, 1998: Scholars Press for South Florida Studies in the History of Judaism).

Describing the Theology of Judaism as Formulated in the Talmud of Babylonia: Where does the Talmud Make Theological Statements and What Are Some of the Important Statements That It Makes?

The Harvest of Hermeneutics: A Theological Reading of the Talmud. I. *Cases in the Division of Appointed Seasons* (Atlanta, 1999: Scholars Press for South Florida Studies in the History of Judaism).

The Harvest of Hermeneutics: A Theological Reading of the Talmud. II. *Cases in the Division of Women* (Atlanta, 1999: Scholars Press for South Florida Studies in the History of Judaism).

The Harvest of Hermeneutics: A Theological Reading of the Talmud. III. *Cases in the Division of Damages* (Atlanta, 2000: Scholars Press for South Florida Studies in the History of Judaism).

The Harvest of Hermeneutics: A Theological Reading of the Talmud. IV. Cases in the Division of Holy Things (Atlanta, 2000: Scholars Press for South Florida Studies in the History of Judaism).

Principles of the Theology of Judaism. I. Theological Ethics. The Judaic Principles of Right and Wrong (Atlanta, 2001: Scholars Press for South Florida Studies in the History of Judaism).

Principles of the Theology of Judaism. II. Theological Anthropology. The Judaic View of Humanity (Atlanta, 2001: Scholars Press for South Florida Studies in the History of Judaism).

Principles of the Theology of Judaism. III. Theological Philosophy. The Judaic View of Truth (Atlanta, 2002: Scholars Press for South Florida Studies in the History of Judaism).

Explaining the Theology of Judaism: The Issue of Continuity and the Unity of the Torah in Rabbinic Literature

From Texts to Theological Matrix: The Torah, One, Entire, and Whole. I. Oral. How Do the Documents of Rabbinic Literature Form a Continuous Statement? (Atlanta, 2003: Scholars Press for South Florida Studies in the History of Judaism).

From Texts to Theological Matrix: The Torah, One, Entire, and Whole. II. Written and Oral. How Do the Two Torahs Form a Single Statement? (Atlanta, 2003: Scholars Press for South Florida Studies in the History of Judaism).

The Unity of the Dual Torah.

At that point, I hope, descriptive and analytical work can give way to a labor of interpretation.

No work of mine can omit reference to the exceptionally favorable circumstances in which I conduct my research. I wrote this book at the University of South Florida, which has afforded me an ideal situation in which to conduct a scholarly life. I express my thanks for the advantage not only of a Distinguished Research Professorship, which must be the best job in the world for a scholar, but also of a substantial research expense fund, ample research time, and some stimulating and cordial colleagues. In the prior chapters of my career, I never knew a university that prized professors' scholarship and publication and treated with respect the professors who actively pursue research. University of South Florida, and nine universities that comprise the Florida State University System as a whole, exemplify the high standards of professionalism that prevail in publicly sponsored higher education in the USA and provide the model that privately sponsored universities would do well to emulate. Here there are rules, achievement counts, and presidents, provosts, and deans honor and respect the university's principal mission: scholarship, scholarship alone – both in the classroom and in publication.

My beloved colleague James Strange read several of the chapters to advise me on whether I was following a model that would accomplish my goals, and I appreciate his goodwill and wise counsel.

JACOB NEUSNER

Distinguished Research Professor of Religious Studies
UNIVERSITY OF SOUTH FLORIDA
Tampa, FL 33620-5550 USA

Part One

CURRENT FINDINGS

1

The Formation of Judaism

The history of the formation of Judaism tells the story of how [1] philosophy became [2] religion, which was then re-presented as [3] theology. The medium of theological re-presentation was hermeneutics, so that, when we know how the Torah is properly read, we discern the theology of Judaism. Before proceeding, I hasten to give a simple definition of hermeneutics, that of Wilhelm Dilthey, since I claim that in its hermeneutics, the Talmud re-presents the Torah: "The methodological understanding of permanently fixed life expressions we call explication...explication culminates in the interpretation of the written records of human existence....The science of this art is hermeneutics."[1] When we know the rules of explication that instruct us on how to interpret the Torah, we gain access to the theology that governs the presentation of the religion, Judaism.

The priority of hermeneutics in the theological venture is not difficult to explain. We deal with a Judaism that affords religious experience – knowledge of God, meeting with God – in particular in books. While that same Judaism, like any other religious system, also meets God in prayer, obedience to the covenant, and right conduct, and expresses the sense of the knowledge of God in music and in art, in pilgrimage and in dance, in rite and in cult, and in most of the ways that religions in general celebrate God, what makes this Judaic system distinctive is its insistence that God is made manifest in, and therefore known through, documents, which preserve and contain the encounter with God that in secular language we call "religious experience." Just as, if the principal medium for meeting God were theater or music, we should search for theology in aesthetics, so since the principal meeting of encounter with God is the Torah, and the Torah is given in writing and oral formulation

---

[1]Cited by K.M. Newton, *Interpreting the Text*, p. 42.

as well, this Judaism promises knowledge of God through the documents of the Torah, and its theological medium will be hermeneutics (as much as philosophy).

The character of the evidence therefore governs. Because the formation of (this particular) Judaism as a religious system is fully exposed in its successive documents, the history of that Judaism's formative age – the first six centuries of the Common Era – comes to us in the right reading of the Torah. In this Judaism, the Torah comprises the holy documents and persons – written and oral documents, and the person of "our sages of blessed memory"; the deeds and teachings of sages take the form of stories and statements preserved in the same documents. Not only so, but because the medium for theology in this Judaism was a fully exposed hermeneutics, the message was conveyed through unarticulated but ubiquitous initiatives of a hermeneutical character. Then theological method consisted in constantly and ubiquitously showing the same few things through that hermeneutics, worked out in the Talmuds for the Oral Torah, and in the Midrash compilations for the Written Torah. But, as we shall see at the end, matters ended up in hardly so simple a way, for the profound hermeneutical problem will emerge only at the end, in the documentary re-presentation of the Torah accomplished by the Talmud of Babylonia, and its hermeneutics is not one of words, phrases, or sentences, but connections and continuities: identifying the questions. The answers flow, once we know what to ask.

Stated in documentary terms, the formative history of Judaism tells a story in three sentences. It shows, first, how the Judaic system emerged in the Mishnah, ca. 200 C.E., and its associated Midrash compilations, ca. 200-300 C.E., as [1] a philosophical structure comprising a politics, philosophy, economics. These categories were defined as philosophers in general understood them: a theory of legitimate violence, an account of knowledge gained through the methods of natural history, and a theory of the rational disposition (and increase) of scarce resources.

This philosophical system then was turned by the Talmud of the Land of Israel and related Midrash compilations, ca. 400-500 C.E., into [2] a religious system. The system was effected through the formation of counterpart categories: an anti-politics of weakness, an anti-economics of the rational utilization of an infinitely renewable resource, a philosophy of truth revealed rather than rules discovered.[2]

---

[2]The characterization of the first two stages in the formation of Judaism is contained within these books of mine: *The Economics of the Mishnah* (Chicago, 1989: University of Chicago Press); *Rabbinic Political Theory: Religion and Politics in the Mishnah* (Chicago, 1991: University of Chicago Press); *Judaism as Philosophy.*

Then, finally, the religious system was restated by the Talmud of Babylonia and its companions of Midrash collection, ca. 500-600 C.E. In those writings it was given [3] theological re-presentation through the recovery of philosophical method for the formulation of religious conceptions. In the great tradition, we may say, the formation of Judaism took place through [3] the final synthesis of [1] the initial thesis and [2] the consequent antithesis. That Hegelian pattern helps make sense of the history of religious expression and ideas that the canonical books of Judaism expose.

Theology is the science of the reasoned knowledge of God, in the case of a Judaism made possible by God's self-manifestation in the Torah. Seen in its whole re-presentation in the Talmud of Babylonia, the theology of Judaism sets forth knowledge of God. This is in two ways. The first (as I just said) is to know God through God's self-revelation in the Torah. This requires that we know what the Torah is, or what torah is (in a generic sense, which can pertain to either message or media or modes of thought). Then knowing how to define and understand the Torah affords access to God's self-revelation. The second is to know through that same self-revelation what God wants of Israel and how God responds to Israel and humanity at large.[3] That specific, propositional knowledge comes through reasoned reading of the Torah, oral and written, the Mishnah and Scripture, represented by the Talmuds and Midrash compilations, respectively.[4] The hermeneutics governing these documents encapsulate that knowledge of reasoned explication.

The priority of hermeneutics in the theological inquiry in a religion expressed through documents (more than, for example, through creeds, institutions, persons, dancing, singing, acting, or laughing, crying, eating, starving, and the like, all of which, as a matter of fact, convey the

---

The Method and Message of the Mishnah (Columbia, 1991: University of South Carolina Press); and *The Transformation of Judaism. From Philosophy to Religion* (Champaign, 1992: University of Illinois Press).

[3] I paraphrase Ingolf Dalferth, "The Stuff of Revelation: Austin Farrer's Doctrine of Inspired Images," in Ann Loades and Michael McLain, eds., *Hermeneutics, the Bible, and Literary Criticism* (London, 1992: MacMillan), p. 71. Dalferth was my colleague when I was Buber Professor of Judaic Studies at the University of Frankfurt, and it was in reading his writing that I began to think along the lines that come to fruition in this theory. Other definitions and premises will yield other ways of reading the theology of the Judaism of the Dual Torah.

[4] And that explains why we still will have to undertake a separate account of the theology yielded by the hermeneutics of the Midrash compilations (not only, or mainly, specific words or phrases or sentences found hither and yon in "The Midrash," as the ignorant conduct the inquiry). The characterization of the hermeneutics of Midrash compilations, early, middle, and late, will stand side by side with the theory set forth here.

systemic statement of this Judaism, too) is then self-evident. Through defining the hermeneutics of the Torah, we learn how the theology of Judaism explains what it means to reason about the Torah, showing how this is to be done in quest of truth about Israel's right action and conviction. The explanation is set forth in the hermeneutics of the Torah, spelled out in the two Talmuds to the Mishnah, and the several Midrash compilations to Scripture. All together, these writings expound the Torah and exemplify the correct hermeneutics for understanding the Torah. The task of describing the theology of Judaism therefore is to identify the correct hermeneutics; and the work of framing statements of normative theology requires proper hermeneutics in the analysis of the Talmud's re-presentation of the Torah: the rules of explication, in Dilthey's definition.

The schematic classifications of the successive, related Judaic systems as philosophical, religious, and theological therefore derive from the character of the successive documents, the Mishnah, Yerushalmi, and Bavli.[5] What makes all the difference in the second Talmud's re-presentation of the Judaic religious system therefore is the character of that Talmud itself. Through analysis of the hermeneutics that conveys the intellectual program of that medium, a religion rich in miscellaneous but generally congruent norms of behavior and endowed with a vast store of varied and episodic but occasionally contradictory ideas was turned into a proportioned and harmonious theology.[6]

Having laid heavy emphasis on the priority of the Bavli, I hasten to qualify matters. As a matter of fact, the process of theological re-presentation went forward in two stages. In the first, in the Talmud of the Land of Israel, the philosophical document that stated that system gained both a vast amplification, in which the categories and methods of the original statement were amplified and instantiated, but also in which took place a remarkable reformulation in counterpart categories. Of the three traits of "tradition," for example, as defined in the tractate Avot in its apologia for the Mishnah – harmony, linearity, and unity – the first of the two Talmuds systematically demonstrated the presence of two: harmony and linearity. The second undertook to demonstrate all three, all together and all at once and everywhere, that is to say, the law behind

---

[5]That is within the qualification that the Yerushalmi did part of the work of theologizing the Mishnah, the work of showing its proportion, composition, harmony, and coherence. The second Talmud did this work, but it also accomplished the far more sophisticated intellectual tasks.

[6]But I maintain that an important part of the theological work was undertaken by the first of the two Talmuds, which means the differentiation between the two Talmuds provides the key, in literary analysis, to the hermeneutical priority of the second of the two.

the laws, meaning, the unity, the integrity of truth. That shown, we know the mind of God, the character of truth.

Viewed as a whole, the result is then to be classified as not philosophical but religious in character and theological in re-presentation. Alongside, earlier Midrash compilations undertook the task of showing the relationship between the two media of the Torah, the oral and the written, by insisting that the Mishnah rested on Scripture. The goal was to show linearity and, of course, harmony. They furthermore began the definition of the Torah – in our terms, the reading of Scripture – by systematizing and generalizing the episodic cases of Scripture. The goal was to demonstrate the comprehensiveness of the Torah: its cases were meant to yield governing rules. The later Midrash compilations continued that reading of Scripture by formulating syllogistic propositions out of the occasional data of Scripture.

The religious writings that formed the second stage in the unfolding of Judaism – Talmud of the Land of Israel, Sifra and the two Sifrés somewhat before, Genesis Rabbah and Leviticus Rabbah somewhat afterward – finally were succeeded, and replaced, by the Talmud of Babylonia and related Midrash compilations, particularly Song of Songs Rabbah, Lamentations Rabbah, and Ruth Rabbah. These were documents that restated in rigorous, theological ways the same religious convictions, so providing that Judaism or Judaic system with its theological statement. In these writings, the religious system was restated in a rigorous and philosophical way. The associated Midrash compilations succeeded in making a single, encompassing statement out of the data of the several books of Scripture they presented.

The re-presentation of the religious system in the disciplined thought of theology took the form of rules of reading the Torah – oral and written – and through those rules exposing the character of the intellectual activity of thinking like God, that is, thinking about the world in the way God thinks. The theology of Judaism – reasoned knowledge of God[7] and God's will afforded by God's self-manifestation in the Torah[8] – affords access in particular to the mind of God, revealed in God's words and the wording of the Torah. Through the Torah, oral and written we work our way back to the intellect of God who gives the Torah. Thus through learning in the Torah in accord with the lessons of the Talmuds and associated Midrash compilations, humanity knows what God personally has made manifest about His mind, that intellect in particular in which "in our image, after our likeness" we, too, are made. That defines the

---

[7]That is a standard definition of theology.

[8]That is my restatement of a standard definition of theology to state what I mean by theology of Judaism.

theology of the Judaism of the Dual Torah and in particular forms the upshot of the Talmud's re-presentation of that theology.

Reading the Mishnah together with one or the other of its Talmudic amplifications, the Talmud of the Land of Israel or the Talmud of Babylonia, or Scripture together with any of the Midrash compilations, on the surface does not convey such an account. The canonical writings – the Mishnah and Talmud of the Land of Israel or the Mishnah and Talmud of Babylonia and their associated Midrash collections – portray not successive stages of the formation of a system but rather a single, continuous Judaism, which everywhere is read as unitary and uniform. Not only so, but in the persons and teachings of sages that same Torah makes part of its statement. But, when examined as single documents, one by one, in the sequence of their closure, to the contrary, matters look otherwise. Each writing then may be characterized on its own, rather than in the continuous context defined by the canon of which it forms a principal part.

Then the formation of Judaism, correctly described, may be stated in a single sentence. [1] The Mishnah, then [2] the first Talmud, then [3] the second Talmud, together with their respective sets of associated Midrash compilations, yield the history of a three-stage formation.

The first tells how the document that set forth the first Judaic system formed a philosophy, utilizing philosophical categories and philosophical modes of thought (philosophy, politics, economics, for categories, Aristotelian methods of hierarchical classification).

The second explains how the categorical formation was recast into religious classifications, from philosophy to Torah, from a politics of legitimate power to an anti-politics of weakness, from an economics of scarce resources to an anti-politics of the abundant resource of Torah learning.

The third then spells out how the received categorical system and structure was restated in its main points in such a way as to hold together the philosophical method and the religious message through a hermeneutical medium. Here I specify the character of that medium and its content. As I have already indicated, I once more stress, lest I be misunderstood, that this division between the second and the third should be shaded somewhat, since, as I shall show, by the operative definition of theology here, part of the theological work was carried on in the second – the Yerushalmi's – stage, part in the third. But, withal, the Bavli formed the summa, holding the whole together and making its own supreme and unique statement.

I have used the terms "philosophy" and "religion" and suggested they be treated as distinct categories of thought. Let me now spell out what I mean by "philosophy" and "religion." By "philosophy" I refer to the category formation, inclusive of categorical definitions, put forth by philosophy in ancient times. By "religion" I refer to the category formation put forth on a wholly-other-than philosophical basis in that same period. The one is secular and worldly in its data, utilizing the methods of natural history for its analytical work; the other is transcendental, finding its data in revelation, utilizing the methods of the exegesis of revelation for its systematic work. Both are exercises of sustained rationality, in the case of this Judaism, of applied reason and practical logic. But the one begins in this world and its facts, which are analyzed and categorized through the traits inherent in them, and the other commences in the world above and its truths, which are analyzed and categorized by the categories of revelation. The one yields philosophy of religion, the other, religious statements, attitudes, convictions, rules of life; the one represents one way of knowing God, specifically, the way through the data of this world, the other, a different way to God altogether, the way opened by God's revelation and self-manifestation, whether through nature or beyond. Let me now spell this distinction out with reference to the systemic results of a reading of the Mishnah and the Yerushalmi.

The Mishnah set forth in the form of a law code a highly philosophical account of the world ("worldview"), a pattern for everyday and material activities and relationships ("way of life"), and a definition of the social entity ("nation," "people," "us" as against "outsiders," "Israel") that realized that way of life and explained it by appeal to that worldview. We have no difficulty in calling this account of a way of life an economics, because the account of material reality provided by the Mishnah corresponds, point for point, with that given in Aristotle's counterpart. The Mishnah moreover sets forth a politics by dealing with the same questions, about the permanent and legitimate institutions that inflict sanctions, that occupy Greek and Roman political thinkers. There is no economics of another-than-this-worldly character, no politics of an inner "kingdom of God." All is straightforward, worldly, material, and consequential for the everyday world. Then the successor documents, closed roughly two centuries later, addressed the Mishnah's system and recast its categories into a connected, but also quite revised, one. The character of their reception of the received categories and of their own category formation, emerging in the contrast between one set of documents and another, justifies invoking the term, "transformation," that is, of one thing into something else. That something else was a religious, as distinct from a philosophical, category formation.

The first Talmud and associated Midrash compilations attest to a system that did more than merely extend and recast the categorical structure of the system for which the Mishnah stands. They took over the way of life, worldview, and social entity defined in the Mishnah's system. And while they rather systematically amplified details, framed a program of exegesis around the requirements of clerks engaged in enforcing the rules of the Mishnah, they built their own system. For at the same time they formed categories corresponding to those of the Mishnah, a politics, a philosophy, an economics. But these categories proved so utterly contrary in their structure and definition to those of the Mishnah that they presented mirror images of the received categories.

The politics, philosophy, and economics of the Mishnah were joined by the Yerushalmi to an anti-politics, an anti-economics, and an utterly transformed mode of learning. In the hands of the later sages, the new mode of Torah study – the definition of what was at stake in studying the Torah – redefined altogether the issues of the intellect. Natural history as the method of classification gave way to a different mode of thought altogether. As a matter of fact the successor system recast not the issues so much as the very stakes of philosophy or science. The reception of the Mishnah's category formations and their transformation therefore stands for the movement from a philosophical to a religious mode of thinking. For the system to which the Mishnah as a document attests is essentially philosophical in its rhetorical, logical, and topical program; the successor system, fundamental religious in these same principal and indicative traits of medium of intellect and mentality.

Given the definitions with which I began, how do I know whether a system is philosophical or religious? The answer is not subjective, nor the criteria, private or idiosyncratic. The indicative traits in both instances, to begin with, derive from and are displayed by documents, for – I take it as axiomatic – the mode of the writing down of any system attests to both the method and the message that sustain that system. From how people express themselves, we work our way backward to their modes of thought: the classification of perceived data, the making of connections between fact and fact, the drawing of conclusions from those connections, and, finally, the representation of conclusions in cogent compositions. All of these traits of mind are to be discerned in the character of those compositions, in the rhetoric that conveys messages in proportion and appropriate aesthetics, in the logic that imparts self-evidence to the making of connections, the drawing of conclusions, and in the representation of sets of conclusions as cogent and intelligible, characteristic of writing and expressed in writing.

In the Yerushalmi (and the Bavli later on) scarce resources, so far as these are of a material order of being, for example, wealth as defined by the Mishnah and Aristotle, are systemically neutral. A definition of scarce resources emerges that explicitly involves a symbolic transformation, with the material definition of scarce resources set into contradiction with an other-than-material one. So we find side by side clarification of the details of the received category and adumbration of a symbolic revision and hence a categorical transformation in the successor writings. The representation of the political structuré of the Mishnah undergoes clarification, but alongside, a quite separate and very different structure also is portrayed. The received structure presents three political classes, ordered in a hierarchy; the successor structure, a single political class, corresponding on earth to a counterpart in Heaven. Here, too, a symbolic transaction has taken place, in which one set of symbols is replicated but also reversed, and a second set of symbols given instead.

The Mishnah's structure comprising a hierarchical composition of foci of power in the Yerushalmi gives way to a structure centered upon a single focus of power. That single focus, moreover, now draws boundaries between legitimate and illegitimate violence, boundaries not conceived in the initial system. So in all three components of the account of the social order the philosophical system gives way to another. The worldview comes to expression in modes of thought and expression – the logic of making connections and drawing conclusions – that are different from the philosophical ones of the Mishnah. The way of life appeals to values expressed in other symbols than those of economics in the philosophical mode. The theory of the social entity comes to concrete expression in sanctions legitimately administered by a single class of persons (institution), rather than by a proportionate and balanced set of classes of persons in hierarchical order, and, moreover, that same theory recognizes and defines both legitimate and also illegitimate violence, something beyond the ken of the initial system. So, it is clear, another system is adumbrated and attested in the successor writings.

The categorical transformation that was under way in the Yerushalmi, signaling the movement from philosophy to religion, comes to the surface when we ask a simple question. Precisely what do the authorships of the successor documents, speaking not about the Mishnah but on their own account, mean by economics, politics, and philosophy? That is to say, to what kinds of data do they refer when they speak of scarce resources and legitimate violence, and exactly how – as to the received philosophical method – do they define correct modes of thought and expression, logic and rhetoric, and even the topical program worthy of sustained inquiry? The components of the initial formation of categories were examined thoughtfully and carefully, paraphrased and augmented and clarified. But the received categories were not continued, not expanded, and not renewed. Preserved merely intact, as they had been handed on, the received categories hardly serve to encompass all of the points of emphasis and sustained development that characterize the successor documents – or, as a matter of fact, any of them. On the contrary, when the framers of the Yerushalmi, for one example, moved out from the exegesis of Mishnah passages, they also left behind the topics of paramount interest in the Mishnah and developed other categories altogether. Here the framers of the successor system defined their own counterparts.

These counterpart categories, moreover, redefined matters, following the main outlines of the structure of the social order manifest in the initial system. The counterpart categories set forth an account of the social order just as did the ones of the Mishnah's framers. But they defined the social order in very different terms altogether. In that redefinition we discern the transformation of the received system, and the traits of the new one fall into the classification of not philosophy but religion. For what the successor thinkers did was not continue and expand the categorical repertoire but set forth a categorically fresh vision of the social order – a way of life, worldview, and definition of the social entity – with appropriate counterpart categories. And what is decisive is that these served as did the initial categories within the generative categorical structure definitive for all Judaic systems. So there was a category corresponding to the generative component of worldview, but it was not philosophical; another corresponding to the required component setting forth a way of life, but in the conventional and accepted definition of economics it was not an economics; and, finally, a category to define the social entity, "Israel," that any Judaic system must explain, but in the accepted sense of a politics it was not politics.

What is the difference between the philosophical and the religious systems? What philosophy kept distinct, religion joined together: that defines the transformation of Judaism from philosophy to religion. The received system was a religious system of a philosophical character; this world data are classified according to rules that apply consistently throughout, so that we may always predict with a fair degree of accuracy what will happen and why. And a philosophical system of religion then systematically demonstrates out of the data of the world order of nature and society the governance of God in nature and supernature: this world's data pointing toward God above and beyond. The God of the philosophical Judaism then sat enthroned at the apex of all things, all being hierarchically classified. Just as philosophy seeks the explanation of things, so a philosophy of religion (in the context at hand) will propose orderly explanations in accord with prevailing and cogent rules. The profoundly philosophical character of the Mishnah has already provided ample evidence of the shape, structure, and character of that philosophical system in the Judaic context. The rule-seeking character of Mishnaic discourse marks it as a philosophical system of religion. But, we shall now see, the successor system saw the world differently. It follows that a philosophical system forms its learning inductively and syllogistically, by appeal to the neutral evidence of the rules shown to apply to all things by the observation of the order of universally accessible nature and society.

A religious system frames its propositions deductively and exegetically by appeal to the privileged evidence of a corpus of truths deemed revealed by God. The difference pertains not to detail but to the fundamental facts deemed to matter. Some of those facts lie at the very surface, in the nature of the writings that express the system. These writings were not free-standing but contingent, and that in two ways. First, they served as commentaries to prior documents, the Mishnah and Scripture, for the Talmud and Midrash compilations, respectively. Second, and more consequential, the authorships insisted upon citing Scripture passages or Mishnah sentences as the centerpiece of proof, on the one side, and program of discourse, on the other. But the differences that prove indicative are not merely formal. More to the point, while the Mishnah's system is steady state and ahistorical, admitting no movement or change, the successor system of the Yerushalmi and Midrash compilations tells tales, speaks of change, accommodates and responds to historical moments. It formulates a theory of continuity within change, of the moral connections between generations, of the way in which one's deeds shape one's destiny – and that of the future as well. If what the framers of the Mishnah want more than anything else is to explain the order and structure of being, then their successors have rejected their generative concern. For what they, for their part, intensely desire to sort out is the currents and streams of time and change, as these flow toward an unknown ocean.

The shift from the philosophical to the religious modes of thought and media of expression – logical and rhetorical indicators, respectively – comes to realization in the recasting of the generative categories of the system as well. These categories are transformed, and the transformation proved so thoroughgoing as to validate the characterization of the change as "counterpart categories." The result of the formation of such counterpart categories in the aggregate was to encompass not only the natural but also the supernatural realms of the social order. That is how philosophical thinking gave way to religious. The religious system of the Yerushalmi and associated documents sets forth the category formation that produced in place of an economics based on prime value assigned to real wealth one that now encompassed wealth of an intangible, impalpable, and supernatural order, but valued resource nonetheless. It points toward the replacement of a politics formerly serving to legitimate and hierarchize power and differentiate among sanctions by appeal to fixed principles by one that now introduced the variable of God's valuation of the victim and the anti-political conception of the illegitimacy of worldly power.

This counterpart politics then formed the opposite of the Mishnah's this-worldly political system altogether. In all three ways the upshot is the same: the social system, in the theory of its framers, now extends its boundaries upward to Heaven, drawing into a whole the formerly distinct, if counterpoised, realms of Israel on earth and the heavenly court above. So if I had to specify the fundamental difference between the philosophical and the religious versions of the social order, it would fall, quite specifically – to state with emphasis – *upon the broadening of the systemic boundaries to encompass Heaven.* The formation of counterpart categories therefore signals not a reformation of the received system but the formation of an essentially new one.

The first fundamental point of reversal, uniting what had been divided, is the joining of economics and politics into a political economy, through the conception of *zekhut,* a term defined presently. The other point at which what the one system treated as distinct the next and connected system chose to address as one and whole is less easily discerned, since to do so we have to ask a question the framers of the Mishnah did not raise in the Mishnah at all. That concerns the character and source of virtue, specifically, the effect, upon the individual, of knowledge, specifically, knowledge of the Torah or Torah study. To frame the question very simply, if we ask ourselves, what happens to me if I study the Torah, the answer, for the Mishnah, predictably is, my standing and status change. Torah study and its effects form a principal systemic indicator in matters of hierarchical classification, joining the *mamzer* disciple of sages in a mixture of opposites, for one self-evident example.

But am I changed within? In vain we look in the hundreds of chapters of the Mishnah for an answer to that question. Virtue and learning form distinct categories, and, overall, I am not changed as to my virtue, my character and conscience, by my mastery of the Torah. And still more strikingly, if we ask, does my Torah study affect my fate in this world and in the life to come, the Mishnah's authorship is strikingly silent about that matter, too. Specifically, we find in the pages of that document no claim that studying the Torah either changes me or assures my salvation. But the separation of knowledge and the human condition is set aside, and studying the Torah deemed the source of salvation, in the successor system. The philosophical system, with its interest in *homo hierarchicus,* proved remarkably silent about the effect of the Torah upon the inner man. The upshot is at the critical points of bonding, the received system proved flawed, in its separation of learning from virtue and legitimate power from valued resources. Why virtue joins knowledge (I call this "the gnostic Torah"), politics links to economics, in the religious system but not in the philosophical one is of course obvious. Philosophy differentiates, seeking the rules that join diverse data; religion integrates, proposing to see the whole all together and all at once, thus (for an anthropology, for example) seeing humanity whole: "in our image, after our likeness." Religion by its nature asks the questions of integration, such as the theory intended to hold together within a single boundary earth and Heaven, this world and the other, should lead us to anticipate.

The second systemic innovation is the formation of an integrated category of political economy, framed in such a way that at stake in politics and economics alike were value and resource in no way subject to order and rule, but in all ways formed out of the unpredictable resource of *zekhut*, sometimes translated as "merit," but, being a matter of not obligation but supererogatory free will, should be portrayed, I think, as "the heritage of virtue and its consequent entitlements." Between those two conceptions – the Torah as a medium of transformation, the heritage of virtue and its consequent entitlements, which can be gained for oneself and also received from one's ancestors – the received system's this-worldly boundaries were transcended, and the new system encompassed within its framework a supernatural life on earth. And appealing to these two statements of worldview, way of life, and social entity, we may as a matter of fact compose a complete description of the definitive traits and indicative systemic concerns of the successor Judaism. It remains to observe very simply: The Bavli in no way innovated in the category formation set forth by the Yerushalmi, and, it follows, no important component of the Bavli's theological statement would have surprised the framers of the Yerushalmi's compositions and compilers of its composites.

My account of the formation of Judaism therefore may be stated in these simple stages, involving method, message, and medium:

[1]   THE METHOD OF PHILOSOPHY: The initial statement of the Judaism of the Dual Torah took the form of a philosophical law code and set forth a philosophical system of monotheism, providing an economics, politics, and philosophy that philosophers in the Aristotelian and Middle- or Neo-Platonic traditions could have understood as philosophical (if they grasped the idiom in which the philosophical system was expressed). That is the point of

my *The Economics of the Mishnah;*[9] *Rabbinic Political Theory: Religion and Politics in the Mishnah;*[10] and *Judaism as Philosophy. The Method and Message of the Mishnah.*[11]

[2] THE MESSAGE OF RELIGION: Through the formation of counterpart categories to economics, politics, and philosophy, the successor system, which came to expression in the Talmud of the Land of Israel and associated Midrash compilations, set forth a religious system and statement of the same Judaism of the Dual Torah. That is the point of my *The Transformation of Judaism. From Philosophy to Religion.*[12]

[3] THE MEDIUM OF THEOLOGY, MELDING METHOD AND MESSAGE: Taking over that system and reviewing its main points, the final Talmud then restated the received body of religion as theology. That then is the point of this chapter, which explains how Judaism came to completion in its definitive statement when [1] the disciplines of philosophy were used to set forth the message of [2] religion so that Judaism stated [3] its theology. The Talmud then re-presented the Judaism of the Dual Torah by joining the method of philosophy to the message of religion. In the context of *Ideengeschichte,* that accounts for the formation of normative Judaism.

---

[9](Chicago, 1989: University of Chicago Press).

[10](Chicago, 1991: University of Chicago Press).

[11](Columbia, 1991: University of South Carolina Press). See also *The Making of the Mind of Judaism* (Atlanta, 1987: Scholars Press for Brown Judaic Studies), and also *The Formation of the Jewish Intellect. Making Connections and Drawing Conclusions in the Traditional System of Judaism* (Atlanta, 1988: Scholars Press for Brown Judaic Studies); and *The Philosophical Mishnah I. The Initial Probe; II. The Tractates' Agenda. From Abodah Zarah to Moed Qatan; III. The Tractates' Agenda. From Nazir to Zebahim;* and IV. *The Repertoire* (Atlanta, 1989: Scholars Press for Brown Judaic Studies).

[12](Champaign-Urbana, 1992: University of Illinois Press).

2

The Feminization of Judaism:
Systemic Reversals and Their Meaning in the Formation of the Rabbinic System

Rabbinic Judaism routinely finds itself represented as a wholly patriarchal, male religious system. One choice example has a self-described "feminist" come under withering criticism because, while alleging the contrary, in fact, "he reconstitutes the masculinist tradition of the rabbis in his choice to emphasize the phallic aspect of Judaism, of penis, foreskin, semen....Yet [his critic points out] circumcision, if it confirms anything about the relationship between body and society, is about a male society in which, at best, women are absent."[1] Certainly, descriptions of Rabbinic Judaism as a male religion, subordinating women in countless ways, adduce in evidence more than ample supporting data. And yet, I shall show, at the systemic center of this patriarchal, male religious system is a deeply feminine conception of relationships.

If we may characterize masculine relationships as assertive, coercive, and aggressive, and feminine ones as suggestive, cooperative, and responsive, then the relationship between God and the human being in Rabbinic Judaism emerges as feminine. God at the center does not coerce humanity, but responds freely to the gift freely given; humanity at the heart of matters does not compel God or engage in acts of force or manipulation. Human gives freely, God responds freely. Masculine relationships are conceived in terms of dominance, women's in terms of mutuality and negotiation. The right relationship with God emerges in the Dual Torah as not coerced, not assertive, not manipulative, but as one

---

[1]Ayala H. Gabriel, review of Howard Eilberg-Schwartz, *The Savage in Judaism,* in *Journal of the American Academy of Religion* 1992, 60:156.

of mutuality and response, the one to the other: a transaction of responsive grace.

I. The Systemic Center: The Conception of *Zekhut*

While people suppose that the Torah forms the symbolic center of Rabbinic Judaism, and study of the Torah, the critical action, so that women, excluded from academies, find no place in Rabbinic Judaism at all, in fact when we reach the systemic center, we find that "the study of Torah" does not outweigh all else, not at all. Even the stories contained in the Talmud of the Land of Israel in which the priority and sanctity of the sage's knowledge of the Torah form the focus of discourse treat study of the Torah as contingent and merely instrumental. Time and again, knowledge of the Torah forms a way station on a path to a more distant, more central goal: attaining *zekhut*, here translated as "the heritage of virtue and its consequent entitlements." Torah study is one means of attaining access to that heritage, of gaining *zekhut*. There are other equally suitable means, and, not only so, but the merit gained by Torah study is no different from the merit gained by any and all other types of acts of supererogatory grace. And still more astonishing, a single remarkable action may produce *zekhut* of the same order as a lifetime of devotion to Torah study, and a simple ass-driver through a noteworthy act of selfless behavior may attain the same level of *zekhut* as a learned sage.

Were such stories as these located other than in the Talmud of the Land of Israel, one might find tempting the thesis that they represented an anti-rabbinic viewpoint. But rabbis told these stories, preserved them, and placed them on exhibition to expose the finest virtue they could imagine. That is why we turn for our integrating conception to that final reversal and revision of the given: just as scarce resources are made abundant, legitimate power deemed only weakness, and facts displaced by revealed truth, so the one-time moment at which *zekhut* is attained from Heaven outweighs a lifetime of Torah learning. *Zekhut* formed the foundation for the Yerushalmi's conception of political economy for the social order of Israel. It and not Torah defined the whole, of which economics and politics comprised mere details. It set forth and accounted for an economics and a politics that made powerlessness into power, disinheritance into wealth. How in fact does *zekhut* function?

Zekhut is gained for a person by an act of renunciation and self-abnegation, such that Heaven responds with an act of grace. As works of supererogation, which Heaven cannot compel but highly prizes, *zekhut* defines the very opposite of coercion. It is an act that no one could anticipate or demand, but an act of such remarkable selflessness that

Heaven finds itself constrained to respond. That is why the systemic center is formed by an act, on Heaven's part, of responsive grace, meaning, grace one by definition cannot demand or compel, but only provoke. When we make ourselves less, Heaven makes us more; but we cannot force our will upon Heaven. When we ask about the feminization of Judaism, our attention rests upon this fact: the right relationship between Israel and God is the relationship that is not coerced, not manipulated, not one defined by a dominant party upon a subordinated one. It is a relationship of mutuality, negotiation, response to what is freely given through what cannot be demanded but only volunteered. The relationship, in other words, is a feminine, not a masculine, one, when measured by the prevailing, conventional stereotypes.

It is where Heaven cannot force its will upon us that *zekhut* intervenes. It is that exquisite balance between our will and Heaven's will that, in the end, brings to its perfect balance and entire fulfillment the exploration of the conflict of God's will and our will that began with Adam and Eve at their last hour in Eden, and our first hour on earth. And, in context, the fact that we may inherit a treasury of *zekhut* from our ancestors logically follows: just as we inherit the human condition of the freedom to practice rebellion against God's word, so we inherit, from former generations, the results of another dimension of the human condition: our power to give willingly what none, even God, can by right or rule compel.

That is why the structure of Israel's political economy rested upon divine response to acts of will consisting of submission, on one's own, to the will of Heaven; these acts endowed Israel with a lien and entitlement upon Heaven. What we cannot by our own will impose, we can by the act of renunciation of our own will evoke. What we cannot accomplish through coercion, we can achieve through submission. God will do for us what we cannot do for ourselves, when we do for God what God cannot make us do. And that means, in a wholly concrete and tangible sense, love God with all the heart, the soul, the might, we have. God then stands above the rules of the created world, because God will respond not to what we do in conformity to the rules alone, but also to what we do beyond the requirement of the rules. God is above the rules, and we can gain a response from God when, on some one, unique occasion, we, too, do more than obey – love, spontaneously and all at once, with the whole of our being. That is the conception of God that *zekhut*, as a conception of power in Heaven and power in humanity, contains. In the relationship between God and humanity expressed in the conception of *zekhut*, we reach the understanding of what the Torah means when it tells us that we are in God's image and after God's likeness: we are then, "in our image," the very mirror image of God.

God's will forms the mirror image of ours: when we are humble, God responds; when we demand, God withdraws.

Since, in the successor system, it is points of integration, not of differentiation, that guide us to the systemic problematic, we must therefore take seriously the contingent status, the standing of a dependent variable, accorded to Torah study in such stories as the following:

Y. Taanit 3:11.IV

C.   There was a house that was about to collapse over there [in Babylonia], and Rab set one of his disciples in the house, until they had cleared out everything from the house. When the disciple left the house, the house collapsed.

D.   And there are those who say that it was R. Adda bar Ahbah.

E.   Sages went and said to him, "What sort of good deeds are to your credit [that you have that much merit]?"

F.   He said to them, "In my whole life no man ever got to the synagogue in the morning before I did. I never left anybody there when I went out. I never walked four cubits without speaking words of Torah. Nor did I ever mention teachings of Torah in an inappropriate setting. I never laid out a bed and slept for a regular period of time. I never took great strides among the associates. I never called my fellow by a nickname. I never rejoiced in the embarrassment of my fellow. I never cursed my fellow when I was lying by myself in bed. I never walked over in the marketplace to someone who owed me money.

G.   "In my entire life I never lost my temper in my household."

H.   This was meant to carry out that which is stated as follows: "I will give heed to the way that is blameless. Oh when wilt thou come to me? I will walk with integrity of heart within my house" (Ps. 101:2).

Striking in this story is that mastery of the Torah is only one means of attaining the *zekhut* that had enabled the sage to keep the house from collapsing. And Torah study is not the primary means of attaining *zekhut*. The question at E provides the key, together with its answer at F. For what the sage did to gain such remarkable *zekhut* is not to master such-and-so many tractates of the Mishnah. It was rather acts of courtesy, consideration, gentility, restraint: *cortesía* in the Spanish sense, *gentilezza* in the Italian. These produced *zekhut*. Now all of these acts exhibit in common the virtue of self-abnegation or the avoidance of power over others and the submission to the will and the requirement of self-esteem of others. Torah study is simply an item on a list of actions or attitudes that generate *zekhut*.

Here, in a moral setting, we find politics replicated: the form of power that the system promises derives from the rejection of power that the world recognizes. Legitimate violence is replaced by legitimation of the absence of the power to commit violence or of the failure to commit violence. And, when we ask, whence that sort of power? the answer lies in the gaining of *zekhut* in a variety of ways, not in the acquisition of *zekhut* through the study of the Torah solely or even primarily. But, we note, the story at hand speaks of a sage in particular. That alerts us once more to the systemic reversal that takes place at the systemic center: the sage has gained *zekhut* by not acting the way sages are commonly assumed to behave but in a humble way. In *zekhut*, a word we clearly cannot translate by an exact counterpart in American, we come to the center of a religious system in which the transformation of the individual through salvific knowledge in the end simply does not provide the compelling answer to the question of personal salvation.

Rabbinic Judaism takes shape by answering a question concerning the theory of the social order, yet we find at the heart of matters an answer addressed to individuals, one that concerns their emotions, attitudes, and sense of personal virtue. The private, the particular, the sentimental, and the emotional – these are commonly portrayed as women's concerns, the public and political, those of men. Here again, the systemic center forms a paradox: a design for an Israel for eternity yields the dimensions of conduct for an Israelite in the here and now of a single, intensely private moment. None can see, none can compel, none will ever know, what he or she performs as an act of uncompelled generosity of spirit. But God knows. And God cares. That most private moment of encounter, the one to the other, with God at hand, is transformed into the most public, the most social, the most political event.

So, we see, a different question stands at center stage, and a different answer altogether defines the dramatic tension of the theatrical globe. At stake is a public and a national question, one concerning Israel's history and destiny, to which the individual and his salvation, while important, are distinctly subordinated. Not Torah study, which may generate *zekhut*, but *zekhut* itself defines what is at issue, the generative problematic of the system, and only when we grasp the answer provided by *zekhut* shall we reach a definition of the question that precipitated the systemic construction and the formation of its categories, principal and contingent alike.

II. The Character of *Zekhut*

When we come to a word that is critical to the system of those who use it and also that is beyond translation by a single, exact counterpart in some other language, we know that we have reached the systemic center, the point at which what the system wishes to say is profoundly particular to that system. *Zekhut* in fact refers to two distinct matters, first, virtue that originates with one's ancestors and that is received from them as a legacy, that is, "original virtue," but, also, power that Heaven accords to people themselves in response to uncoerced acts of grace done by those people. *Zekhut* then is scarce or common as our capacity for uncoerced action dictated, puissant or supine as our strength to refrain from deeds of worldly power decided.

That protean conception formed into a cogent political economy for the social order of Israel the economics and the politics that made powerlessness into power, disinheritance into wealth. Acts of will consisting of submission, on one's own, to the will of Heaven endowed Israel with a lien and entitlement upon Heaven. What we cannot by will impose, we can by will evoke. What we cannot accomplish through coercion of Heaven, trading deed for deed, we can achieve through submission, hoping for response to our freely given act of feeling, sentiment, emotion of self-renunciation. God will do for us what we cannot do for ourselves, when we do for God what God cannot make us do. In a wholly concrete and tangible sense, it is to love God with all the heart, the soul, the might, that we have. That systemic statement justifies classifying the successor system as religious in as profound and complete a way as the initial system had been wholly and restrictedly philosophical. Here, too, we move from the relationship in which one party dominates the other, to one in which each party gives what cannot be coerced, so that both parties will join freely and willingly together: one of mutuality and cooperation.

The final step in the path that began with God's profession of love for Israel, the response of the freely given, uncoerced act of love, *zekhut* stands for the empowerment, of a supernatural character, that derives from the virtue of one's ancestry or from one's own virtuous deeds of a very particular order. No single word in English bears the same meaning, nor is there a synonym for *zekhut* in the canonical writings in the original either. The difficulty of translating a word of systemic consequence with a single word in some other language (or in the language of the system's documents themselves) tells us we deal with what is unique, beyond comparison and therefore contrast and comprehension. What is most particular to, distinctive of, the systemic structure and its functioning requires definition through circumlocution: "the heritage of virtue and its consequent entitlements."[2]

---

[2]The commonly used single word, "merit," does not apply, since "merit" bears the sense of reward for carrying out an obligation, e.g., by doing such and such, he merited so and so. *Zekhut*, by contrast, commonly refers to acts of supererogatory free will, and therefore while such acts are meritorious in the

Accordingly, the systemic centrality of *zekhut* in the structure, the critical importance of the heritage of virtue together with its supernatural entitlements – these emerge in a striking claim. It is framed in extreme form – another mark of the unique place of *zekhut* within the system. Even though a man was degraded, one action sufficed to win for him that heavenly glory to which rabbis in lives of Torah study aspired. The mark of the system's integration around *zekhut* lies in its insistence that all Israelites, not only sages, could gain *zekhut* for themselves (and their descendants). A single remarkable deed, exemplary for its deep humanity, sufficed to win for an ordinary person the *zekhut* that elicits supernatural favor enjoyed by some rabbis on account of their Torah study.

III. Systemic Remission: *Zekhut* over Torah Learning

When we come to the way in which *zekhut* is set forth, we find ourselves in a set of narratives of a rather special order. What is special about them is that women play a critical role, appear as heroines, win the attention and respect of the reader or listener. It is difficult to locate in Rabbinic literature before the Talmud of the Land of Israel – the Mishnah, the Tosefta, Sifra, for instance – stories in which women figure at all. So to take up a whole series of stories in which women are key players comes as a surprise. But there is more. The storyteller on the surface makes the man the hero; he is the center of the narrative. And yet a second glance at what is coming shows us that the woman precipitates the tale, and her action, not the man's, represents the gift that cannot be compelled but only given; she is the one who freely sacrifices, and she also is represented as the source of wisdom. So our systemic reversal – something above the Torah and the study of the Torah takes priority – is matched by a still-less-predictable shift in narrative quality, with women portrayed as principal actors.

In all three instances that follow and define what the individual must do to gain *zekhut*, the point is that the deeds of the heroes of the story make them worthy of having their prayers answered, which is a mark of

---

sense of being virtuous (by definition), they are not acts that one owes but that one gives. And the rewards that accumulate in response to such actions are always miraculous or supernatural or signs of divine grace, e.g., an unusually long life, the power to prevent a dilapidated building from collapsing. Note the fine perception of S. Levy, *Original Virtue and Other Studies*, pp. 2-3: "Some act of obedience, constituting the Ascent of man, is the origin of virtue and the cause of reward for virtue....What is the conspicuous act of obedience which, in Judaism, forms the striking contrast to Adam's act of disobedience, in Christianity? The submission of Isaac in being bound on the altar...is regarded in Jewish theology as the historic cause of the imputation of virtue to his descendants."

the working of *zekhut*. It is supererogatory, uncoerced deeds, those well beyond the strict requirements of the Torah, and even the limits of the law altogether, that transform the hero into a holy man, whose holiness served just like that of a sage marked as such by knowledge of the Torah. The following stories should not be understood as expressions of the mere sentimentality of the clerks concerning the lower orders, for they deny in favor of a single action of surpassing power sages' lifelong devotion to what the sages held to be the highest value, knowledge of the Torah:

Y. Taanit 1:4.I

F. A certain man came before one of the relatives of R. Yannai. He said to him, "Rabbi, attain *zekhut* through me [by giving me charity]."

G. He said to him, "And didn't your father leave you money?"

H. He said to him, "No."

I. He said to him, "Go and collect what your father left in deposit with others."

J. He said to him, "I have heard concerning property my father deposited with others that it was gained by violence [so I don't want it]."

K. He said to him, "You are worthy of praying and having your prayers answered."

The point of K, of course, is self-evidently a reference to the possession of entitlement to supernatural favor, and it is gained, we see, through deeds that the law of the Torah cannot require but must favor: what one does on one's own volition, beyond the measure of the law. Here is the opposite of sin. A sin is what one has done by one's own volition beyond all limits of the law. So an act that generates *zekhut* for the individual is the counterpart and opposite: what one does by one's own volition that also is beyond all requirements of the law.

In the continuation of these stories, we should not miss an odd fact. The story tells about the *zekhut* attained by a humble, poor, ignorant man. It is narrated to underline what he has done. But what provokes the event is an act of self-abnegation far greater than that willingly performed by the male hero, which is, the woman's readiness to sell herself into prostitution to save her husband. That is not a focus of the story but the given. But nothing has compelled the woman to surrender her body to save her husband; to the contrary, the marital obligations of a woman concern only conventional deeds, which indeed the Mishnah's law maintains may be coerced; failure to do these deeds may result in financial penalties inflicted on the woman in the settlement of her marriage contract. So the story of the uncoerced act of selflessness is told about a man, but occasioned by a woman, and both actors in the story exhibit one and the same virtue.

When Torah stories are told, by contrast, the point is, a man attains *zekhut* by study of the Torah, and a woman attains *zekhut* by sending her sons and her husband off to study the Torah and sitting home alone – not exactly commensurate action. Only *zekhut* stories represent the act of the woman as the counterpart and equivalent to the act of the man; and, in fact, even here, the fact that the woman's uncoerced gift is far greater than the man's – her body, merely his ass – should not go unnoticed. Once more, we find ourselves at the systemic center, where everything is reversed:

L.   A certain ass-driver appeared before the rabbis [the context requires: in a dream] and prayed, and rain came. The rabbis sent and brought him and said to him, "What is your trade?"

M.   He said to them, "I am an ass-driver."

N.   They said to him, "And how do you conduct your business?"

O.   He said to them, "One time I rented my ass to a certain woman, and she was weeping on the way, and I said to her, 'What's with you?' and she said to me, 'The husband of that woman [me] is in prison [for debt], and I wanted to see what I can do to free him.' So I sold my ass and I gave her the proceeds, and I said to her, 'Here is your money, free your husband, but do not sin [by becoming a prostitute to raise the necessary funds].'"

P.   They said to him, "You are worthy of praying and having your prayers answered."

The ass-driver clearly has a powerful lien on Heaven, so that his prayers are answered, even while those of others are not. What he did to get that entitlement? He did what no law could demand: impoverished himself to save the woman from a "fate worse than death."

Q.   In a dream of R. Abbahu, Mr. Pentakaka ["Five sins"] appeared, who prayed that rain would come, and it rained. R. Abbahu sent and summoned him. He said to him, "What is your trade?"

R.   He said to him, "Five sins does that man [I] do every day, [for I am a pimp:] hiring whores, cleaning up the theater, bringing home their garments for washing, dancing, and performing before them."

S.   He said to him, "And what sort of decent thing have you ever done?"

T.   He said to him, "One day that man [I] was cleaning the theater, and a woman came and stood behind a pillar and cried. I said to her, 'What's with you?' And she said to me, 'That woman's [my] husband is in prison, and I wanted to see what I can do to free him,' so I sold my bed and cover, and I gave the proceeds to her. I said to her, 'Here is your money, free your husband, but do not sin.'"

U.   He said to him, "You are worthy of praying and having your prayers answered."

Q moves us still further, since the named man has done everything sinful that one can do, and, more to the point, he does it every day. So the singularity of the act of *zekhut*, which suffices if done only one time, encompasses its power to outweigh a life of sin – again, an act of *zekhut* as the mirror image and opposite of sin. Here again, the single act of saving a woman from a "fate worse than death" has sufficed.

V.   A pious man from Kefar Imi appeared [in a dream] to the rabbis. He prayed for rain and it rained. The rabbis went up to him. His householders told them that he was sitting on a hill. They went out to him, saying to him, "Greetings," but he did not answer them.

W.   He was sitting and eating, and he did not say to them, "You break bread, too."

X.   When he went back home, he made a bundle of faggots and put his cloak on top of the bundle [instead of on his shoulder].

Y.   When he came home, he said to his household [wife], "These rabbis are here [because] they want me to pray for rain. If I pray and it rains, it is a disgrace for them, and if not, it is a profanation of the Name of Heaven. But come, you and I will go up [to the roof] and pray. If it rains, we shall tell them, 'We are not worthy to pray and have our prayers answered.'"

Z.   They went up and prayed and it rained.

AA.   They came down to them [and asked], "Why have the rabbis troubled themselves to come here today?"

BB.   They said to him, "We wanted you to pray so that it would rain."

CC.   He said to them, "Now do you really need my prayers? Heaven already has done its miracle."

DD.   They said to him, "Why, when you were on the hill, did we say hello to you, and you did not reply?"

EE.   He said to them, "I was then doing my job. Should I then interrupt my concentration [on my work]?"

FF.   They said to him, "And why, when you sat down to eat, did you not say to us, 'You break bread, too'?"

GG.   He said to them, "Because I had only my small ration of bread. Why would I have invited you to eat by way of mere flattery [when I knew I could not give you anything at all]?"

HH.   They said to him, "And why when you came to go down, did you put your cloak on top of the bundle?"

II.   He said to them, "Because the cloak was not mine. It was borrowed for use at prayer. I did not want to tear it."

JJ.   They said to him, "And why, when you were on the hill, did your wife wear dirty clothes, but when you came down from the mountain, did she put on clean clothes?"

KK.   He said to them, "When I was on the hill, she put on dirty clothes, so that no one would gaze at her. But when I came home from the hill, she put on clean clothes, so that I would not gaze on any other woman."

LL.   They said to him, "It is well that you pray and have your prayers answered."

Here the woman is at least an equal player; her actions, as much as her husband's, prove exemplary and illustrate the ultimate wisdom. The pious man of V, finally, enjoys the recognition of the sages by reason of his lien upon Heaven, able as he is to pray and bring rain. What has so endowed him with *zekhut*? Acts of punctiliousness of a moral order: concentrating on his work, avoiding an act of dissimulation, integrity in the disposition of a borrowed object, his wife's concern not to attract other men and her equal concern to make herself attractive to her husband.

We note that, at the systemic center, women find entire equality with men; with no role whatever in the study of the Torah and no possibility of attaining political sagacity, women find a critical place in the sequence of actions that elicit from Heaven the admiring response that *zekhut* embodies. Indeed, a second reading of the stories shows that the hero is second to the heroine; it is the woman who, in each case, precipitates the occasion for the man's attainment of *zekhut*, and she, not he, exemplifies the highest pinnacle of selfless virtue. It follows, once more, that those reversals that signal the systemic center culminate in the (for so male a system as this one) ultimate reversal: woman at the height. Just as Torah learning is subordinated, so man is subordinated; *zekhut*, the gift that can be given but not compelled, like love, in an unerring sense must be called the female virtue that sits atop a male system and structure.

IV. The Yerushalmi's Household of Israel and the Heritage of *Zekhut*

In the Talmud of the Land of Israel, Israel the people emerges above all as a family, the social metaphors of people, nation, kingdom, giving way to the one social metaphor that a feminine Judaism must select for itself. Coming to the Talmud of the Land of Israel and associated Midrash compilations, we turn first to the conception of the *zekhut* that has been accumulated by the patriarchs and been passed on to Israel, their children. The reason is that the single distinctive trait of *zekhut*, as we have seen it to this point, is its transitive quality: one need not earn or merit the supernatural power and resource represented by the things you can do if you have *zekhut* but cannot do if you do not have it. One can inherit that entitlement from others, dead or living. Moses not only attains *zekhut* but he also imparts *zekhut* to the community of which he is leader, and the same is so for any Israelite.

Zekhut speaks of not legitimate but illegitimate violence, not power but weakness. In context, time and again, we observe that *zekhut* is the power of the weak. People who through their own merit and capacity can accomplish nothing can accomplish miracles through what others do for them in leaving a heritage of *zekhut*. And, not to miss the stunning message of the triplet of stories cited above, *zekhut* also is what the weak and excluded and despised can do that outweighs in power what the great masters of the Torah have accomplished. In the context of a system that represents Torah as supernatural, that claim of priority for *zekhut* represents a considerable transvaluation of power, as much as of value. And, by the way, *zekhut* also forms the inheritance of the disinherited: what you receive as a heritage when you have nothing in the present and have gotten nothing in the past, that scarce resource that is free and unearned but much valued. So let us dwell upon the definitive character of the transferability of *zekhut* in its formulation, *zekhut abot*, the *zekhut* handed on by the ancestors, the transitive character of the concept and its standing as a heritage of entitlements.

It is in the successor documents that the concept of *zekhut* is joined with *abot*, that is, the *zekhut* that has been left as Israel's family inheritance by the patriarchs or ancestors, yielding the very specific notion, defining the systemic politics, its theory of the social entity, of Israel not as a (mere) community (for example, as in tractate Abot's reference to Moses' bestowing *zekhut* upon the community) but as a family, with a history that takes the form of a genealogy, precisely as Genesis has represented that history. Now *zekhut* was joined to the metaphor of the genealogy of patriarchs and matriarchs and served to form the missing link, explaining how the inheritance and heritage were transmitted from them to their heirs. Consequently, the family, called "Israel," could draw upon the family estate, consisting of the inherited *zekhut* of matriarchs and patriarchs in such a way as to benefit today from the heritage of yesterday. This notion involved very concrete problems. If "Israel, the family" sinned, it could call upon the "*zekhut*" accumulated by Abraham and Isaac at the binding of Isaac (Gen. 22) to win forgiveness for that sin. True, "fathers will not die on account of the sin of the sons," but the children may benefit from the *zekhut* of the forebears. That concrete expression of the larger metaphor imparted to the metaphor a practical consequence, moral and theological, that was not at all neglected.

The *zekhut* deriving from the patriarchs, or *zekhut abot*, emerges in a statement of the legitimate power – sufficient to achieve salvation, which, in this context, always bears a political dimension – imparted by the *zekhut* of the ancestors. That *zekhut* will enable them to accomplish the political goals of Israel: its attaining self-rule and avoiding government by gentiles. This statement appeals to the binding of Isaac as the source of the *zekhut*, deriving from the patriarchs and matriarchs, which will in the end lead to the salvation of Israel. What is important here is that the *zekhut* that is inherited joins together with the *zekhut* of one's own deeds; one inherits the *zekhut* of the past, and, moreover, if one does what the progenitors did, one not only receives an entitlement out of the past, one secures an entitlement on one's own account. So the difference between *zekhut* and sin lies in the sole issue of transmissibility:

Genesis Rabbah LVI:II.5

A. Said R. Isaac, "And all was on account of the *zekhut* attained by the act of prostration.

B. "Abraham returned in peace from Mount Moriah only on account of the *zekhut* owing to the act of prostration: '...and we will worship [through an act of prostration] and come [then, on that account] again to you' (Gen. 22:5).

C. "The Israelites were redeemed only on account of the *zekhut* owing to the act of prostration: And the people believed...then they bowed their heads and prostrated themselves' (Ex. 4:31).

D. "The Torah was given only on account of the *zekhut* owing to the act of prostration: 'And worship [prostrate themselves] you afar off' (Ex. 24:1).

E. "Hannah was remembered only on account of the *zekhut* owing to the act of prostration: 'And they worshipped before the Lord' (1 Sam. 1:19).

F. "The exiles will be brought back only on account of the *zekhut* owing to the act of prostration: 'And it shall come to pass in that day that a great horn shall be blown and they shall come that were lost...and that were dispersed...and they shall worship the Lord in the holy mountain at Jerusalem' (Isa. 27:13).

G. "The Temple was built only on account of the *zekhut* owing to the act of prostration: 'Exalt you the Lord our God and worship at his holy hill' (Ps. 99:9).

H. "The dead will live only on account of the *zekhut* owing to the act of prostration: 'Come let us worship and bend the knee, let us kneel before the Lord our maker' (Ps. 95:6)."

The entire history of Israel flows from its acts of worship ("prostration") beginning with that performed by Abraham at the binding of Isaac. Every sort of advantage Israel has ever gained came about through that act of worship done by Abraham and imitated thereafter. Israel constitutes a family and inherits the *zekhut* laid up as a treasure for the descendants by the ancestors. It draws upon that *zekhut* but, by doing the deeds they did, it also enhances its heritage of *zekhut* and leaves to the descendants greater entitlement than they would enjoy by reason of their own actions. But their own actions – here, prostration in worship – generate *zekhut* as well.

VI. Responsive Grace

Zekhut comes about through deeds of a supererogatory character – to which Heaven responds by deeds of a supererogatory character: supernatural favor to this one, who through deeds of ingratiation of the other or self-abnegation or restraint exhibits the attitude that in Heaven precipitates a counterpart attitude, hence generating *zekhut*, rather than to that one, who does not. The simple fact that rabbis cannot pray and bring rain, but a simple ass-driver can, tells the whole story. The relationship measured by *zekhut* – Heaven's response by an act of uncoerced favor to a person's uncoerced gift, for example, act of gentility, restraint, or self-abnegation – contains an element of unpredictability for which appeal to the *zekhut* inherited from ancestors accounts. So while one cannot coerce Heaven, he or she – for women as much as men enjoy full access to *zekhut*, though they do not to the study of the Torah – can through *zekhut* gain acts of favor from Heaven, and that is by doing what Heaven cannot require of me. Heaven then responds to one's attitude in carrying out his or her duties – and more than those duties. That act of pure disinterest – giving the woman one's means of livelihood – is the one that gains for me Heaven's deepest interest.

So *zekhut* forms the political economy of the religious system of the social order put forward by the Talmud of the Land of Israel, Genesis Rabbah, Leviticus Rabbah, and related writings. Here we find the power that brought about the transvaluation of value, the reversal of the meaning of power and its legitimacy. *Zekhut* expresses and accounts for the economic valuation of the scarce resource of what we should call moral authority. *Zekhut* stands for the political valorization of weakness, that which endows the weak with a power that is not only their own but their ancestors'. It enables the weak to accomplish goals through not their own power, but their very incapacity to accomplish acts of violence – a transvaluation as radical as that effected in economics. And *zekhut* holds together both the economics and the politics of this Judaism: it makes the same statement twice.

VII. The World Upside Down and Right Side Up: The Power of the Weak

Here we find the ultimate reversal, which the moves from scarcity of real estate to abundance of Torah learning, the legitimacy of power to the legitimacy of weakness, in perspective are shown merely to adumbrate. "Make God's wishes yours, so that God will make your wishes his.... Anyone from whom people take pleasure, God takes pleasure" (Abot 2:4). These two statements hold together the two principal elements of the conception of the relationship to God that in a single word *zekhut* conveys. Give up, please others, do not impose your will but give way to the will of the other, and Heaven will respond by giving a lien that is not coerced but evoked. By the rationality of discipline within, we have the power to form rational relationships beyond ourselves, with Heaven; and that is how the system expands the boundaries of the social order to encompass not only the natural but also the supernatural world.

Treating every deed, every gesture as capable of bringing about enchantment, the successor system imparted to the givens of everyday life – at least in their potential – remarkable power. The conviction that, by dint of special effort, one may so conduct himself or herself as to acquire an entitlement of supernatural power turns one's commonplace circumstance into an arena encompassing Heaven and earth. God responds to an individual's – and holy Israel's – virtue, filling the gap – so to speak – about oneself and about one's entire family that is left when one forebears, withdraws, and gives up what is one's own: one's space, one's self. When one does so, then God responds; one's sacrifice then evokes memories of Abraham's readiness to sacrifice Isaac; devotion to the other calls up from Heaven what by demanding one cannot coerce. What imparts critical mass to the conception of *zekhut*, that gaining of supernatural entitlements through the surrender of what is mine, is the recasting, in the mold and model of that virtue of surrender, of the political economy of Israel in the Land of Israel. That accounts for the definition of legitimate power in politics as only weakness, economics as the rational increase of resources that are, but need not be, scarce, valued things that are capable of infinite increase.

God here gains what the philosophical God of the Mishnah lacks, which is personality, active presence, pathos and empathy. The God of the religious system breaks the rules, accords an entitlement to this one, who has done some one remarkable deed, but not to that one, who has done nothing wrong and everything right. So a life in accord with the rules – even a life spent in the study of the Torah – in Heaven's view is outweighed by a single moment, a gesture that violates the norm, extending the outer limits of the rule, for instance, of virtue. And who but a God who, like us, feels, not only thinks, responds to impulse and sentiment, can be portrayed in such a way as this?

> "So I sold my ass and I gave her the proceeds, and I said to her, 'Here is your money, free your husband, but do not sin [by becoming a prostitute to raise the necessary funds].'"
>
> They said to him, "You are worthy of praying and having your prayers answered."

No rule exhaustively describes a world such as this. Here the law of love is transcended, for love itself is now surpassed. Beyond love is the willing, uncoerced sacrifice of self: love of the other more than the love of self, love of the Other most of all. Feminine Judaism relates to God as lovers relate to one another: giving not in order to receive, receiving only in order to give.

What is asked of Israel and of the Israelite individual now is truly godly restraint, supernatural generosity of soul that is "in our image, after our likeness": that is what sets aside all rules. And, since as a matter of simple fact, that appeal to transcend the norm defined not personal virtue but the sainthood of all Israel, living all together in the here and in the now, we must conclude that, within Israel's society, within what the Greco-Roman world would have called its *polis*, its political and social order, the bounds of earth have now extended to Heaven. In terms of another great system composed in the same time and in response to a world-historical catastrophe of the same sort, Israel on earth dwells in the city of God. And, it must follow, God dwells with Israel, in Israel: "Today, if you will it."

Life in conformity with the rule, obligatory but merely conventional, did not evoke the special interest of Heaven. Why should it? The rules describe the ordinary. But (in language used only in a later document) "the All-Merciful really wants the heart," and that is not an ordinary thing. Nor was the power to bring rain or hold up a tottering house gained through a life of merely ordinary sanctity. Special favor responded to extraordinary actions, in the analogy of special disfavor, misfortune deemed to punish sin. And just as culpable sin, as distinct from mere error, requires an act of will, specifically, arrogance, so an act of extraordinary character requires an act of will. But, as mirror image of sin, the act would reveal in a concrete way an attitude of restraint, forbearance, gentility, and self-abnegation. A sinful act, provoking Heaven, was one that one did deliberately to defy Heaven. Then an act that would evoke Heaven's favor, so imposing upon Heaven a lien that Heaven freely gave, was one that, equally deliberately and concretely, displayed humility.

Zekhut is the power of the powerless, the riches of the disinherited, the valuation and valorization of the will of those who have no right to will. *Zekhut* arms Israel with the weapons of woman: the strength of weakness, the power of patience and endurance, the coercion that comes about through surviving, come what may. This feminine Judaism's Israel is a family, its God a lover and beloved, its virtue uncoerced, its wisdom uncompelled – this Judaism served for those long centuries in which Judaism addressed a people that could not dominate, but only reason; that could not manipulate, but only hope; that could not guarantee results, but only trust in what would be. In the context of Christian Palestine, Jews found themselves on the defensive. Their ancestry called into question, their supernatural standing thrown into doubt, their future denied, they called themselves "Israel," and the land, "the Land of Israel." But what power did they possess, legitimately, if need be through violence, to assert their claim to form "Israel"? And, with the Holy Land passing into the hands of others, what scarce resource did they own that could manage to take the place of that measure of value that now no longer was subjected to their rationality? Asserting a politics in which all violence was illegitimate, an economics in which nothing tangible, even real property in the Holy Land, had value, the system through its counterpart categories made a single, simple, and sufficient statement.

We now appreciate the entire systemic reversal that we find at the very heart of Rabbinic Judaism. Study of the Torah, which only men could do, emerges as contingent; the life of obedience to the commandments proves necessary but not sufficient; Israel's relationship to God finds its definition not in what it must do, but in what it alone can decide to do, not commanded, not coerced, but also not so positioned as to dominate or manipulate. This Judaism values relations that are mutual and negotiated, cooperative, suggestive, not assertive, coercive, or aggressive. The conception of *zekhut* came to the fore to integrate the system's theory of the way of life and of the social order, its economics, together with its account of the social entity of the social order, its politics. The remarkable actions – perhaps those of omission more than those of commission – that produced *zekhut* yielded an increase in the scarcest of all resources, supernatural favor, and at the same time endowed a person rich in entitlements to heavenly intervention with that power to evoke that vastly outweighed the this-worldly power to coerce in the accomplishment of one's purpose. It is no wonder that, at the systemic apex, woman and the virtue that is natural to her situation now sits enthroned. The right relationship to God is one of responsive grace and love freely given, one that is not subject to conditions, but that embodies perfect commitment.

3

How the Mishnah Expresses
Its Philosophy

While some religions, Christianity and Islam, for example, are rich in theological writings, and others in myth, still others make their general statements about the abstract principles, for instance, the nature of being and of the realm of the sacred, primarily through law. In the Mishnah, ca. 200, which, after Scripture, is the first document of the Judaism of the Dual Torah, we have a considerable corpus of laws which prescribe the way things are done but make no effort to interpret what is done. Accordingly, the Mishnah has been classified as a mere collection of laws, and the description of Judaism set forth by that Mishnah frequently alleges that that Judaism had no theology, on the one side, or shared with every other writing a common theology but said nothing distinctive to itself, on the other.[1] These rules or laws are then alleged to constitute ritual entirely lacking in mythic, let along theological, explanation.

At stake in this presentation is not the particular proposition, but the mode of discourse in which the proposition is set forth. What we shall see in striking ways is a way of expressing a principle and of exploring conflicting positions that is quite odd. Our authorship, specifically, talks only in picayune details. Great issues of philosophy are spelled out in exchanges on matters of no consequence. Only when we see the whole do we perceive that, through arguments about nothing very much, our authorship has laid forth a variety of positions on a fundamental issue, a concern that animates the entire system they propose to construct.

---

[1]Most currently, E.P. Sanders, *Judaism. From 63 B.C.E. to 66 C.E.* (Philadelphia, 1992: Trinity Press International) rejects the former view and maintains the latter. In my view he phrases the matter as he does because he does not grasp the philosophical substrate of Mishnaic thought.

A proper reading of the Mishnah shows that it was through the details of the laws that the sages of Judaism took positions on profound issues of philosophical concern.[2] Here we shall examine one example of that fact, concerning the matter of intentionality, a subdivision of the larger analysis of the character and effects of responsibility.[3] The way in which the matter of intentionality bears theological messages requires explanation. In fact, it is at the point of intentionality that God and the human being meet. For one fundamental principle of the system of Judaism attested in the Mishnah is that God and the human being share traits of attitude and emotion. They want the same thing. For example, it is made clear in Mishnah-tractate Maaserot, man and God respond in the same way to the same events, since they share not only ownership of the Land but also viewpoint on the value of its produce. When the farmer wants the crop, so, too, does God. When the householder takes the view that the crop is worthwhile, God responds to the attitude of the farmer by forming the same opinion.

Through its analysis of intentionality, in quite abstract terms as a matter of fact, the Mishnah's theological anthropology brings God and the householder into the same continuum and indeed prepares the way for understanding what makes the entire Mishnaic system work. But in what kind of language, and precisely through what sort of discourse, does the authorship of the Mishnah set forth principles that motivate the entire system of the Mishnah? Here I shall show that through little that authorship says much, and in discourse on matters of no consequence at all, indeed, matters that, in the setting of the writers of the document, had no practical bearing at all, principal conceptions emerge.

The Mishnah's authorship's discussion on intention works out several theories concerning not God and God's relationship to humanity but the nature of the human will, a decidedly philosophical topic. The human being is defined as not only sentient but also a volitional being, who can will with effect, unlike beasts and, as a matter of fact, angels (which do not, in fact, figure in the Mishnah at all). On the one side, there is no consideration of will or attitude of animals, for these are null. On the other side, will and attitude of angels, where these are

---

[2]I have discussed these matters in a more systematic way in the following: *The Philosophical Mishnah* (Atlanta, 1989: Scholars Press for Brown Judaic Studies). I. *The Initial Probe*. II. *The Tractates' Agenda. From Abodah Zarah to Moed Qatan*. III. *The Tractates' Agenda. From Nazir to Zebahim*. IV. *The Repertoire;* see especially *Judaism as Philosophy. The Method and Message of the Mishnah* (Columbia, 1991: University of South Carolina Press).

[3]For the philosophical issues set forth in the context of Aristotle's thought, see Richard Sorabji, *Necessity, Cause, and Blame. Perspectives on Aristotle's Theory* (London, 1980: Duckworth).

represented in later documents, are totally subservient to God's wishes. Only the human being, in the person of the farmer, possesses and also exercises the power of intentionality. And it is the power that intentionality possesses that forms the central consideration. Because a human being forms an intention, consequences follow, whether or not given material expression in gesture or even in speech. An account of the Mishnah's sages' philosophical anthropology – theory of the structure of the human being – must begin with the extraordinary power imputed by the Mishnah's system to the will and intentionality of the human being.

But that view comes to expression with regard to human beings of a particular sort. The householder-farmer (invariably represented as male) is a principal figure, just as the (invariably male) priest in the Temple is another. The attitude of the one toward the crop, like that of the other toward the offering that he carries out, affects the status of the crop. It classifies an otherwise unclassified substance. It changes the standing of an already classified beast. It shifts the status of a pile of grain, without any physical action whatsoever, from one category to another. Not only so, but as we shall now so, the attitude or will of a farmer can override the effects of the natural world, for example, keeping in the status of what is dry and so insusceptible to cultic uncleanness a pile of grain that in fact has been rained upon and wet down. An immaterial reality, shaped and reformed by the householder's attitude and plan, overrides the material effect of a rain storm. And that example brings us to the way in which these profound, philosophical issues are explored. It is in the remarkable essay on theories of the relationship between action and intention worked out in Mishnah-tractate Makhshirin and exemplified by Chapter Four of that tractate.[4]

The subject matter that serves as the medium for sages' theories of human will and intention hardly appears very promising. Indeed, the topic of the tractate before us on its own hardly would have led us to anticipate what, in fact, will interest sages. The subject matter of tractate Makhshirin, to which we now turn, is the effect of liquid upon produce. The topic derives from the statement of Lev. 11:37: "And if any part of their carcass [a dead creeping thing] falls upon any seed for sowing that is to be sown, it is clean; but if water is put on the seed and any part of their carcass falls on it, it is unclean for you." Sages understand this statement to mean that seed that is dry is insusceptible to uncleanness, while seed that has been wet down is susceptible. They further take the

---

[4]It goes without saying, however, that numerous other chapters of the Mishnah yield the same fundamental concern with the matter of how intentionality relates to action, much as Sorabji's discussion shows Aristotle's interest in assigning blame through a consideration of responsibility and causation.

view – and this is the point at which intention or human will enters in – that if seed, or any sort of grain, is wet down without the assent of the farmer who owns the grain, then the grain remains insusceptible, while if seed or grain is wet down with the farmer's assent, then the grain is susceptible to uncleanness. The upshot is that that grain that a farmer wets down and that is touched by a source of uncleanness, for example, a dead creeping thing, is then deemed unclean and may not be eaten by those who eat their food in a state of cultic cleanness in accord with the laws of the book of Leviticus pertaining to the priests' food in the Temple.

Once we agree that what is deliberately wet down is susceptible and what is wet down not with the farmer's assent or by his intention is insusceptible, then we work out diverse theories of the interplay between intention and action. And that is the point, over all, at which the authorship of Mishnah-tractate Makhshirin enters in and sets forth its ideas. Tractate Makhshirin is shown to be formed of five successive layers of generative principles, in sequence:

1. Dry produce is insusceptible, a notion which begins in the plain meaning of Lev. 11:34, 37.

2. Wet produce is susceptible only when *intentionally* wet down, a view expressed in gross terms by Abba Yosé as cited by Joshua.

3. Then follow the refinements of the meaning and effects of *intention,* beginning in Aqiba's and Tarfon's dispute, in which the secondary matter of what is tangential to one's primary motive is investigated.

4. This yields the contrary views, assuredly belonging to second-century masters, that what is essential imparts susceptibility and what is peripheral to one's primary purpose does not; and that both what is essential and what is peripheral impart susceptibility to uncleanness. (A corollary to this matter is the refinement that what is wet down under constraint is not deemed wet down by deliberation.)

5. The disputes on the interpretation of intention – Is it solely defined by what one actually does or modified also by what one has wanted to do as well as by what one has done? – belonging to Yosé and Judah and his son Yosé conclude the tractate.

We see from this catalogue of successive positions, assigned to authorities who lived in successive generations, that the paramount theme of the tractate is the determination of the capacity of the eligible liquids to impart susceptibility to uncleanness. The operative criterion, whether or not the liquids are applied intentionally, obviously is going to emerge in every pericope pertinent to the theme. If I now summarize the central and generative theme of our tractate, we may state matter as follows.

First, liquids are capable of imparting susceptibility to uncleanness only if they are useful to men, for example, drawn with approval, or otherwise subject to human deliberation and intention. The contrary view is that however something is wet down, once it is wet, if falls within the rule of Lev. 11:34, 38, and is subject to uncleanness.

Second, if we begin with the fundamental principle behind the tractate, it is

[1]   that which is given in the name of Abba Yosé-Joshua (M. Makhshirin 1:3M):   Water imparts susceptibility to uncleanness only when it is applied to produce intentionally or deliberately. This yields a secondary and derivative rule:

[2]   Aqiba's distinction at M. Makhshirin 4:9 and M. Makhshirin 5:4:   Water intrinsic to one's purpose is detached with approval, but that which is not essential in accomplishing one's primary purpose is not under the law, If water be put. What Aqiba has done is to carry to its logical next stage the generative principle. If water applied with approval can impart susceptibility to uncleanness, then, it follows, only *that part* of the detached and applied water essential to one's intention is subject to the law, If water be put. Items in the name of second-century authorities that develop Aqiba's improvement of Abba Yosé's principle raise interesting questions:

[3]   What is the relationship between intention and action? Does intention to do something govern the decision in a case, even though one's action has produced a different effect? For example, if I intend to wet down only part of an object, or make use of only part of a body of water, but then wet down the whole or dispose of the whole, is the whole deemed susceptible? Does my consequent action revise the original effects of my intention?

Aristotle would not have taken much interest in such issues of enchantment and cult; but reframed as a consideration of the relationship between intentionality and act, cause and result, intent and responsibility, he would have found himself at home. For the deep

thought on the relationship between what one does and what one wants
to see happen explores the several possible positions. Judah and his son,
Yosé, take up the position that ultimate deed or result is definitive of
intention. What happens is retrospectively deemed to decide what I
wanted to happen (M. Makhshirin 3:5-7). Other Ushans, Yosé in
particular (M. Makhshirin 1:5), maintain the view that, while
consequence plays a role in the determination of intention, it is not
exclusive and definitive. What I wanted to make happen affects the
assessment of what actually has happened. Now the positions on the
interplay of action and intention are these:

[1]   Judah has the realistic notion that a person changes his mind,
      and therefore we adjudge a case solely by what he does and
      not by what he says he will do, intends, or has intended, to
      do. If we turn Judah's statement around, we come up with
      the conception predominant throughout his rulings: *A case is
      judged in terms solely of what the person does.* If he puts on
      water, that water in particular that he has deliberately
      applied imparts susceptibility to uncleanness. If he removes
      water, only that water he actually removes imparts
      susceptibility to uncleanness, but water that he intends to
      remove but that is not actually removed is not deemed
      subject to the person's original intention. And, it is fair to
      add, we know it is not subject to the original intention,
      because the person's action has not accomplished the
      original intention or has placed limits upon the original
      intention. What is done is wholly determinative of what is
      originally intended, and that is the case whether the result is
      that the water is deemed capable or incapable of imparting
      susceptibility to uncleanness. We move from effect to cause
      to intentionality: responsibility is the obvious outcome.

[2]   Yosé at M. Makhshirin 1:5 expresses the contrary view.
      Water that has been wiped off is detached with approval.
      But water that has remained on the leek has not conformed
      to the man's intention, and that intention is shown by what
      the man has actually done. Accordingly, the water
      remaining on the leek is not subject to the law, If water be
      put. The upshot is to reject the view that what is done is
      wholly determinative of what is originally intended. We sort
      things out by appeal to nuances of effect. Once, in assessing
      blame, we invoke the consideration of intentionality, then
      matters become more complicated.

[3]   Simeon's point at M. Makhshirin 1:6 is that the liquid left on the palm of the hand is not wanted and not necessary to the accomplishment of one's purpose. Simeon's main point is that liquid not essential in accomplishing one's purpose is not taken into account and does not come under the law, If water be put. Why not? Because water is held to be applied with approval *only* when it serves a specific purpose. That water which is incidental has not been subjected to the man's wishes and therefore does not impart susceptibility to uncleanness. Only that water that is necessary to carry out the farmer's purpose imparts susceptibility to uncleanness. If a pile of grain has been wet down, then water that the farmer has deliberately applies effects susceptibility to uncleanness to that part of the grain pile that it has touched. But water that is incidental and not subject to the farmer's initial plan has no effect upon the grain, even though, as a matter of fact, grain at some other point in the pile may be just as wet as grain the farmer has deliberately watered.

Simeon and Yosé deem water to have been detached and applied with approval only when it serves a person's essential purpose, and water that is not necessary in accomplishing that purpose is not deemed subject to the law, If water be put. That is why Simeon rules as he does. Yosé states a different aspect of the same conception. Water that actually has dripped of the leek in no way has fallen under the person's approval. This is indicated by the facts of the matter, the results of the person's actual deed. And this brings us to the concrete exposition of the chapter at hand. With the positions and principles just now outlined, the reader can follow the discussion with little difficulty. We begin with the simple distinction between water that I want for the accomplishment of my purpose, and water that I do not want, and that category of water does not have the power to impart susceptibility to uncleanness.

The recurrent formula, "If water be put," alludes to Lev. 11:34, 37, and refers to the deliberate watering down of seed or produce. But at stake is the classification of the water. The kind of water to which allusion is made is in the category of "If water be put," meaning that that water, having served the farmer's purpose, has the power to impart susceptibility to uncleanness should it fall on grain. Water that is not in the category of "If water be put," should it fall on grain by some sort of accident, does not impart susceptibility to uncleanness to grain that is otherwise kept dry. It remains to observe that the reason the farmer wets down grain is that the grain is going to be milled, and milling grain requires some dampening of the seed. Accordingly, we have the counterpart to the issue of tithing. When the farmer plans to make use of the (now-tithed) grain, and indicates the plan by wetting down the grain, then the issue of cultic cleanness, that is, preserving the grain from the sources of cultic uncleanness listed in Leviticus Chapters Eleven through Fifteen, is raised. Before the farmer wants to use the produce, the produce is null. The will and intentionality of the farmer, owner of the grain, are what draws the produce within the orbit of the immaterial world of uncleanness and cleanness.

Now to the actual texts I have chosen for illustrating not only the issues but the way in which the issues are set forth and analyzed: arguments about very picayune questions indeed, and, furthermore, questions lacking all concrete relevance in the world in the second century in which the Mishnah's philosophers actually lived.

M. Makhshirin 4:1

A.   He who kneels down to drink –

B.   the water that comes up on his mouth and on his moustache is under the law, If water be put. [That water imparts susceptibility to uncleanness should it drip on a pile of grain, since the farmer has accomplished his purpose – getting a drink – by stirring up that water and getting it into his mouth or on his moustache.]

C.   [The water that comes up] on his nose and on [the hair of] his head and on his beard is not under the law, If water be put. [That water does not have the power to impart susceptibility to uncleanness should it fall on a pile of dry produce.]

D.   He who draws [water] with a jug –

E.   the water that comes up on its outer parts and on the rope wound round its neck and on the rope that is needed [in dipping it] – lo, this is under the law, If water be put.

F.   And how much [rope] is needed [in handling it]?

G.   R. Simeon b. Eleazar says, "A handbreadth."

H.   [If] one put it under the water-spout, [the water on its outer parts and on the rope, now not needed in drawing water] is not under the law, If water be put.

What must get wet in order to accomplish one's purpose is deemed wet down by approval. But water not needed in one's primary goal is not subject to approval. The pericope consists of A-C and D-H, the latter in two parts, D-E + F-G, and H. The point of A-C is clear. Since, D-E, in dipping the jug into the water, it is not possible to draw water without wetting the outer parts and the rope, water on the rope and the outer parts is deemed affected by one's wishes. Simeon b. Eleazar glosses. At H one does not make use of the rope and does not care to have the water on the outer parts, since he can draw the water without recourse to either. Accordingly, water on the rope and on the outer parts does not impart susceptibility to uncleanness.

M. Makhshirin 4:2

A. He on whom rains fell,

B. even [if he is] a Father [principal source] of uncleanness –

C. it [the water] is not under the law, If water be put [since even in the case of B, the rainfall was not wanted].

D. But if he shook off [the rain], it [the water that is shaken off] is under the law, If water be put.

E. [If] he stood under the water-spout to cool off,

F. or to rinse off,

G. in the case of an unclean person [the water] is unclean.

H. And in the case of a clean person, [the water] is under the law, If water be put.

The pericope is in two parts, A-D and E-H, each in two units. The point of A + C is that the rain does not come under the person's approval. Therefore the rain is not capable of imparting susceptibility to uncleanness. If by some action, however, the person responds to the rain, for example, if he shook off his garments, then it falls under his approval. B is certainly a gloss, and not an important one. The principal source of uncleanness, for example, the *Zab* of Leviticus, Chapter Fifteen, derives no benefit from the rain and therefore need not be explicitly excluded. At E, however, the person obviously does want to make use of the water. Therefore it is rendered both susceptible to uncleanness and capable of imparting susceptibility to other things. G makes the former point, H, the latter. Perhaps it is G that has generated B, since the distinction between unclean and clean is important at G-H and then invites the contrast between A + B and E + G, that is, falling rain versus rainwater pouring through the water-spout and deliberately utilized.

M. Makhshirin 4:3

A. He who puts a dish on end against the wall so that it will rinse off, lo, this [water that flows across the plate] is under the law, If water be put.

B. If [he put it there] so that it [rain] should not harm the wall, it [the water] is not under the law, If water be put.

The established distinction is repeated one more, with reference to an inanimate object. Now we make use of the water for rinsing off the plate. Accordingly, the water is detached with approval. But if the plate is so located as to protect the wall, then the water clearly is not wanted and therefore does not have the capacity to impart susceptibility to uncleanness.

M. Makhshirin 4:4

I. A. A jug into which water leaking from the roof came down –

B. the House of Shammai say, "It is broken."

C. The House of Hillel say, "It is emptied out."

D.   And they agree that he puts in his hand and takes pieces of fruit from its inside, and they [the drops of water, the pieces of fruit] are insusceptible to uncleanness.

M. Makhshirin 4:5

II.   F.   A trough into which the rain dripping from the roof flowed [without approval] –

G.   [water in the trough and (GRA)] the drops [of water] that splashed out and those that overflowed are not under the law, If water be put.

H.   [If] one took it to pour it out –

I.   the House of Shammai say, "It is under the law, If water be put." [Since he poured the water away only when the tub was moved to another place, it may be said that he did not object to the water when the tub was in its original place.]

J.   The House of Hillel say, "It is not under the law, If water be put." [His pouring away showed that he did not want the water even in the tub's original place.]

III.   K.   [If] one [intentionally] left it out so that the rain dripping from the roof would flow into it –

L.   the drops [of water] that splashed out and those that overflowed –

M.   the House of Shammai say, "They are under the law, If water be put" [all the more so what is in the trough].

N.   The House of Hillel say, "They [the drops that splashed or overflowed] are not under the law, If water be put."

O.   [If] one took it in order to pour it out, these and those agree that [both kinds of water] are under the law, If water be put. [For since the owner did not empty it where it stood, the water is deemed to be detached with his approval.]

P.   He who dunks the utensils, and he who washes his clothing in a cave [pond] –

Q.   the water that comes up on his hands is under the law, If water be put.

R.   [And the water that comes up] on his feet is not under the law, If water be put.

S.   R. Eleazar says, "If it is impossible for him to go down [into the water] unless his feet become muddy, even [the drops of water] that come up on his feet are under the law, If water be put [since he wants to clean his feet]."

The composite is in the following parts: A-D, a complete and well-balanced Houses' dispute, in which the apodosis exhibits exact balance in the number of syllables, F-G, which set the stage for the second Houses' dispute, at H-J; K-L, the protasis for the third dispute, which depends upon F (+ G = L) – a trough that happens to receive rain versus one deliberately left out to collect rain – and the standard apodosis, M-N; and a final agreement, O, parallel to D. R-S form a separate pericope entirely. The issue of A-D is this: We have left a jug containing fruit in such a position that water leaking from the roof fills it. We want to empty the fruit out of the jug. But we want to do so in such a way that the water in the jug does not receive the capacity to impart susceptibility to uncleanness to the fruit contained in the jug. There are these considerations.

[1]   Clearly, in is present location, the water is insusceptible. Why? Because it did not fall into the jug with approval.

[2]   If then we break the jug, we accomplish the purpose of treating the water as unwanted and this is what the Shammaites say we should to (B).

[3]   But if we merely empty out the fruit, we stir the water with approval; the fruit in the jug forthwith is wet down by the water, with approval, and becomes susceptible.

The Hillelites (C) say that if we pour out the fruit, that suffices. Why? Because the man wants the fruit, not the water. So the water does not have the capacity to impart susceptibility to uncleanness. In its original location it is not subject to approval. The Shammaites and Hillelites agree that, so long as the fruit in the jug is unaffected by the water, the fruit is insusceptible to uncleanness. It is not made susceptible even by the water which is removed with the fruit. Maimonides (*Uncleanness of Foodstuffs*, 12:7) at the italicized words adds a valuable clarification:

> If a jar is full of fruit and water leaking from the roof drips into it, the owner may pour off the water from the fruit, and it does not render the fruit susceptible, *even though it was with his approval that the water remained in the jar until he should pour it off the fruit.*

Accordingly, Maimonides not only follows the Hillelite position but (quite reasonably) imposes that position upon the Shammaite agreement at D.

The second Houses' dispute, F-J, goes over the ground of the first. There is no significant difference between water that has leaked into the jug and water that has fallen into the trough, A/F. But the issue, G, is different. Now we ask about water that overflows. Does this water flow with approval? Certainly not, both parties agree. None of this water is wanted. What if the man then takes up the trough with the intention of pouring the water out? We already know the Hillelite position. It is the same as at C. There is no reason to be concerned about moving the trough in order to empty it. The man pours out the water. By his deed he therefore indicates that he does not want it. The Shammaites are equally consistent. The man has raised the trough to pour out the water. In moving the water, he (retrospectively) imparts the stamp of approval on the original location of the water. The reference at G is only to set the stage for K-L, since the water in the trough of F itself is insusceptible.

At K the problem is that the man deliberately does collect the water. Accordingly, he certainly has imparted his approval to it. The problem of L is that part of the water splashes out or overflows. Clearly, the man wanted the water and therefore, what overflowed or splashed out has not conformed to his original wishes. That is, if he shook the tree to bring down the water, all parties agree that the water that falls is subject to the man's approval. But the water that does not fall is a problem. Here, too, the Shammaites say that what has been in the trough and overflowed has been subject to the man's intention. Therefore, like the water in the trough, the drops that splash out or overflow are under the law, If water be put. But the House of Hillel maintain that the water not in the location where the man has desired it is not subject to his wishes, and therefore does not impart susceptibility to uncleanness.

O completes the elegant construction by bringing the Hillelites over to the Shammaite position. If the man lifted up a trough of water that he *himself* has collected, then this is water that at one point in its history has surely conformed to the man's wishes and therefore has the capacity to impart insusceptibility to uncleanness. The Hillelites of N clearly will agree that the water in the trough is subject to the law, If water be put, just as the Shammaites at L-M will maintain the same. The dispute of M-N concerns only the liquid referred to at L. P-R go over the ground of M. 4:1. That is, water necessary to accomplish the man's purpose is subject to the law, If water be put. That which is not important in the accomplishment of his purpose is not subject to the law. Eleazar's gloss, S, adds that if the man's feet grow muddy in the process of getting the water, then he will want to clean his feet, and even the water on his feet therefore is subject to the law, If water be put. There is nothing surprising in this unit, but the exposition is elegant indeed.

M. Makhshirin 4:6

A.   A basket that is full of lupines and [that happens to be] placed into an immersion pool –

B.   one puts out his hand and takes lupines from its midst, and they are insusceptible to uncleanness.

C.   [If] one took them out of the water [while still in the basket] –

D.   the ones that touch the [water on the sides of the] basket are susceptible to uncleanness.

E.   And all the rest of the lupines are insusceptible to uncleanness.

F.   A radish that is in the cave [water] –

G.   a menstruant rinses it off, and it is insusceptible to uncleanness.

H.   [If] she brought it out of the water in any measure at all, [having been made susceptible to uncleanness in the water,] it is unclean.

We go over the point at which the Houses agree at M. Makhshirin 4:4D. The lupines in the basket are wet on account of the water in the pool, but that does not render them susceptible to uncleanness. Accordingly, since the water is not detached with approval, when one takes the lupines out of the basket, they remain insusceptible. The water on the basket, however, is detached with approval, since presumably the basket has been immersed to render it clean from uncleanness. (The lupines – being food – in any event cannot be cleaned in the pool.) Accordingly, at C, the ones in the basket that touch the sides of the basket are in contact with water capable of imparting susceptibility to uncleanness, having been used with approval. The others, however, although wet, remain clean. Why? Because they have not touched water that has been detached with approval. The sentence structure is slightly strange, since A sets the stage for a thought, but the thought begins afresh at B. This is then extreme apocopation at A-B, less clear-cut apocopation at C-D.

The same form is followed at F-H. The radish in the water is insusceptible to uncleanness. The menstruant rinses it off. While the radish is in the water, it remains insusceptible. But the woman has rinsed her hands and the radish. Accordingly, the water on the radish is detached with approval. It renders the radish susceptible to uncleanness, and as soon as the radish is taken out of the water, the woman's touch imparts uncleanness.

M. Makhshirin 4:7

A.   Pieces of fruit that fell into a water channel –

B.   he whose hands were unclean reached out and took them –

C.   his hands are clean, and the pieces of fruit are insusceptible to uncleanness.

D.   But if he gave thought that his hands should be rinsed off [in the water], his hands are clean, and the [water on the] pieces of fruit is under the law, If water be put.

The pericope is in the severe apocopation characteristic of the present set, A, B, and C being out of clear syntactical relationship to one another. We should have to add, at A *as to pieces...*, then at B, *if he whose hands...*, and C would follow as a complete sentence. But A is not continued at B-C. Rather, we have apocopation. We have a further illustration of the principle of the foregoing. The owner wants to retrieve the fruit. Even though his hands are unclean, he reaches out and takes the fruit. What is the result? The hands are made clean by the water flow. But the fruit remains insusceptible to uncleanness. Why? Because it was not the man's intent to rinse off his hands in the water channel and so to clean them. If, D adds, that was his intent, then his hands of course are clean, but the fruit now has been rendered susceptible to uncleanness.

M. Makhshirin 4:8

A.   A [clay] dish that is full of water and placed in an immersion pool,
B.   and into [the air space of] which a Father of uncleanness put his hand,
C.   is unclean [but the water remains clean].
D.   [If he was unclean only by reason of] contact with unclean things, it is clean.
E.   And as to all other liquids – they are unclean.
F.   For water does not effect cleanness for other liquids.

The present pericope is not phrased in the expected apocopation, for C refers to the dish and so completes the thought of A. We have an exercise in several distinct rules. First, a clay pot is made unclean only by a Father of uncleanness. Second, it is not cleaned by immersion in the pool but only by breaking. But the sides of the pot are porous, as at M. Makhshirin 3:2. Therefore, third, the water in the pot is deemed in contact with the immersion pool. The dish is touched by a Father of uncleanness and is therefore made unclean. But, D, someone in the first remove of uncleanness is not able to contaminate the pot. The liquid in the pot is not referred to at A-D, but E demands that we understand the liquid in A-C and D to be clean. Why? Because the water referred to at A certainly is cleaned and kept clean in the pool, along the lines of M. Makhshirin 4:6-7. E then simply registers the fact that liquids apart from those enumerated at M. Makhshirin 6:4 are not cleaned in an immersion pool. E-F should also tell us that if other liquids are in the pot, the pot also is unclean, because liquids in the first remove of uncleanness do impart uncleanness to clay or earthenware utensils. Accordingly, E-F form either a slightly awry gloss, taking for granted that A-C have said *the water is clean, even though it* [the pot] *is unclean,* or they belong to a pericope other than the present one, which is highly unlikely.

M. Makhshirin 4:9

A.   He who draws water with a swape-pipe [or bucket] [and pieces of fruit later fell into the moisture or water remaining in the pipe or bucket],
B.   up to three days [the water] imparts susceptibility to uncleanness. [Afterward it is deemed to be unwanted (Maimonides).]
C.   R. Aqiba says, "If it has dried off, it is forthwith incapable of imparting susceptibility to uncleanness, and if it has not dried off, up to thirty days it [continues to] impart susceptibility to uncleanness."

The dispute poses A-B against C. We deal now with a wooden pipe or bucket. Do we deem the bucket to be dried off as soon as it is empty?

No, B says, the water in the bucket, detached with approval (by definition) remains able to impart susceptibility for three days. 'Aquiba qualifies the matter. If the water drawn with approval was dried out of the bucket, whatever moisture then is found in the bucket is not wanted; the man has shown, by drying out the bucket or pipe, that he does not want moisture there. If it is not dried out, then whatever liquid is there is deemed to be detached from the pool with approval and therefore able to impart uncleanness for a very long time. Only after thirty days do we assume that the wood is completely dry of the original water detached with approval.

M. Makhshirin 4:10

A. Pieces of wood on which liquids fell and on which rains fell –

B. if [the rains] were more [than the liquids], [the pieces of wood] are insusceptible to uncleanness.

C. [If] he took them outside so that the rains might fall on them, even though they [the rains] were more [than the liquids], they [the pieces of wood] are [susceptible to uncleanness and] unclean.

D. [If] they absorbed unclean liquids, even though he took them outside so that the rains would fall on them, they are clean [for the clean rain has not had contact with the unclean absorbed liquid].

E. But he should kindle them only with clean hands alone [to avoid contaminating the rainwater of D].

F. R. Simeon says, "If they were wet [freshly cut] and he kindled them, and the liquids [sap] that exude from them were more than the liquids that they had absorbed, they are clean."

The pericope is in the following parts: A-B balanced by C; and D, qualified by E. F is an important gloss of D-E. The point of A-B is familiar from M. Makhshirin 2:3. If we have a mixture of unclean and clean liquids, we determine matters in accord with the relative quantity of each. If the clean liquids are the greater part, the whole is deemed clean. Accordingly, since the rain, which is insusceptible and does not impart susceptibility to uncleanness unless it falls with approval, forms the greater part, B, the liquids on the pieces of wood are deemed clean. But if, C, the man deliberately arranged for the rain to fall on the pieces of wood, then the rain falls on the wood with approval, and the wood is susceptible to uncleanness and is made unclean by the unclean liquids already on the wood.

D raises a separate question: What if pieces of wood have absorbed unclean liquids? The answer is that what is absorbed does not have contact with what is on the surface – that is the meaning of absorption. Therefore if rain falls on wood that has absorbed unclean liquids, the rain does not impart susceptibility to uncleanness if it has not fallen with approval. D does not treat that matter; it wishes to say something additional. Even if the rain falls with approval, the wood remains clean.

Why? Because nothing has made the rain unclean. That secondary point then invites E – or E imposes the detail, *even if,* on D: Even though he took them outside, so the rain falls with approval, E adds, since the rain *has* fallen with approval, it is susceptible to uncleanness. Accordingly, the man should kindle the wood only with clean hands, lest he make the rainwater unclean.

Simeon deals then with a still further point. If the wood is freshly cut when kindled, then the unclean absorbed liquids are deemed neutralized by the sap. If the exuded liquid caused by the heat is more than the still absorbed liquid, then the clean, exuded liquid forms the greater part, and the whole is clean, just as at A-B. Simeon, Maimonides says, differs from D (+ E). We hold, as at A-D, that if unclean liquids are absorbed by the wood, they are deemed clean and do not impart uncleanness to the oven, *only* in the case in which the wood is wet. Then, when it is heated, it produces sap in greater quantity than the unclean liquids that it absorbed. But if not, the wood imparts uncleanness to the oven when it is heated because of the unclean liquid that has been absorbed.

Now if we reflect on the detailed rules we have observed, one thing will have struck the reader very forcefully. What Scripture treats as unconditional the authorship of the Mishnah has made contingent upon the human will. Specifically, when Scripture refers at Lev. 11:34, 37 to grain's being made wet, it makes no provision for the attitude of the owner of the grain, his intention in having wet the grain, or his will as to its disposition. What is wet is susceptible, what is dry is insusceptible. The effect of the water is *ex opere operato.* Yet, as we see, that very matter of the attitude of the householder toward the grain's being made wet forms the centerpiece of interest. The issue of intentionality thus forms the precipitating consideration behind every dispute we have reviewed, and, it is clear, the priestly authors of Leviticus could not have conceived such a consideration. The introduction of that same concern can be shown to characterize the Mishnah's treatment of a variety of biblical rules and to form a systemic principle of profound and far-reaching character. We may draw a simple and striking contrast, for instance, between the following bald statements:

1.   "Whatever touches the altar shall become holy" (Ex. 29:37).

It would be difficult to find a less ambiguous statement. But here is the rule of the Mishnah's sages:

2.   "The altar sanctifies that which is appropriate to it" (M. Zebahim 9:1)....And what are those things which, even if they have gone up, should go down [since they are not

offered at all and therefore are not appropriate to the altar]? "The flesh for the priests of Most Holy Things and the flesh of Lesser Holy Things [which is designated for priestly consumption]" (M. Zeb. 9:5).

To understand the conflict between statement No. 1 and statement No. 2 we have to understand how an animal enters the category of Most Holy Things or Lesser Holy Things. It is by the action of the farmer, who owns the beast and designates it for a purpose, within the cult, that imparts to the beast that status of Most Holy Things or Lesser Holy Things. In both cases, the rule is that such a beast yields parts that are burned up on the alter, and other parts that are given to the priests to eat or to the farmer, as the case may be.

Now the point is that it is the farmer who has designated a beast owned by him for sacrifice in the status of Most Holy Things or Lesser Holy Things. His disposition of the offering then places that offering into the classification that yields meat for the officiating priest out of the carcass of the sacrificial beast. Here is, in principle, something that is *surely* appropriate to the altar. But because of the designation, that is, the realization of the act of intentionality, of the householder, the owner of the beast, the beast has fallen into a classification that must yield meat to be eaten, and that meat of the carcass that is to be eaten is taken off the altar, though it is fit for being burnt up as an offering to God, and given to the owner or to the priest, as the rule may require.

It would be difficult to find a more profound difference, brought about by a keen appreciation for the power of the human will, between the Scripture's unnuanced and uncontingent rule and the Mishnah's clear revision of it. It would carry us far afield to catalogue all of the innumerable rules of the Mishnah in which intentionality forms the central concern. The rather arcane rules of Mishnah-tractate Makhshirin show us how sages thought deeply and framed comprehensive principles concerning will and intentionality and then applied these principles to exceedingly picayune cases, as we should, by now, expect. A simple conclusion seems well justified by the chapter we have examined in its broader conceptual context.

From the cases at hand, we may generalize as follows: Will and deed constitute those actors of creation which work upon neutral realms, subject to either sanctification or uncleanness: the Temple and table, the field and family, the altar and hearth, woman, time, space, transactions in the material world and in the world above as well. An object, a substance, a transaction, even a phrase or a sentence is inert but may be made holy, when the interplay of the will and deed of the human being arouses or generates its potential to be sanctified. Each may be treated as ordinary or (where relevant) made unclean by the neglect of the will and inattentive act of the human being. Just as the entire system of uncleanness and holiness awaits the intervention of the human being, which imparts the capacity to become unclean upon what was formerly inert, or which removes the capacity to impart cleanness from what was formerly in its natural and puissant condition, so in the other ranges of reality, the human being is at the center on earth, just as is God in heaven. And all of this comes to us in arguments about the status of some drops of water.

The upshot is very simple. A central problem in the interpretation of the Mishnah, the foundation document of Judaism, is to explain this very strange mode of discourse. Specifically, we want to know why its philosophical authorship has chosen such a strikingly concrete and unphilosophical manner for the expression of what clearly are abstract and profoundly reflective philosophical positions on the nature of human intention in relationship to metaphysical reality. To answer that question, it seems to me, sustained attention to modes of philosophical discourse in the age of the Mishnah, which is to say, the second century, will be required. Here then is a task awaiting attention: to explain why philosophers have chosen the petty and banal mode of discourse of rule-making bureaucrats. I cannot even imagine an answer to that question.

4

Comparing Judaic and Zoroastrian Law: The Pahlavi Rivayat Accompanying the Dadestan i Denig and the Talmud of Babylonia

The Pahlavi Rivayat Accompanying the Dadestan i Denig is found among the manuscripts associated with the Dadestan i Denig of Manushchihr, high priest of Pars and Kirman, and forms part of that writing down of the great tradition that took place in the ninth century under his sponsorship.[1] At that same time, Sherira, a principal authority of Judaism in Babylonia, was explaining that the Talmud of Babylonia was written down to preserve the great, originally oral tradition from disappearance. So both legal documents were assigned the same purpose.

The Bavli's authors would have found much of Pahlavi Rivayat analogous to their own Talmud. That is the part of this rivayat made up of questions and answers, whether of legal or theological character. In general, most of the chapters "are in some ways answers either to a question, explicit or implied, or to a predicament." It is "neither speculative, philosophical, nor in any narrow sense theological; it is pedagogical, for here, above all, the doctrines of purity, righteousness, and just, meritorious action are extolled to the reader by every available means. Clearly, the voice is that of a priest."[2] Then the colloquy between

---

[1]All translations are by A.V. Williams, *The Pahlavi Rivayat Accompanying the Dadestan i Denig* (Copenhagen, 1990: The Royal Danish Academy of Sciences and Letters through Munksgaard). Williams, 1:8: "[It] is placed in the manuscripts with works by authors from one well-known family of learned priests and it is likely that a member of the family might have compiled this Rivayat."
[2]Williams, 1:9.

Zoroaster and God is the priest's recording of the received tradition, as much as the Mishnah represents Judah the Patriarch's allegation of having preserved in fixed and readily memorized form – thus published in an odd way – the received tradition.

Closer to the trait of the Bavli still, this rivayat contains numerous citations of prior, authoritative writings. So the work is traditional in another sense parallel to the Bavli: received authoritative writings are the sources for much that is said, so Williams: "Much of the material appears to come directly from a knowledge of the Pahlavi versions of the Avesta with the Zand, either oral or written." Williams comments:

> [The text] was addressed to Zoroastrians living in Muslim Iran, at a time of great insecurity for those who adhered to the older religion. The text was intended not only to impart information, whether practical, ritual, or theological, to the community; rather it intends to preach solidarity and faithfulness in the community.[3]

In this context, Williams cites Jacques de Menasce's comment:

> "The documents of this type do not generally insist on what, in a faith, is the most current and the most actual. Interest is turned more on what is in danger of being forgotten and on what is the object of controversy. Thus one will not find a balanced and complete account."

Whether or not the same may be said in specific passages of the Bavli, the highly contentious and argumentative character of the Bavli's unique writing (as distinct from kinds of writing it shares with other documents, for example, the Mishnah, not only cited but imitated in authoritative formulations of law) points to the same intentionality. Let us undertake the comparison of episodic points of law, at which the two codes intersect.

I. The Transmission of Uncleanness

The Rivayat forms only a part of a much larger set of writings, and its rules testify to only one component of a complete legal and theological system. The severely limited range of comparison, to be sure, is not because, even at their most arcane, the two writings do not cover the same ground in the same way. The contrary is the fact. Anyone familiar with the Judaic law of uncleanness will find himself at home in a statement such as the following, concerning the transmission of uncleanness through being affected by the motion of, without direct contact with, the source of uncleanness:

> If they are carrying a dead (body) over a bridge of wood or of stone,
> if it trembles, if everyone who is standing on the bridge (is standing) still

---

[3]Williams, 1:10.

(they are) not polluted, but if anyone keeps going he will indeed be polluted.

The principle here is that the corpse uncleanness is conveyed through motion, but not at rest; the criterion (who has to be moving) is, the person who is a candidate for contamination.

Let me paraphrase the Iranian rule. If a corpse is carried across the bridge, and if others are moving on it, too, if the bridge trembles under the weight of the corpse, then all other persons on the bridge are made unclean, the movement of the bridge transmitting the corpse uncleanness to third parties if they, too, are moving. But if they are not moving, then the uncleanness is null. It then follows that [1] if the bridge is firm and does not shift, [2] and if occupants of the bridge also do not move, then others standing on the bridge are unaffected. The upshot is simple. Corpse uncleanness is transmitted through the motion of an object that bears its weight.

In the following the same principle of the physics of the transmission of uncleanness pertains, though it works itself out somewhat differently. The datum is the category of uncleanness described at Lev. 15, called in Hebrew the *Zab*, a person afflicted with flux uncleanness. Such a person transmits uncleanness to objects that bear his weight, even though not touching those objects – just as the corpse does in the Zoroastrian case – if the other party also is in motion by reason of the same cause, the movement of the ship or the raft or the beast.

Mishnah-tractate Zabim 3:1

A. The Zab and the clean person who sat in a ship or on a raft,
B. or who rode [together] on a beast,
C. even though their clothes do not touch –
D. lo, these are unclean with midras uncleanness.
E. [If] they sat on a plank, or on a bench, or on a bed frame, and on the beam,
F. when they are infirm –
G. [if] they climbed up on a tree which was shaky,
H. on a branch which was shaky on a firm tree –
I. [if they climbed up] on an Egyptian ladder when it is not fastened with a nail,
J. on the bridge,
K. and on the beam,
L. and on the door,
M. when they are not fastened with clay –
N. they are unclean.
O. R. Judah declares clean.

At Eff. we come to precisely the case before us: the *Zab* and the clean person are on the same plank, bench, bed frame, or beam or tree or ladder or bridge; if these are shaky, then the clean person is made unclean. Why? Because the uncleanness of the *Zab* is transmitted to the clean person through the motion of the infirm bridge or other object. And that is the exact counterpart to the Zoroastrian detail, if the persons on the bridge are moving, too. The point of difference proves equally obvious: for the Mishnaic law, it is the bridge that is moving, for the Zoroastrian, the afflicted parties. For the one, the uncleanness is transmitted by the movement of the weight-bearing component of the tableau, for the other, the movement of the candidate for uncleanness. In the following, we find the same principle:

M. Negaim 13:7

A.   The unclean [person] stands under the tree, and the clean person passes –
B.   he is unclean.
C.   The clean person stands under the tree, and the unclean passes –
D.   he is clean.
E.   If he stood, he is unclean.
F.   And so with the stone which is afflicted with plague – he is clean.
G.   And if he put it down, lo, this one is unclean.

Now if the unclean person is at rest (put the corpse down on the bridge) and the clean person walks by (add: and overshadows it, in line with Num. 19), then the clean person contracts uncleanness. The opposite is also the rule: if the uncleanness is in motion and the clean person or object at rest, then the clean person or object remains clean. So the distinction recurs, and makes the same difference, but, for the Judaic system, in reverse. The point of this arcane exercise should not be missed: we can readily identify, even in the most remote and hermetic chapters of the law of uncleanness of Iran and Israel, more than a few points of intersection, where the same principles and the same cases generate decisions that are either the same or the opposite: a fine problem for comparison and contrast indeed. And, I am sure readers will agree to stipulate, a search through the ninth-century documents (all the more so prior ones) will yield countless points of parallel and even intersection.[4] But until we have formed a theory of the whole, each

---

[4]A systematic comparison of the two systems' purity rules, encompassing the entirety of their respective canons (on the side of the Mishnah and Talmuds, Leviticus and Numbers and the Tosefta, for instance) would certainly yield a hypothesis on how the entirety of the two systems compare. One can work from details to the whole – and has to. Nonetheless, episodic intersection such as what is before us leaves open too many variables to allow for the forming of a hypothesis on the comparison and contrast of the systems at hand. A fine preliminary effort in just the right direction is in A.V. Williams, "Zoroastrian and Jewish Purity Laws. Reflections on the Viability of a Sociological Interpretation," to be published in a future volume of *Irano-Judaica*.

system compared in its entirety to the other, these details remain inert facts, generating nothing beyond themselves. That is why, for the present purpose, a clear view of what we wish to find out has always to remain in plain sight. It is to compare the two traditions when they go over the same theme and reach comparable conclusions, a comparison that, once more, shows us how the documents differ where they are alike.

II. Master-Disciple Relationships

Certainly the two systems' orbits come close in their address to the relationship prized by each, that is, the one upon which the formulation and transmission of the great tradition ultimately depends: the relationship between master and disciple. That is how God's word has come down in both traditions. The myth of the Oral Torah, beginning with Moses at Sinai, rests upon that relationship; the claim of the ninth-century priests to set down the great tradition depends upon it as well.

In the Judaic case, it is through the chain of master-disciple relationships, extending forward from Sinai, that the tradition is formulated and transmitted. In the Zoroastrian case, in the two rivayat writings before us and also in the Pursishniha, the literary form – question, answer – and much of the contents as well presuppose the relationship of master and disciple, the one answering, the other asking questions. And in both cases, the model derives from the original moment of revelation: God instructing Moses at Sinai, Ohrmazd instructing Zoroaster. The Bavli's presentation – functioning as counterpart to the colloquy language utilized by our rivayat – is as follows:

Bavli Erubin 54B-55A

43.   A.   *Our rabbis have taught on Tannaite authority:*
      B.   What is the order of Mishnah teaching? Moses learned it from the mouth of the All-powerful. Aaron came in, and Moses repeated his chapter to him and Aaron went forth and sat at the left hand of Moses. His sons came in and Moses repeated their chapter to them, and his sons went forth. Eleazar sat at the right of Moses, and Itamar at the left of Aaron.
      C.   R. Judah says, "At all times Aaron was at the right hand of Moses."
      D.   Then the elders entered, and Moses repeated for them their Mishnah chapter. The elders went out. Then the whole people came in, and Moses repeated for them their Mishnah chapter. So it came about that Aaron repeated the lesson four times, his sons three times, the elders two times, and all the people once.
      E.   Then Moses went out, and Aaron repeated his chapter for them. Aaron went out. His sons repeated their chapter. His sons went

out. The elders repeated their chapter. So it turned out that everybody repeated the same chapter four times....

What we see here is characteristic of the Bavli: presentation of the fact, then systematic analysis of that fact.

Not only in myth, but also in law, the master-disciple relationship proves of critical interest to both traditions. For instance, the merit of a disciple accrues to the master; not only so, but if the disciple then teaches other disciples, "the merit of teaching the disciple to teach other disciples shall verily be unto the teacher. Unto those who shall so practice it, just as it is." Even those acts which the other teacher performs, it is just as if they perform [i.e., that which the disciple performs goes over to the teacher, and that which goes over to the disciple from other persons does not go over to the teacher].[5] In the Judaic counterpart, the teacher enters into the status of the father and deserves the respect owing to the disciple's father by the disciple; and takes precedence over the father. The principle is the same, the details, diverse.

In that context, we compare rules of conduct delivered by masters to disciples. The form is essentially the same: an instruction by a named master to a disciple, consisting in both cases of a long set of rules of proper attitude and action. I find the "counsels of Adurbad" and those of the Judaic sages in tractate Abot to serve the same purpose and to take the same form. For the sake of brevity, I give only the initial part of Adurbad's counsels, also abbreviating the repertoire in tractate Abot:

Chapter Sixty-Two
Counsels of Adurbad, Son of Mansarspand, from the Sayings of His Teacher Mihr Ohrmazd

There was a disciple of Adurbad of immortal soul, son of Mannsarspand; he was with Adurbad for a long time.

And this indeed he said to Adurbad: "Instruct me, so that when I go forth from the presence of the teacher instruction of my soul can then (proceed) better on account of that."

Adurbad said: "Be certain (in faith) in the yazads. Keep your thought, speech and action honest and true. Neither think nor speak nor do any sin whatsoever, and may you be blessed."

And the disciple said: "O teacher, I am not perfect in this, give me special instruction, so that I shall practice it and I shall be blessed."

Adurbad said: "Consider the twenty-two precepts of Mihr Ohrmazd, my teacher; understand all (of them), put them into practice and may you be blessed!"

---

[5]See Kaikhusroo M. Jamaspa and Helmut Humbach, *Pursishniha. A Zoroastrian Catechism* (Wiesbaden, 1971: Otto Harrassowitz), Part I. *Text, Translation, Notes,* pp. 29-31.

The disciple said: "If you consider me as worthy, please tell (me the precepts), so that I may understand and practise (accordingly)."

Adurbad said in reply: "The precepts (are) these three kinds of generosity, fourth truthfulness, fifth virtuousness, sixth diligence, seventh intercession, eighth trustworthiness, ninth peace seeking, tenth law-abidingness, eleventh union, twelfth laying down of weapons, thirteenth moderation, fourteenth lowliness, fifteenth humility, sixteenth modesty, seventeenth pleasantness, eighteenth completeness (of mind), nineteenth patience, twentieth love for people, twenty-first contentedness, twenty-second oneness (of mind).

"The best generosity: first, he who is not asked but gives; second, he who is asked (and) gives immediately; third, he who is asked and fixes a time and does (his giving) on time. He (is) best, who, when he gives, entertains no hope as regards that (receiver of his generosity, thinking): 'He will give (it) back to me'; he does not give for the sake of acquiring trade, nor for the sake of covetousness...."

What we have is a catalogue of virtues, systematically expounded as a handbook for the good life. I fail to see any material differences, in the chosen form of transmitting a tradition on good attitude and action, from the mode of tractate Abot, in the following (also abbreviated) reprise:

Tractate Abot Chapter Three
Chapter Four

Ben Zoma says, "Who is a sage? He who learns from everybody, as it is said, From all my teachers I have gotten understanding (Ps. 119:99). Who is strong? He who overcomes his desire, as it is said, He who is slow to anger is better than the mighty, and he who rules his spirit than he who takes a city (Prov. 16:32). Who is rich? He who is happy in what he has, as it is said, When you eat the labor of your hands, happy will you be, and it will go well with you (Ps. 128:2). ("Happy will you be – in this world, and it will go well with you – in the world to come.") Who is honored? He who honors everybody, as it is said, For those who honor me I shall honor, and they who despise me will be treated as of no account (1 Sam. 2:30)."

In both cases an important component of the master-disciple relationship is the transmission of wisdom on proper conduct. In both instances, the master is named, and in both cases, a liturgy is tacked on to the end of the catalogue of virtuous attitudes and behavior. To be sure, this kind of writing would have presented no surprise to sages and disciples who flourished from the remotest times of writing onward; Sumerian, Akkadian, Egyptian, not to mention Greek and Roman writers recorded the same kind of advice, and even much the same advice (recommendations of arrogance are vastly outnumbered in the literature by the counsel of humility, but, to be sure, praise of masters' humility is outweighed in volume by complaints about their arrogance). But in the Zoroastrian and Judaic writings, the master-disciple relationship finds definition in not only generalizations but detailed rules, and that is what makes the comparison particular to the two cases and distinctive as well.

III. Father-Son or Master-Disciple Relationships

The comparison of the relationship of father to son and master to disciple comes to expression in this rivayat in the revelation by Ohrmazd to Zoroaster on the rule – parallel in the two relationships – governing law suits between persons of said classifications. The tradition tells the judge how to adjudicate a case in which each party presents evidence of the same weight as that of the other. In that case, the judge is to favor the master or the father, who has nurtured him. Indeed, the father, and, by extension, the master, owns the earnings of the son or disciple and the merit of his good deeds, as though the father or the master had done those deeds himself:

Chapter Twenty-Nine
The Privileges of Seniority

This also (is) revealed, Ohrmazd said to Zoroaster: "If a father is engaged in a lawsuit with his son, or a herbad with his pupil, or a father-in-law with his son-in-law, and if the father (has) one witness on his side, and the son one witness on his, make the decision in favour of the father, and entrust the property (at stake) to the father, for this reason that the good that the father does for his son, the son can never repay that goodness. He has nurtured him from childhood and immaturity until that (time) when he becomes an adult. Indeed according to this saying: 'Until a son is 15 years old his nurture (comes) from his father,' then also so long as he [i.e., the father] (is) alive the (son's) earnings belong to the father, and all the good deeds which the son does will thus belong to the father as if he had done them with his own hands."

What attracts our attention is two facts, first, the reason – the father has nurtured the son, and the master is in the status of the father and so is deemed to have nurtured him, too – and second the consequence, the father or master owns the son's earnings and merits. We find the same issue worked out along intersecting lines in the following:

Mishnah-tractate Baba Mesia 2:11

A. [If one has to choose between seeking] what he has lost and what his father has lost,
B. his own takes precedence.
C. [If he has to choose between seeking] what he has lost and what his master has lost,
D. his own takes precedence.
E. [If he has to choose between seeking] what his father has lost and what his master has lost,
F. that of his master takes precedence.

G. For his father brought him into this world.

H. But his master, who has taught him wisdom, will bring him into the life of the world to come.

I. But if his father is a sage, that of his father takes precedence.

J. [If] his father and his master were carrying heavy burdens, he removes that of his master, and afterward removes that of his father.

K. [If] his father and his master were taken captive,

L. he ransoms his master, and afterward he ransoms his father.

M. But if his father is a sage, he ransoms his father, and afterward he ransoms his master.

The issue is framed in different terms, of course, since it is the son who has the decision to make, not the judge. And the son has to give priority to his own interest, for a reason that the Talmud would immediately want to uncover. At issue is when he (not the judge) has to choose between his father and his master. The answer, however, would have interested the author of our rivayat, since the Mishnah rule carries forward the same principle as the Zoroastrian one: the master enters into the status of the father. The Mishnah cannot imagine that the master or father will take over the property or the merit of good deeds of the son.

But the framer of the Bavli wants to know why the son's interests take priority, and that is, I assume, in light of the commandment to honor father and mother. The answer follows:

I.1 A. What is the scriptural source of this rule ["his own takes precedence"]?

B. Said R. Judah said Rab, "Said Scripture, 'Except that there shall be no poor among you' (Deut. 15:4). Your own takes precedence over anybody else's."

C. But said R. Judah said Rab, "Whoever treats himself in such a way will end up in such a condition [of poverty]."

II.1 A. [If] his father and his master were carrying heavy burdens, he removes that of his master, and afterward removes that of his father.

B. Our rabbis have taught on Tannaite authority:

C. "The master of which they have spoken is the one who taught him wisdom, not the master who taught him Scripture or Mishnah," the words of R. Meir.

D. R. Judah says, "It is anyone from whom he has gained the greater part of his learning."

E. R. Yosé says, "Even someone who has enlightened his eyes in his repetition of a single Mishnah paragraph – lo, this is his master" [T. B.M. 2:30D-F].

F. Said Raba, "For example, R. Sehorah, who explained to me the meaning of the words that stand for a certain utensil [at M. Kel. 13:2]."

II.2 A. Samuel tore his garment as a mark of mourning for one of the rabbis, who had merely taught him the meaning of the phrase, **one** of the keys goes into the duct as far as the armpit and the other opens the door directly [M. Tam. 3:6E].

II.3   A.   Said Ulla, "Disciples of sages who are located in Babylonia stand up in respect to one another and tear their garments in mourning for one another.

        B.   "But as to returning a lost object, in a case in which there is a choice between his father [and his master], he goes first of all in search of his master only when it is his principal teacher."

The Bavli's initial contribution, as is commonly the case, links the Mishnah's rule to a source in the Written Torah. The proof is such as to eliminate the possibility that the father or master owns the son's or disciple's property. The Talmud's next step is to enrich the discussion through the qualification produced by Tosefta's supplement: defining the master who counts. Here we recall the rivayat's distinction between a disciple who does not teach others and the one who does; the master gets credit for the good deeds of the disciple who teaches others. We find ourselves moving in the reverse direction: the identification of the master who enjoys the status that is subject to discussion here. No. 3 pursues the same matter. The difference in the presentation of the rule becomes apparent here: the rivayat gives rules, the Bavli undertakes a systematic analysis of them. Information by itself is insufficient; sustained, applied reason and practical logic transform information into truth and insight. The next point of intersection yields the same formal contrast between the two writings.

IV. Husband-Wife Relationships: The Wife's Perfect Obedience

The Zoroastrian code finds it possible to say in a few words precisely what the wife owes the husband, which is perfect and unquestioning obedience to his will in all matters; and anyhow, she shouldn't torment him. Between the ritual ideal, on the one side, and the concession to the everyday, on the other, presumably lies what can be expected. On the Judaic side, the same thing is spelled out in more concrete ways, the Mishnah being a far more detailed document than the two rivayats before us (or the Pursishniha, for that matter):

Chapter Thirty-Nine
Wife and Husband

This (question): how should a wife behave towards her husband?

The wife of *padixsay* (status) should consult her husband three times every day saying: "What do you require when I think and speak and act, for I do not know what is required when I think and speak and act, tell (me), so that I will think and speak and act as you require?" Then she must do everything that the righteous husband tells her, and she should refrain from tormenting and afflicting her husband.

The concrete obligations of the woman to the man in Judaism convey the same attitude, but because of their specificity, place some (few) limits on the husband's caprice:

Mishnah-tractate Ketubot 5:5

A.   These are the kinds of labor which a woman performs for her husband:

B.   she (1) grinds flour, (2) bakes bread, (3) does laundry, (4) prepares meals, (5) gives suck to her child, (6) makes the bed, (7) works in wool.

C.   [If] she brought with her a single slave girl, she does not (1) grind, (2) bake bread, or (3) do laundry.

D.   [If she brought] two, she does not (4) prepare meals and does (not 5) feed her child.

E.   [If she brought] three, she does not (6) make the bed for him and does not (7) work in wool.

F.   If she brought four, she sits on a throne.

G.   R. Eliezer says, "Even if she brought him a hundred slave girls, he forces her to work in wool,

H.   "for idleness leads to unchastity."

I.   Rabban Simeon b. Gamaliel says, "Also: He who prohibits his wife by a vow from performing any labor puts her away and pays off her marriage contract. For idleness leads to boredom."

The Bavli's reading of the rule follows, in abbreviated form. The traits we have found characteristic recur here.

I.1 A.   **Grinds flour:**

      B.   *Under what circumstances [can we imagine that a woman would grind flour, which involves moving heavy machinery]?*

      C.   *Read:* taking charge of the grinding.

      D.   And if you prefer: grinding with a hand mill.

I.2 A.   *Our Mishnah paragraph is not in accord with R. Hiyya, for R. Hiyya set forth the following Tannaite rule:*

      B.   [Marrying] a woman is only for her beauty, only for children.

      C.   *And R. Hiyya set forth the following Tannaite rule:*

      D.   A wife is for wearing women's ornaments.

      E.   *And R. Hiyya set forth the following Tannaite rule:*

      F.   He who wants his wife to be attractive should dress her in linen clothes. He who wants his daughter to have a bright skin should feed her young chicken and give her plenty of milk to drink as she comes toward her first period.

II.1 A.   **Gives suck to her child:**

      B.   *May one say that this does not accord with the position of the House of Shammai? For it has been taught on Tannaite authority:*

      C.   **If she took a vow not to give suck to her child,**

      D.   **the House of Shammai say, "She pulls her teats from the child's mouth."**

      E.   **And the House of Hillel say, "He can force her to give suck to her child."**

F.   If she was divorced, however, they do not force her to give suck to him.

G.   If her son recognized her as his mother, they give her a wage, and she gives suck to him, because of the danger to the child's life. The husband cannot force his wife to give suck to the child of his fellow, and the wife cannot force her husband to permit her to give suck to the child of her girlfriend [T. Ket. 5:5A-H].

H.   *Well, you may even maintain that the House of Shammai stand behind our Mishnah paragraph. Here with what case do we deal? It is a case in which she took the oath and he confirmed it for her. The House of Shammai take the view that he has put his finger between her teeth [the vow is his fault], and the House of Hillel maintain that she put her finger between his teeth....*

III.1 A.   **[If] she brought with her a single slave girl, she does not (1) grind, (2) bake bread, or (3) do laundry:**

B.   *But the rest of the duties she has to do.*

C.   *But why can't she say to him, "I brought you another woman in my place [for all manner of work, not just for this]"?*

D.   *Because he can say to her, "That slave girl works for me and for herself, who's going to work for you?"*

IV.1 A.   **[If she brought] two, she does not (4) prepare meals and does not (5) feed her child:**

B.   *But the rest of the duties she has to do.*

C.   *But why can't she say to him, "I brought you another woman in my place [for all manner of work, not just for this], and she's going to work for me and for her, and the first one will work for you and for herself"?*

D.   *Because he can say to her, "So who's going to work for our guests and visitors?"*

V.1   A.   **[If she brought] three, she does not (6) make the bed for him and does not (7) work in wool:**

B.   *But the rest of the duties she has to do.*

C.   *But why can't she say to him, "I brought you a third one still, to work for our guests and visitors"?*

D.   *Because he can say to her, "The bigger the household, the more numerous the guests and the visitors."*

E.   *If so, then even if she brought in four, you could have the same colloquy!*

F.   *If there are four, since they are that many, they help one another.*

This drastically abbreviated presentation of the Bavli's analysis points in an obvious direction, which we may discern by noting that what is of special interest to us in the Bavli is not the rule, but the mode of representing it. Here, clearly, we come to the principal point of difference between this Rivayat and the Bavli, when the two writings intersect.

To state the difference in a simple way: What should we have found in the Rivayat, had the words, "The wife of *padixsay* (status) should consult her husband three times every day saying: 'What do you require when I think and speak and act, for I do not know what is required when

I think and speak and act, tell (me), so that I will think and speak and act as you require,'" been followed by:

[1]   what is the source [in the Avesta or Gathas] of this rule? or

[2]   under what circumstances?

[3]   this rule is not in accord with the following, known in some other compilation?

Then again, if we had the same rule, followed by, "may we say this does not accord with the position of...," followed by a contrary view in some other source, what should the rivayat have looked like? Or if we had, "if the husband said...," and then, "but does she have to do no more?" what shape would the writing have taken? The answer is simple: we should have had something very like the Bavli. And we do not have anything like the Bavli.

V. Commercial Relationships: True Value

Our final specific comparison of the two traditions as they intersect on the same matter concerns the conception of true value. That theory maintains that an object possesses an intrinsic and inherent value, which is distinct from the price that the market sets on the same object (that is, what an informed buyer and informed seller are willing to pay and to receive for the object to change hands). The notion of true value logically belongs together with the conception of money as an item of barter or meant merely to facilitate barter, because both notions referred to the single underlying conception of the economy as a steady-state entity in which people could not increase wealth but only exchange it. Fraud involves not adulteration of a product or misrepresentation of the character or quality of merchandise, such as we should grasp, but simply charging more than something is worth, and that can only mean, than something is worth intrinsically.

The Zoroastrian formulation maintains that if an object has a true value of four, and one sells it elsewhere for ten, he may not retain six; he may keep the four that he paid, plus his expenses and his wages, and the rest of the profit goes to a meritorious purpose. Now the given is that, in that other place, the object has a true value of ten. Then the man is governed by the criterion of the true value set by the place in which he bought the object, not the place in which he sold it.

Trading and Acquisition of Wealth

This (question): how should trading take place so that there will be no sin in it?

When (a trader) buys for four drachms a single piece of clothing, worth four drachms, and he takes it to another town, and (in) the place where he takes it it is worth ten drachms, he sells it for ten drachms, and takes out of it wages and daily sustenance for himself and his horse, and he gives away what remains (of it) as a righteous gift, it is a (work of) great merit.

"True value" then is negotiated in relationship to market value. That is, the "true value" of four, set at the time of purchase, has to be brought into relationship with the true value of ten, which the market has placed on the object in that other place. We take account of the difference between the true value, which is the purchase price where the trader lives, and the market value, by refunding the difference between the market price and the true value in acts of piety.

The Mishnah expresses the identical notion, that an object possesses a true value. But it sets forth the idea in a different context. It speaks of an "overcharge," meaning, what the market has paid for an item that exceeds true value; true value then is a fixed and known value, and "fraud" or overreaching is whatever the market pays over and above that value, which is anything more than 16.667 percent above true value. The difference has to be refunded:

Mishnah-tractate Baba Mesia 4:3

A.   Fraud [overreaching] is an overcharge of four pieces of silver out of twenty-four pieces of silver to the sela –

B.   one-sixth of the purchase price.

C.   For how long is it permitted to retract [in the case of fraud]?

D.   So long as it takes to show [the article] to a merchant or a relative [who will know the true value of the object that one has bought].

Fraud here is simply a charge higher than the intrinsic worth of the object permits. That definition rejects the conception of "free" and "market," that redundancy that insists upon the market as the instrument of the rationing of scarce resources. If an object has a true value of twenty-four and the seller pays twenty-eight, he has been defrauded and may retract. Tarfon gave and took, E-K. What is expressed here are, first, the notion of a just price, second, the emphasis upon barter. The reason is that the logic of the one demanded the complementary logic of the other. Once we impute a true value to an object or commodity, we shall also dismiss from consideration all matters of worth extrinsic to the object or commodity; hence money is not an abstract symbol of worth but itself a commodity, and, further, objects bear true value.

The Talmud's amplification of the matter addresses ambiguities in the Mishnah's rule – once more the point of departure of the Talmud from the Rivayat:

I.1   A.   It has been stated:
       B.   Rab said, "What we have learned to repeat in the Mishnah is, 'a six
             of the purchase price [reckoned at true value]' [**one-sixth of the
             purchase price**]."
       C.   And Samuel said, "A sixth of the money paid also was taught."
       D.   *Obviously if something worth six was sold for five or seven, all parties
             concur that we follow the purchase price and if there was overreaching by
             one-sixth, [the law of fraud is invoked]. Then what is at issue? It would
             be a case in which something worth five or seven was sold for six.*
       E.   *As to Samuel, who has said that we follow the money paid as well, in both
             instances there is a valid claim of fraud.*
       F.   *But in the view of Rab, who has said that we follow only the purchase
             price, then if something worth five went for six, the sale is invalid, but if
             something worth seven is sold for six [so it is only a seventh of the true
             value of the purchase price,] then the seller is deemed to have renounced
             part of what is really coming to him.*
       G.   *And Samuel said, "When do we maintain that there is renunciation by the
             seller or invalidation of the sale? Only if there is not a sixth of variation
             from true value on either side [whether we regard the true purchase price
             or the money paid (Freedman)], but if there is a sixth of variation on one
             side, then it is a case of fraud."*

Enough of the Talmud is before us to show how a sustained analysis of
the secondary issue raised by Rab and Samuel is set forth. So the simple
rule at hand requires amplification and clarification. Had this Rivayat's
author wished to address the problem, he could well have given us an
entirely factual statement along the same lines; he certainly could have
told us how to calculate the overcharge, if his formulation (4/10) had left
any point of unclarity. So in comparison, the issue is not where the
presentations of the rule differ, rather, it is the mode of discourse. When
the two great traditions make the same or similar points, they do so in
strikingly different ways, and that fact points to the paramount definitive
trait of the Judaism put forth by the Talmud of Babylonia. Any account
of the history of Judaism must answer the simple question: How shall we
account for the remarkable power of that Talmud to define Judaism? In
this comparison one answer is adumbrated.[6] One point is clear from the

---

[6]In the following monograph in seven parts I have given my answer to this larger
question in a systematic comparison of the two Talmuds and an identification of
how the second is intellectually unique: *The Bavli's Unique Voice. A Systematic
Comparison of the Talmud of Babylonia and the Talmud of the Land of Israel. I. Bavli
and Yerushalmi Qiddushin Chapter One Compared and Contrasted; II. Yerushalmi's,
Bavli's, and Other Canonical Documents' Treatment of the Program of Mishnah-Tractate
Sukkah Chapters One, Two, and Four Compared and Contrasted. A Reprise and
Revision of* The Bavli and Its Sources; *III. Bavli and Yerushalmi to Selected Mishnah
Chapters in the Division of Moed. Erubin Chapter One, and Moed Qatan Chapter Three;
IV. Bavli and Yerushalmi to Selected Mishnah Chapters in the Division of Nashim.
Gittin Chapter Five and Nedarim Chapter One; V. Bavli and Yerushalmi to Selected*

comparison at hand: the Bavli conveys its messages at two levels, one, on the surface, a message of rules, regulations, theological requirements; another, beneath the surface, a measure conveyed through hermeneutics.[7] Now, when we come to hermeneutics, we return to our starting point: the fine scholarly record of Lou H. Silberman, who carried forward the Talmudic tradition of saying one thing, but conveying many, through the depth of thought set forth in clear and lucid ways.

Mishnah Chapters in the Division of Neziqin. Baba Mesia Chapter One and Makkot Chapters One and Two; VI. Bavli and Yerushalmi to a Miscellany of Mishnah Chapters. Gittin Chapter One, Qiddushin Chapter Two, and Hagigah Chapter Three; VII. What Is Unique about the Bavli in Context? An Answer Based on Inductive Description, Analysis, and Comparison.

[7]And this second clearly forms a theological statement of considerable profundity, made through the medium of hermeneutics. This I spell out in my *Judaism States Its Theology: The Talmudic Re-Presentation* (in press).

Part Two

ISSUES OF METHOD

5

The Documentary History of Judaism and the Problem of Dating Sayings

During a long period in the history of scholarship on history of religion in general, and Judaism in particular, the premises of learning in the rabbinic literature of late antiquity joined new historical interest with a received theological conviction. The former wished to describe in context ideas that had formerly been assigned no context at all: they were "Torah," and now were to be the history of ideas. The latter maintained that the documents of the rabbinic corpus were essentially seamless and formed one vast Dual Torah, Oral and Written; and that all attributions were valid, so that if a given authority was supposed to have made a statement, he really made it. On the basis of that received conviction, imputing inerrancy to the attributions (as well as to the storytellers) just as had many generations of the faithful, but asking questions of context and development that were supposed to add up to history, the great figures of the first three-quarters of the twentieth century set forth their accounts of what they conceived to be Judaism in historical context, hence, the history of Judaism.

But what if we recognize that documentary formulations play a role in the representation of compositions, so that the compositors' formulation of matters takes a critical place in the making of the documentary evidence? And what if, further, we no longer assume the inerrancy of the Oral Torah's writings, so that attributions are no longer taken at face value, stories no longer believed unless there are grounds for disbelief (as the Jerusalem canard has it)? Then the fundamental presuppositions of the received method of studying the history of Judaism prove null. And that fact bears in its wake the further problem: Since we cannot take their answers at face value, can we pursue their questions any more? In my judgment, the answer is negative. All work

71

in the history of the formative age of the Judaism of the Dual Torah that treats documentary lines as null and attributions as invariably valid must be dismissed as a mere curiosity; a collection and arrangement of this and that, bearing no compelling argument or proposition to be dealt with by the new generation.

Let me now reframe the question in a manner which will make clear the right way in which to work. The question that demands a response before any historical issues can be formulated is this: How are we to determine the particular time and circumstance in which a writing took shape, and how shall we identify the generative problems, the urgent and critical questions, that informed the intellect of an authorship and framed the social world that nurtured that same authorship? Lacking answers to these questions, we find our work partial, and, if truth be told, stained by sterile academicism. Accordingly, the documentary method requires us to situate the contents of writings into particular circumstances, so that we may read the contents in the context of a real time and place. How to do so? I maintain that it is by reference to the time and circumstance of the closure of a document, that is to say, the conventional assignment of a piece of writing to a particular time and place, that we proceed outward from context to matrix.

Overall, scholars have tended simply to take at face value attributions of sayings to particular authorities and interpret what is said as evidence of the time and place in which the cited authorities flourished. When studying topics in the Judaism of the sages of the rabbinic writings from the first through the seventh centuries, people routinely cite sayings categorized by attribution rather than by document. That is to say, they treat as one group of sayings whatever is assigned to Rabbi X. This is without regard to the time of redaction of the documents in which those sayings occur or to similar considerations of literary context and documentary circumstance. The category defined by attributions to a given authority furthermore rests on the premise that the things given in the name of Rabbi X really were said by him. No other premise would justify resorting to the category deriving from use of a name, that alone. Commonly, the next step is to treat those sayings as evidence of ideas held, if not by that particular person, then by people in the age in which the cited authority lived. Once more the premise that the sayings go back to the age of the authority to whom they are attributed underpins inquiry. Accordingly, scholars cite sayings in the name of given authorities and take for granted that those sayings were said by the authority to whom they were attributed and, of course, in the time in which that authority flourished. By contrast, in my method of the documentary study of Judaism, I treat the historical sequence of sayings only in accord with the order of the documents in which they first occur.

Let me expand on why I have taken the approach that I have, explain the way the method works, and then, as before, set forth an example of the method in action.[1]

Since many sayings are attributed to specific authorities, why not lay out the sayings in the order of the authorities to whom they are attributed, rather than in the order of the books in which these sayings occur, which forms the documentary method for the description of the matrix of texts in context? It is because the attributions cannot be validated, but the books can. The first of the two principles by which I

---

[1] My example is drawn from a whole series of books in which I worked on the histories of specific conceptions or problems, formulated as I think correct, out of the sequence of documents. These are in the following works of mine, which are now summarized in my *Introduction to Rabbinic Judaism* (New York, 1995: Doubleday Anchor Reference Library):

The Idea of Purity in Ancient Judaism. The Haskell Lectures, 1972-1973 (Leiden, 1973: E.J. Brill). [This was a most preliminary work, which made me aware of the problems to be addressed later on. The documentary theory of the history of ideas was worked out only in the earlier 1980s.]

Judaism and Story: The Evidence of The Fathers According to Rabbi Nathan (Chicago, 1990: University of Chicago Press).

The Foundations of Judaism. Method, Teleology, Doctrine (Philadelphia, 1983-85: Fortress Press), I-III. I. *Midrash in Context. Exegesis in Formative Judaism* (second printing, Atlanta, 1988: Scholars Press for Brown Judaic Studies).

The Foundations of Judaism. Method, Teleology, Doctrine (Philadelphia, 1983-85: Fortress Press), I-III. II. *Messiah in Context. Israel's History and Destiny in Formative Judaism* (second printing, Lanham, 1988: University Press of America), Studies in Judaism series.

The Foundations of Judaism. Method, Teleology, Doctrine (Philadelphia, 1983-85: Fortress Press), I-III. III. *Torah: From Scroll to Symbol in Formative Judaism* (second printing, Atlanta, 1988: Scholars Press for Brown Judaic Studies).

The Foundations of Judaism (Philadelphia, 1988: Fortress). Abridged edition of the foregoing trilogy.

Vanquished Nation, Broken Spirit. The Virtues of the Heart in Formative Judaism (New York, 1987: Cambridge University Press). Jewish Book Club selection, 1987.

Editor with William Scott Green, *Judaisms and Their Messiahs in the Beginning of Christianity* (New York, 1987: Cambridge University Press).

Judaism in the Matrix of Christianity (Philadelphia, 1986: Fortress Press; British edition, Edinburgh, 1988: T. & T. Collins).

Judaism and Christianity in the Age of Constantine. Issues of the Initial Confrontation (Chicago, 1987: University of Chicago Press).

Judaism and Its Social Metaphors. Israel in the History of Jewish Thought (New York 1988: Cambridge University Press).

The Incarnation of God: The Character of Divinity in Formative Judaism (Philadelphia, 1988: Fortress Press).

Editor with William Scott Green *The Christian and Judaic Invention of History* (Atlanta, 1989: Scholars Press for American Academy of Religion). Studies in Religion series. All of the papers in this collection are worked out within the basic thesis of the documentary history of ideas.

describe the matrix that defines the context in which texts are framed is that we compose histories of ideas of the Judaism of the Dual Torah in accord with the sequence of documents that, in the aggregate, constitute the corpus and canon of the Judaism of the Dual Torah. And those histories set forth dimensions of the matrix in which that Judaism, through its writings, is to be situated for broader purposes of interpretation. Documents reveal the system and structure of their authorships, and, in the case of religious writing, out of a document without named authors we may compose an account of the authorship's religion: a way of life, a worldview, a social entity meant to realize both. Read one by one, documents reveal the interiority of intellect of an authorship, and that inner-facing quality of mind inheres even when an authorship imagines it speaks outward, toward and about the world beyond. Even when set side by side, moreover, documents illuminate the minds of intersecting authorships, nothing more.

Then why not simply take at face value a document's *own* claims concerning the determinate situation of its authorship? Readers have already noted innumerable attributions to specific authorities. One obvious mode of determining the matrix of a text, the presently paramount way, as I said, is simply to take at face value the allegation that a given authority, whose time and place we may identify, really said what is attributed to him, and that if a writing says something happened, what it tells us is not what its authorship thought happened, but what really happened. That reading of writing for purposes of not only history, but also religious study, is in fact commonplace. It characterizes all accounts of the religion, Judaism, prior to mine, and it remains a serious option for all those outside of my school and circle.[2] Proof of that fact is to be shown, lest readers who find accommodation in more contemporary intellectual worlds, where criticism and the active intellect reign, doubt my judgment of competing methods and differing accounts. Accordingly, let me characterize the prevailing way of determining the historical and religious matrix of texts, and then proceed to explain my alternate mode for answering the question of what is to be learned, from within a piece of writing, about the religious world beyond.

---

[2]That is why people can still read Urbach or Moore or Sanders as though we learned anything of historical and not merely ad hoc exegetical interest from their compilations of sayings under their various rubrics. In this regard Urbach's various asides are quite interesting, even though not a single account of the history and context of an idea can stand; and the straight historical chapters – e.g., on the social role of sages, on the life of Hillel, on the history of the time – are not only intellectually vulgar, they are a travesty of scholarship, even for the time and within the premises in which they were written.

In historical study, we gain access to no knowledge a priori. All facts derive from sources correctly situated, for example, classified, comprehensively and completely described, dispassionately analyzed, and evaluated. Nothing can be taken for granted. What we cannot show, we do not know. These simple dogmas of all historical learning derive not from this writer but go back to the very beginnings of Western critical historical scholarship, to the age of the Renaissance. But all historical and religious-historical scholarship on the documents of the Judaism of the Dual Torah in its formative age, except for mine and for that of a very few others, ignores the canons of criticism that govern academic scholarship. Everyone in the past and many even now take for granted that pretty much everything they read is true – except what they decide is not true.

Since colleagues in other areas of the study of religion will naturally find implausible my description of the intellectually primitive character of the use of Rabbinic writings for history and history of religions, I have to provide compelling evidence that I have not exaggerated the state of affairs. So let me spell out, in terms of a concrete case, the sort of controversy that is precipitated when, in the field of the study of Judaism, the settled principles of critical historical method are introduced. My example takes the form of a narrative of an incident of the suppression of critical debate in Jerusalem. Ten years ago, in 1983, I got an invitation to address the Historical Society of Israel on the occasion of its fiftieth anniversary celebration of its journal, *Ziyyon* (Zion). A month later, I got myself disinvited. That fact tells us all we need to know about academic freedom in Jewish Studies in the State of Israel: you're free to say what they want you to say, but nothing else. Unfortunately, raised in the American tradition of academic freedom, I didn't know the rules. In our academic community the task of learning is criticism; our tradition comes to us from the French Enlightenment and the German tradition of objective science (*Wissenschaft*) and the British tradition of pragmatism and insistence on hard evidence. But what defines the American academic tradition is the powerful commitment to freedom of speech, expression, and thought.

Let me digress a moment to explain why the Israel Historical Society thought it quite proper to do what elsewhere is deemed utterly disreputable. The reason derives from the foundations of the secular, academic study of Judaism in the Israeli academy. Specifically, there is a reason that Judaic studies in Israeli universities do not share that commitment. In the humanities and particularly the Judaic humanities, Israel's academic tradition, such as it is, draws on two sources, one imperfectly understood, the other, alas, a wraithlike presence. The founders of Israeli university studies of Judaism come from the tradition of *Wissenschaft des Judentums,* that is, "the science of Judaism." When called upon to found universities, first in Jerusalem, then elsewhere, they took as their model the only universities they knew, the German ones. The other tradition of Jewish learning, the Yeshiva one, they knew equally superficially: violent argument and the ritual conflict of personalities; but they did not grasp what was at stake at all.

So they formed out of the German and Yeshiva traditions an academy of their own. The latter they aped in its appalling manners. The former defined their professional self-image. The authentic professor would then be an inflated, self-important brute. The reason is that, never having been professors, they imitated what they remembered of the professors of their youth: the pomposity, the union of high self-esteem and (correspondingly) modest solid achievement, the overweening demand of entitlement, confusion of the power of sustained thought and political preferment. Immature students in general see the externals: they perceive professors as powerful, and reduce power to politics and personalities. That memory of Germany formed the first generation of Israel Herr Professor Doktors and accounts for the character of Israeli universities in this field: unproductive, politicized, obsessed with gossip about personalities.

Consequently, when called upon to create a university field of Jewish learning for the nascent Jewish state, the founders, moving out of their high-school teaching positions (Yehezqel Kaufman), or the post offices (Ephraim Urbach), or the stores, or the synagogues and yeshivas, where they had earned their livings, had no authentic academic model. But they did have a spurious one: their own memories of yeshivas, where by definition they were undistinguished, having apostatized; and the German universities, where they were outsiders. So what they remembered was, run things your own way, conduct scholarship as a blood sport, suppress what you cannot control, boycott whom you cannot subvert or surpass, and exercise the thought control that threat effects.

When the Israel Historical Society asked me for a keynote address on "method in Talmudic history," I accepted. This was, after all, an academic society, which published a reputable journal. True, the journal is dull and its articles mere displays of information, hardly at the frontiers of learning. But, on the other hand, the then president was someone I knew and (mistakenly) trusted as an authentic and honorable scholar, Menahem Stern. I accepted the invitation. Since I planned to speak in English, I also agreed to send a copy of the lecture some months in advance, for translation into Hebrew. The paper was scheduled for July 2, 1984. The invitation came in late autumn; I mailed the paper to Jerusalem on January 27, 1984. In those days an exchange of letters took about a month. A letter dated March 5, 1984, disinvited me, no reason given; the disinvitation came by what amounted to return mail. When I complained to Stern, then president, he did not answer my letter, though he had been my guest at Brown University only a year earlier.

The excerpt given presently explains what was at stake. As readers will see, there I patiently spell out precisely why their work in the field is gullible and therefore unscholarly: they believe everything they read, except what they decide they don't believe: no method, no system, no criticism. Now I cannot say I blame the Israelis in my field for not liking the message that everything they have done in the field they call "Talmudic history" is historically worthless. I did not imagine I would get a medal for telling them that they were not up to the state of the art. I paid the Israel Historical Society the high, but in the USA and Europe, quite routine, compliment of believing it was a professional and academic body, not a theological cabal of sectarians and know–nothings. It simply did not occur to me that, in exchange for the honor of the invitation, I was supposed to bring to Jerusalem the pretense that one can negotiate serious difference on fundamental questions of method. These are not political questions and they are not subject to negotiation, only evidence, argument, analysis, sustained and hard work of trying things one way rather than some other. Here is an excerpt from the lecture the Israel Historical Society refused to hear. Should I have been disinvited? Readers will judge for themselves.

Methodology in Talmudic History

When we speak of methodology, we may mean many things. To specify the very few things under discussion here, let us begin with the simplest possible definition. The method by which we work tells us the questions we choose to pose and the means we use to find the answers. Our method tells us what we want to know and how we can find it out. Method then testifies to the point at which we begin, the purpose for which we work. A sound method will guide us to questions both pertinent to the sources under study and also relevant to broader issues of the day. The one without the other is merely formal, on the one side, or impressionistic and journalistic, on the other. Proper method will tell us what sources we must read and how to interpret them. Above all, sound method will match the issues we raise to the information at hand, that is, will attend especially to questions of historical epistemology: *what we know and how we know it.*

We cannot raise in the abstract the issues of historical methodology in Talmudic history. Talmudic history is a field that people practice. We cannot ignore what people actually do in favor of some preferred theory of what we think they should do. It furthermore would defy the honorable occasion at hand, to speak about Talmudic history without paying appropriate attention to the journal we celebrate here and now. Accordingly, let us first of all turn our attention to *Zion* itself and ask how Talmudic history is practiced in its pages: the methodology demonstrated here.

The answer is in three parts. First, Talmudic history constitutes a strikingly unimportant field in *Zion*. From 1935 (Vol. 1) to 1983 (Vol. 48), the journal published 476 articles, at the rate of approximately 10 per volume. Of these, no more than 28 in all fall into the category of Talmudic history, approximately one article for every two volumes. Talmudic history accounts, in all, for little more than 5 percent of all articles published in the 50 years we celebrate – a strikingly small proportion. Yet, in fact, these figures overstate the importance accorded to Talmudic history in the journal. How so? Of the 28 articles at hand, seven deal with Second Temple times, using rabbinic literature for the treatment of the period before 70 (five of the seven by Y. Baer, as a matter of fact). Now since a vast range of sources, outside of the Talmud, pertain to the period before 70, and since the bulk of the Talmudic writings do not speak of that period, we can hardly concur that that period falls into Talmudic history at all. Strictly speaking, Talmudic history encompasses the period from the second century A.D. onward. Accordingly, when we ask how many articles in *Zion* dealt with problems on which the Talmuds and related documents provide first-hand evidence, rather than merely referring to things that happened long ago of which the authors have no direct knowledge of their own, and on which (by definition) the Talmuds constitute the principal corpus of evidence, the figures change. Specifically, only 21 of the 476 articles – 4 percent of the total, at the rate of somewhat less than one article every two years attend to the field at hand. So we see in a rather dramatic way that Talmudic history – the history of the Jewish people in its formative centuries beyond 70 and up to the rise of Islam – enjoys little attention in *Zion*. I need hardly add that were we to examine other scholarly journals in this country [*viz.*, the State of Israel, where the paper was supposed to be presented] and overseas, the proportions might change somewhat, but the picture would emerge pretty much the same.

The second and third observations about the status and methodology of Talmudic history in *Zion* require less exposition. The second is that when people practice Talmudic history in *Zion*, they limit their discussion to Talmudic history in particular. The field does not encompass its period, but only one set of sources emergent from its period. While many of the scholars represented in *Zion* draw upon *sources* outside the Talmud, none of the articles deals with a *problem* outside the Talmud. Accordingly, Talmudic history in the journal at hand finds definition as the study of historical problems pertinent to a given *source*, rather than to a chronological *period* to which that source attests. (In this regard, Baer's articles form an exception to the rule.) It follows that Talmudic history severely limits itself, in *Zion*, to literary evidence. While, once again, we may find allusion to archaeological data, no article in the past half-century has entered the category of inquiry in which archeology, as much as literature, defines the problem or contributes to its solution.

The third observation is that the methodology of reading the literary sources, which define the problems and solutions of Talmudic history in *Zion*, begins in an assumption universally adopted by the scholars of the journal (and not only there). Whatever the Talmud says happened happened. If the Talmud attributes something to a rabbi, he really said it. If the Talmud maintains that a rabbi did something, he really did it. So among the 21 articles under discussion, I find not a single one that asks the basic critical questions with which historical study normally commences: How does the writer of this source know what he tells me? How do I know that he is right? On the contrary, the two Talmuds serve, in *Zion*, as encyclopedias of facts about rabbis and other Jews in the Land of Israel and Babylonia. The task of the historian is to mine the encyclopedias and come up with important observations on the basis of the facts at hand. The work of the historian then is the collection and arrangement of facts, the analysis of facts, the synthesis of facts. It is not in the inquiry into the source and character of the facts at hand. Just as, for the literary scholar, the text constitutes the starting point of inquiry, so for the historian, the text at hand defines the facts and dictates the character of inquiry upon them. This is the case, beginning and end, from Allon to Kimelman.

Whether it is G. Alon, telling us what Yohanan ben Zakkai meant in his conversation with Vespasian in August 70, on the assumption that Vespasian and Yohanan were attended by secretaries who wrote down their every word, or whether it is Kimelman, telling us about the politics of the priesthood and exilarchate as reported by a story in Yerushalmi Shabbat 12:3, the method is the same. Now I hasten to add that the prevailing assumption need not deprive of all interest and value a given study in *Zion*. For instance, where the meaning of a story is subject to interpretation, without attention to whether or not the story took place, the article stands on its own, as in the case of Wasserstein on Gamaliel and Proclus and Israi on Abbahu's saying. Again, when the author deals with events on which the Talmud by definition constitutes a primary source, as in the case of Goodblatt's study of the Babylonian Yeshivot, we deal with a very high level of critical acumen. But the bulk of the articles could not have been written in the way that they were written had the authors first of all taken up the critical program of contemporary historical scholarship....

Now I focus discussion on the concrete errors that render useless for historical purposes nearly all work on the Talmud, with the two exceptions specified earlier, namely, interpretation of Talmudic texts in historical context...and study of Talmudic institutions in historical reality....The bulk of the articles in *Zion*, as well as elsewhere, have taken for granted that the numerous specific stories concerning what given rabbis and other Jews actually said and did under specific circumstances – on a given day, at a given place, in a given setting – tell us *exactly the way things were*. I speak, then, of a species of the genus, fundamentalism.

The philological fundamentalists have generally supposed that once we have established a correct text of a rabbinic work and properly interpreted its language, we then know a set of historical facts. The facticity will be proportionately greater the earlier the manuscript and the better its condition. These suppositions are correct. But these facts will concern *only* what the compiler of the text wished to tell us.

Whether or not the original text was veracious is to be settled neither by textual criticism nor by philological research, valuable though both of these ancillary sciences are for the historical inquiry.

The fundamentalists further suppose that any story, whether occurring early or late in the corpus of rabbinic literature, may well contain valuable information, handed on orally from generation to generation, until it was finally written down. I cannot accept the unexamined opinion held in rabbinical circles, both scholarly and traditional, that all rabbinical material was somehow sent floating into the air, if not by Moses, then by someone in remote antiquity (the Men of the Great Assembly, the generation of Yavneh); that it then remained universally available until some authority snatched it down from on high, placed his name on it, and so made it a named tradition and introduced it into the perilous processes of transmission. By this thesis nothing is older than anything else: "there is neither earlier nor later in the Torah."

...the primary conviction of fundamentalism is that the story supplies an accurate account of what actually happened. It is difficult to argue with that conviction. A study of rabbinic sources will provide little, if any, evidence that we have eyewitness accounts of great events or stenographic records of what people actually said. On the contrary, it is anachronistic to suppose the Talmudic rabbis cared to supply such information to begin with. Since they did not, and since they asserted that people had said things of which they had no sure knowledge, we are led to wonder about the pseudepigraphic mentality. By the time we hear about a speech or an event, it has already been reshaped for the purpose of transmission in the traditions. It is rarely possible to know just what, if anything, originally was said or done. Sometimes we have an obvious gloss, which tells us the tradition originated before the time the glossator made his addition. But knowing that a tradition was shaped within half a century of the life of the man to whom it was attributed helps only a little bit. It is very difficult to build a bridge from the tradition to the event, still more difficult to cross that bridge. The fact is that the entire Babylonian Talmud is a completely accurate record of the history of those who are responsible for it. But the specification of those people, the recognition of the viewpoint of a particular group, place, and time to which the Talmud's various facts pertain – these remain the fundamental task still facing us....

This excerpt conveys the flavor of the lecture. I thought it moderate and civil, if uncompromising and vigorous. I cannot find a word that I should today revise, and I cannot identify a line that is not today still a propos to Israeli (and American Rabbinical School) scholarship in the study of ancient Judaism.

In retrospect I realize, that refusal to listen and debate, which I could never have anticipated, formed a high compliment indeed: they really got the message and could not think of a reply other than suppression. Among the many honors that have come my way, with more than a dozen honorary degrees and academic medals, I have to regard the one conferred in its rather brutal manner by the Israel Historical Society to be the highest award of all. What they stated in reply to my lecture is, they had no reply to make, so therefore they had to suppress my lecture and boycott me. In the academy, then and now, campaigns of character assassination and demonization, ostentatious "ignoring," boycott and conspiracy – these form the defense of the know-nothings. What they attest is the power of ideas, the priority of rationality, and the preferment accorded, in the end, solely to solid achievement. Absent these, you disinvite. The disinvitation confessed that the Jerusalem "school" in "Jewish history" could not cope.

The pertinence of this illustration derives from a single unfortunate fact. Nothing said in this (suppressed) speech has lost its pertinence today. Israeli "scholarship" in this field persists in its capricious and wholly uncritical use of fables for history. Overseas reviews of books written in the Jerusalem fashion patiently instruct the Israelis in the rules of critical learning – of the nineteenth century. In the world at large, in this field, Israeli scholarship enjoys no hearing, let alone imitation and influence. Protected by high walls of political protection, it thrives in a ghetto of its own making.

Let me now generalize on the case at hand. Those who today claim to write history on the basis of the ancient rabbinic writings cannot and do not raise the question of whether an authorship knows what it is talking about, and they do not address the issue of the purpose of a text: historical or imaginative, for example. For them the issue always is history, namely, what really happened, and that issue was settled, so to speak, at Sinai: it is all true (except, on an episodic basis, what is not true, which the scholars somehow know instinctively). They exhibit the credulity characteristic of the believers, which in the circle of piety is called faith, and rightly so, but in the center of academic learning is mere gullibility. The fundamentalists in the Talmudic academies and rabbinical seminaries and Israeli universities take not only as fact but at face value everything in the holy books. "Judaism" is special and need not undergo description, analysis, and interpretation in accord with a shared and public canon of rules of criticism. "We all know" how to do the work, and "we" do not have to explain to "outsiders" either what the work is or why it is important. It is a self-evidently important enterprise in the rehearsal of information. Knowing these things the way "we" know them explains the value of knowing these things.

Scholarship formed on the premise that the sources' stories are to be believed at face value does not say so; rather, it frames questions that implicitly affirm the accuracy of the holy books, asking questions, for example, that can only be answered in the assumption that the inerrant Scriptures contain the answers – therefore, as a matter of process, do not err. By extension holy books that tell stories produce history through the paraphrase of stories into historical language: this is what happened, this is how it happened, and here are the reasons why it happened. If the Talmud says someone said something, he really said it, then and there. That premise moreover dictates their scholarly program, for it permits these faithful scholars to describe, analyze, and interpret events or ideas held in the time in which that person lived. Some of these would deny the charge, and all of them would surely point, in their writing, to evidence of a critical approach. But the premise remains the old gullibility. Specifically, the questions they frame to begin with rest on the assumption that the sources respond to these questions. The assumption that, if a story refers to a second-century rabbi, then the story tells us about the second century, proves routine. And that complete reliance merely on the allegations of sayings and stories constitutes perfect faith in the facticity of fairy tales.

The operative question facing anyone who proposes to translate writing into religion, that is, accounts of "Judaism," as George F. Moore claims to give, or "The Sages," that Ephraim E. Urbach imagines he has made, or the charming, if puerile, "harmony of the sources" – all sources, from every age and venue – into a single unitary and wholly harmonistic "Judaism" that E.P. Sanders has just now presented to the world as "the book he has always wanted to write," is the historical one: How do you know exactly what was said and done, that is, the history that you claim to report about what happened long ago? Specifically, how do you know he really said it? And if you do not know that he really said it, how can you ask the questions that you ask, which have as their premise the claim that you can say what happened or did not happen?

The wrong, but commonplace, method is to assume that if a given document ascribes an opinion to a named authority the opinion actually was stated in that language by that sage. On this assumption a much richer history of an idea, not merely of the literary evidences of that idea, may be worked out without regard only to the date of the document at hand. Within this theory of evidence, we have the history of what individuals thought on a common topic. I have already set forth the reason that we cannot proceed to outline the sequence of ideas solely on the basis of the sequence of the sages to whom ideas are attributed. We simply cannot demonstrate that a given authority really said what a document assigns to him. Let me list the range of uncertainty that necessitates this fresh approach, which I have invented.

First, if the order of the documents were fully sound and the contents representative of rabbinical opinion, then the result would be a history of the advent of the idea at hand and the development and articulation of that idea in formative Judaism. We should then have a fairly reliable picture of ideas at hand as these unfolded in orderly sequence. But we do not know that the canonical history corresponds to the actual history of ideas. Furthermore, we cannot even be sure that the order of documents presently assumed in scholarly convention is correct. Second, if a rabbi really spoke the words attributed to him, then a given idea would have reached expression within Judaism *prior* to the redaction of the document. Dividing things up by documents will tend to give a later date and thus a different context for interpretation to opinions held earlier than we can presently demonstrate. Third, although we are focusing upon the literature produced by a particular group, again we have no clear notion of what people were thinking outside of that group. We therefore do not know how opinions held by other groups or by the Jewish people in general came to shape the vision of rabbis. When, for example, we note that there also existed poetic literature and translations of Scriptures characteristic of the synagogue worship, we cannot determine whether the poetry and most translations spoke for rabbis or for some quite different group.

For these reasons I have chosen to address the contextual question within the narrow limits of the canon. That accounts for my formulation of the episteme as "the canonical history of ideas," and explains, also, why I have carefully avoided claiming that a given idea was broadly held only at a given time and place. All I allege is that a given document underscores the presence of an idea for that authorship – that alone. Obviously, if I could in a given formulation relate the appearance of a given idea to events affecting rabbis in particular or to the life of Israel in general, the results would be exceedingly suggestive. But since we do not know for whom the documents speak, how broadly representative they are, or even how comprehensive is their evidence about rabbis' views, we must carefully define what we do and do not know. So for this early stage in research the context in which a given idea is described, analyzed, and interpreted is the canon. But this first step alone carries us to new territory. I hope that in due course others will move beyond the limits which, at the moment, seem to me to mark the farthest possible advance. Now let us turn to the specific case meant to illustrate the method.

Let me now explain in some greater detail the alternative, which I call the documentary history of ideas. It is a mode of relating writing to religion through history through close attention to the circumstance in which writing reached closure. It is accomplished, specifically, by assessing shifts exhibited by a sequence of documents and appealing to the generally accepted dates assigned to writings in explaining those shifts. In this way I propose to confront questions of cultural order, social system, and political structure, to which the texts respond explicitly and constantly. Confronting writings of a religious character, we err by asking questions of a narrowly historical character: what did X really say on a particular occasion, and why. These questions not only are not answerable on the basis of the evidence in hand. They also are trivial, irrelevant to the character of the evidence. What strikes me as I review the writings just now cited is how little of real interest and worth we should know, even if we were to concede the historical accuracy and veracity of all the many allegations of the scholars we have surveyed. How little we should know – but how much we should have *missed* if that set of questions and answers were to encompass the whole of our inquiry.

If we are to trace the unfolding, in the sources of formative Judaism, of a given theme or ideas on a given problem, the order in which we approach the several books, that is, components of the entire canon, gives us the sole guidance on sequence, order, and context, that we are apt to find. As is clear, we have no way of demonstrating that authorities to whom, in a given composition, ideas are attributed really said what is assigned to them. The sole fact in hand therefore is that the framers of a given document included in their compilation sayings imputed to named authorities. Are these dependable? Unlikely on the face of it. Why not? Since the same sayings will be imputed to diverse authorities by different groups of editors, of different books, we stand on shaky ground indeed if we rely for chronology upon the framers' claims of who said what. More important, attributions by themselves cannot be shown to be reliable. And, it goes without saying, assuming without corroboration that we have *ipsissima verba* merely because a saying is attached to a name simply contradicts the basic premises of all contemporary historical scholarship.

What we cannot show we do not know.[3] Lacking firm evidence, for example, in a sage's own, clearly assigned writings, or even in writings redacted by a sage's own disciples and handed on among them in the discipline of their own community, we have for chronology only a single fact. It is that a document, reaching closure at a given time, contains the allegation that Rabbi X said statement Y. So we know that people at the time the document reached closure took the view that Rabbi X said statement Y. We may then assign to statement Y a position, in the order of the sequence of sayings, defined by the location of the document in the order of the sequence of documents. The several documents' dates, as is clear, all constitute guesses. But the sequence explained in the prologue, Mishnah, Tosefta, Yerushalmi, Bavli for the exegetical writings on the

---

[3]See now *What We Cannot Show, We Do Not Know: Rabbinic Literature and the New Testament* (Philadelphia, 1993: Trinity Press International), and *Judaic Law from Jesus to the Mishnah. A Systematic Reply to Professor E.P. Sanders* (Atlanta, 1993: Scholars Press for South Florida Studies in the History of Judaism).

Mishnah is absolutely firm and beyond doubt. The sequence for the exegetical collections on Scripture Sifra, the Sifrés, Genesis Rabbah, Leviticus Rabbah, the Pesiqtas and beyond is not entirely sure. Still the position of the Sifra and the two Sifrés at the head, followed by Genesis Rabbah, then Leviticus Rabbah, then Pesiqta deRab Kahana and Lamentations Rabbati and some related collections, seems likely.

What are the canonical main beams that sustain the history of ideas as I propose to trace that history? Three principal periods presently delineate the canonical sequence: the Mishnah's, in the first two centuries; the Yerushalmi's, in the next, ca. 200-400; and the Bavli's, in the third, ca. 400-600. The formative age of Judaism is the period marked at the outset by the Mishnah, taking shape from sometime before the Common Era and reaching closure at ca. 200 C.E., and at the end by the Talmud of Babylonia, ca. 600 C.E. In between these dates, two streams of writings developed, one legal, explaining the meaning of the Mishnah, the other theological and exegetical, interpreting the sense of Scripture. The high points of the former come with tractate Abot, which is the Mishnah's first apologetic, the Tosefta, a collection of supplements ca. 300 C.E., the Talmud of the Land of Israel ca. 400 C.E., followed by the Babylonian Talmud. The latter set of writings comprise compositions on Exodus, in Mekilta attributed to R. Ishmael and of indeterminate date, Sifra on Leviticus, Sifré on Numbers, and another Sifré, on Deuteronomy at a guess to be dated at ca. 300 C.E., then Genesis Rabbah ca. 400 C.E., Leviticus Rabbah ca. 425 C.E., and at the end, Pesiqta deRab Kahana, Lamentations Rabbati, and some other treatments of biblical books, all of them in the fifth or sixth centuries. The so-called Tannaitic Midrashim, Mekhilta, Sifra, the two Sifrés, form transitional documents, between the Mishnah and the Yerushalmi and its Midrash companions, Genesis Rabbah, Leviticus Rabbah, and Pesiqta deRab Kahana. Alongside the Bavli are its Midrash associates, Lamentations Rabbah, Song of Songs Rabbah, Esther Rabbah I, and Ruth Rabbah. These books and some minor related items together form the canon of Judaism as it had reached its definitive shape by the end of late antiquity.

If we lay out these writings in the approximate sequence in which – according to the prevailing consensus – they reached closure beginning with the Mishnah, the Tosefta, then Sifra and its associated compositions, followed by the Talmud of the Land of Israel, and alongside Genesis Rabbah and Leviticus Rabbah, then Pesiqta deRab Kahana and its companions, and finally the Talmud of Babylonia, we gain what I call "canonical history." This is, specifically, the order of the appearance of ideas when the documents, read in the outlined sequence, address a given idea or topic. The consequent history consists of the sequence in which a given statement on the topic at hand was made (early, middle, or late) in the unfolding of the canonical writings. To illustrate the process, what does the authorship of the Mishnah have to say on the theme? Then how does the compositor of Abot deal with it? Then the Tosefta's compositor's record comes into view, followed by the materials assembled in the Talmud of the Land of Israel, alongside those now found in the earlier and middle ranges of compilations of scriptural exegeses, and as always, the Talmud of Babylonia at the end. The results, for the history of ideas, of the documentary method are set forth in various monographs of mine, and now are fully put together into a single account as well.[4]

So, in sum, this story of continuity and change rests upon the notion that we can present the history of the treatment of a topical program in the canonical writings of that Judaism. I do not claim that the documents represent the state of popular or synagogue opinion. I do not know whether the history of the idea in the unfolding official texts corresponds to the history of the idea among the people who stand behind those documents. Even less do I claim to speak about the history of the topic or idea at hand outside of rabbinical circles, among the Jewish nation at large. All these larger dimensions of the matter lie wholly beyond the perspective of this book. The reason is that the evidence at hand is of a particular sort and hence permits us to investigate one category of questions and not another. The category is defined by established and universally held conventions about the order in which the canonical writings reached completion. Therefore we trace the way in which matters emerge in the sequence of writings followed here.

We trace the way in which ideas were taken up and spelled out in these successive stages in the formation of the canon. Let the purpose of the exercise be emphasized. *When we follow this procedure, we discover how, within the formation of the rabbinical canon of writings, the idea at hand came to literary expression and how it was then shaped to serve the larger purposes of the nascent canonical system as a whole.*

That exercise then defines the first task in trying to understand the relationship between the history of the ideas of a Judaism and the social history of that same Judaism in late antiquity. By knowing the place and uses of the topic under study within the literary evidences of the

---

[4] Two such monographs are *Judaism and Its Social Metaphors. Israel in the History of Jewish Thought* and *The Incarnation of God: The Character of Divinity in Formative Judaism,* cited above. My summaries of the documents as a whole and the history of Judaism are in my Doubleday Anchor Research Library volumes, *Introduction to Rabbinic Literature* (New York, 1994) and *Introduction to Rabbinic Judaism* (New York, 1995). I mean the latter to answer the same question as does Moore's *Judaism,* Urbach's *The Sages,* Sanders's *Paul and Palestinian Judaism* and his *Judaism. 63 B.C.E. – 67 C.E.,* respectively.

rabbinical system, we gain a better understanding of the formative history of that system. What do we not learn? Neither the condition of the people at large nor the full range and power of the rabbinical thinkers' imagination comes to the fore. About other larger historical and intellectual matters we have no direct knowledge at all. Consequently we claim to report only what we learn about the canonical literature of a system evidenced by a limited factual base. No one who wants to know the history of a given idea in all the diverse Judaisms of late antiquity, or the role of that idea in the history of all the Jews in all parts of the world in the first seven centuries of the Common Era will find it here.

In order to understand the documentary method we must again underline the social and political character of the documentary evidence presented. These are public statements, preserved and handed on because people have adopted them as authoritative. The sources constitute a collective, and therefore official, literature. All of the documents took shape and attained a place in the canon of the rabbinical movement as a whole. None was written by an individual in such a way as to testify to personal choice or decision. Accordingly, we cannot provide an account of the theory of a given individual at a particular time and place. We have numerous references to what a given individual said about the topic at hand. But these references do not reach us in the authorship of that person, or even in his language. They come to us only in the setting of a *collection* of sayings and statements, some associated with names, other unattributed and anonymous. The collections by definition were composed under the auspices of rabbinical authority – a school or a circle. They tell us what a group of people wished to preserve and hand on as authoritative doctrine about the meaning of the Mishnah and Scripture. The compositions reach us because the larger rabbinical estate chose to copy and hand them on. Accordingly, we know the state of doctrine at the stages marked by the formation and closure of the several documents.

We follow what references we find to a topic in accord with the order of documents just now spelled out. In this study we learn the order in which ideas came to expression in the canon. We begin any survey with the Mishnah, the starting point of the canon. We proceed systematically to work our way through tractate Abot, the Mishnah's first apologetic, then the Tosefta, the Yerushalmi, and the Bavli at the end. In a single encompassing sweep, we finally deal with the entirety of the compilations of the exegeses of Scripture, arranged, to be sure, in that order that I have now explained. Let me expand on the matter of my heavy emphasis on the order of the components of the canon. The reason for that stress is simple. We have to ask not only what documents viewed whole and all at once ("Judaism") tell us about our theme. In tracing the order in which ideas make their appearance, we ask about the components in sequence ("history of Judaism") so far as we can trace the sequence. Then and only then shall we have access to issues of *history*, that is, of change and development. If our theme makes its appearance early on in one form, so one set of ideas predominate in a document that reached closure in the beginnings of the cannon and then that theme drops out of public discourse or undergoes radical revision in writings in later stages of the canon, that fact may make considerable difference. Specifically, we may find it possible to speculate on where, and why a given approach proved urgent, and also on the reasons that that same approach receded from the center of interest.

In knowing the approximate sequence of documents and therefore the ideas in them (at least so far as the final point at which those ideas reached formal expression in the canon), a second possibility emerges. What if – as is the case – we find pretty much the same views, treated in the same proportion and for the same purpose, yielding the same message, early, middle, and late in the development of the canon? Then we shall have to ask why the literature remains so remarkably constant. Given the considerable shifts in the social and political condition of Israel in the Land of Israel as well as in Babylonia over a period of more than four hundred years, that evident stability in the teachings for the affective life will constitute a considerable fact for analysis and interpretation. History, including the history of religion, done rightly thus produces two possibilities, both of them demanding sustained attention. Things change. Why? Things do not change. Why not? We may well trace the relationship between the history of ideas and the history of the society that holds those same ideas. We follow the interplay between society and system – worldview, way of life, addressed to a particular social group – by developing a theory of the relationship between contents and context, between the world in which people live and the world which people create in their shared social and imaginative life. When we can frame a theory of how a system in substance relates to its setting, of the interplay between the social matrix and the mode and manner of a society's worldview and way of life, then we may develop theses of general intelligibility, theories of why this, not that, of why, and why not and how come.

The story of continuity and change rests upon the notion that we can present the history of the treatment of a topical program in the canonical writings of that Judaism. I do not claim that the documents represent the state of popular or synagogue opinion. I do not know whether the history of the idea in the unfolding official texts corresponds to the history of the idea among the people who stand behind those documents. Even less do I claim to speak about the history of the topic or idea at hand outside of rabbinical circles, among the Jewish nation at large. All these larger dimensions of the matter lie wholly beyond the perspective of this book. The reason is that the evidence at hand is of a particular sort and hence permits us to investigate one category of questions and not another. The category is defined by established and universally held conventions about the order in which the canonical writings reached completion. Therefore we trace the way in which matters emerge in the sequence of writings followed here. We trace the way in which ideas were taken up and spelled out in these successive stages in the formation of the canon. When we follow this procedure, we discover how, within the formation of the rabbinical canon of writings, the idea at hand came to literary expression and how it was then shaped to serve the larger purposes of the nascent canonical system as a whole.

What do I conceive to be at stake in the documentary history of Judaism? It is to set forth the history of the formation of Judaism, as the canonical writings of late antiquity allow us to trace that history. Let me explain. Between 200 and 400 Judaism changed from a philosophy to a religion. In current work I explain the meaning of that simple sentence, starting with the subject, Judaism.[5] Defining the word Judaism in this

---

[5]The monographic foundations for this account of the transformation of the Judaic system from philosophy to religion are complete:

A History of the Mishnaic Law of Purities (Leiden, 1977: E.J. Brill), XXI. *The Redaction and Formulation of the Order of Purities in the Mishnah and Tosefta.*

A History of the Mishnaic Law of Purities (Leiden, 1977: E.J. Brill), XXII. *The Mishnaic System of Uncleanness. Its Context and History.*

The Mishnah before 70 (Atlanta, 1987: Scholars Press for Brown Judaic Studies). [Reprise of pertinent results of *A History of the Mishnah Law of Purities*, vols. III, V, VIII, X, XII, XIV, XVI, XVII, and XVIII.]

A History of the Mishnaic Law of Holy Things (Leiden, 1979: E.J. Brill), VI. *The Mishnaic System of Sacrifice and Sanctuary.*

A History of the Mishnaic Law of Women (Leiden, 1980: E.J. Brill), V. *The Mishnaic System of Women.*

A History of the Mishnaic Law of Appointed Times (Leiden, 1981: E.J. Brill), V. *The Mishnaic System of Appointed Times.*

A History of the Mishnaic Law of Damages (Leiden, 1985: E.J. Brill), V. *The Mishnaic System of Damages.*

Uniting the Dual Torah: Sifra and the Problem of the Mishnah (Cambridge and New York, 1989: Cambridge University Press).

Judaism. The Evidence of the Mishnah (Chicago, 1981: University of Chicago Press).

The Making of the Mind of Judaism (Atlanta, 1987: Scholars Press for Brown Judaic Studies).

The Economics of the Mishnah (Chicago, 1989: University of Chicago Press).

The Formation of the Jewish Intellect. Making Connections and Drawing Conclusions in the Traditional System of Judaism (Atlanta, 1988: Scholars Press for Brown Judaic Studies).

The Mishnah. An Introduction (Northvale, New Jersey, 1989: Jason Aronson, Inc.).

context involves the understanding of a religion as an account of a system of the social order formed (whether in fact or in imagination) by the believers, an account portrayed in writing. The problem I address concerns the transformation by continuator documents of a Judaic system of the social order, fully set forth in its initial document. That problem therefore directs attention to systemic description, analysis, and interpretation of documentary evidence, for by comparing one set of writings with another I compare one system to another. This work is carried out in my *Transformation of Judaism. From Philosophy to Religion.*[6]

Since the word "system" occurs throughout my account of the formation of Judaism, let me define it. Writings that are read all together, such as those of the unfolding canon of Judaism in late antiquity, are deemed to make a cogent and important statement. I call that encompassing, canonical picture a "system," when it is composed of three necessary components: an account of a worldview, a prescription of a corresponding way of life, and a definition of the social entity that finds definition in the one and description in the other. When those three fundamental components fit together, they sustain one another in explaining the whole of a social order, hence constituting the theoretical account of a system.

Systems defined in this way work out a cogent picture, for those who make them up, of *how* things are correctly to be sorted out and fitted together, of *why* things are done in one way, rather than in some other, and of *who* they are that do and understand matters in this particular way. When, as is commonly the case, people invoke God as the foundation for their worldview, maintaining that their way of life corresponds to what God wants of them, projecting their social entity in a particular relationship to God, then we have a religious system. When, finally, a religious system appeals as an important part of its

---

The Politics of the Mishnah. The Initial Structure and System, submitted to University of Chicago Press. Sixth draft to be filed: 7.1.89.

The Philosophical Mishnah. I. The Initial Probe (Atlanta, 1989: Scholars Press for Brown Judaic Studies).

The Philosophical Mishnah. II. The Tractates' Agenda. From Abodah Zarah to Moed Qatan (Atlanta, 1989: Scholars Press for Brown Judaic Studies).

The Philosophical Mishnah. III. The Tractates' Agenda. From Nazir to Zebahim (Atlanta, 1989: Scholars Press for Brown Judaic Studies).

The Philosophical Mishnah. IV. The Repertoire (Atlanta, 1989: Scholars Press for Brown Judaic Studies).

The Philosophy of Judaism. The First Principles, under consideration by Johns Hopkins University Press and University of Illinois Press.

From Literature to Theology in Formative Judaism. Three Preliminary Studies (Atlanta, 1989: Scholars Press for Brown Judaic Studies).

[6](Champaign-Urbana, 1992: University of Illinois Press).

authoritative literature or canon to the Hebrew Scriptures of ancient Israel or "Old Testament, we have a Judaism.

Let me specify what I conceive to be at stake in this approach to the reading of the formation of the Judaism of the Dual Torah. I am trying to find out how to describe that "Judaism" beyond the specific texts, moving beyond the text and the context and toward the matrix of all of the canonical texts. What is it that each document takes for granted but no document spells out? To answer that question I have to describe the processes of category formation, to specify the categorical imperative in the description of a Judaism. That accounts for the focus on the re-formation of received categories and the formation of new ones, wholly congruent to the received ones but also entirely fresh, as well.

The categories that I bring to the study are those of the social order: philosophy or science, politics, and economics. These correspond to worldview, theory of the social entity, and way of life, or ethos, ethnos, and ethics. The reason it is legitimate to describe the categorical unfolding of Judaism within the categories of political economy is simple. The Mishnah, the foundation document, after Scripture, of the canonical corpus we study here, in point of fact sets forth a full account of the social order, to which philosophy, politics, and economics are integral, just as philosophy, politics, and economics are integral to the social order conceived by Greco-Roman philosophy in the tradition of Aristotle. These deal with the worldview (in philosophy), the way of life (in economics), and the definition of the social entity (in politics) of the (imagined, or real) social order portrayed in documents identified as canonical.

Then at stake in systemic description is the reading of written evidence as the evidence has been combined to form an authoritative statement. Then I ask, in the analysis at hand, what happened, in the unfolding of the canon, to these categories of description of the social order, the issues of the way of life, worldview, and definition of the social entity, that all together form the social system imagined by the authors or authorships of authoritative writings? I know how to answer that question.

These three inquiries of Greco-Roman political economy, philosophy, politics, and economics set forth only the initial system of Judaism, the one to which the Mishnah attests. But that Judaism in many important ways hardly turned out wholly symmetrical with the final system of Judaism that emerged from the formative age and defined matters to the present day. The economics, politics, and philosophy of the initial formation of Judaism set the agenda and formed the court of appeal. But successors and continuators picked and chose, and, it follows, they framed a fresh definition for the social foundations of the world they proposed to invent. The philosophy, politics, and economics of the next phase in the formation of Judaism, seen on their own but also in relationship with the initial theories, will therefore demand sustained description, analysis, and interpretation. That explains why I know how the initial system was revised and adapted by later system makers. What is at stake, in all, is how intellectuals defined the rationalities of Judaism as a social composition: a theory of the society of Israel, the holy people of God.

Now to return to the definition of Judaism. By Judaism I mean a Judaic system, which is a cogent account of the social order, comprising a worldview, way of life, and theory of the social entity, "Israel," all together setting forth a response to a question deemed urgent and encompassing an answer found self-evidently valid. The Jews' long history has witnessed the formation of a variety of such Judaic systems. In the first seven centuries of the Common Era (=A.D.) one such system, the one that has predominated since that time, took shape. That is the Judaic system the transformation of which is under discussion here. I describe that system through the canonical writings produced by sages bearing the title "rabbis."

The ultimate system of Judaism itself formed during those seven centuries in three distinct stages, marked in each case by the distinctive traits of the literature that reached closure at the end of each successive stage, as I shall explain. More to the point, each stage produced a Judaic system. Formed in the first two hundred years and represented by the Mishnah and its associated writings, the first is utterly free-standing. The second, taking shape from 200 to 400 and represented by the Talmud of the Land of Israel and its companions, is connected to the first but essentially distinct from it. The third, expressed in documents that reached closure between 400 and 600 within and around the Talmud of Babylonia, is connected to the second but in important traits distinct from it as well. These three systems, autonomous when viewed synchronically but connected when seen diachronically, ultimately, at the end of their formative age, formed a single, wholly and utterly continuous structure, that one we call Judaism. But in their successive stages of autonomy, then autonomy and connection, the three distinct systems may be classified, respectively, as philosophical, religious, and theological. Judaism then took shape in a passage from a philosophical, to a religious, and finally to a theological system, each one taking over and revising the definitive categories of the former and framing its own fresh, generative categories as well. The formative history of Judaism then is the story of the presentations and re-presentations of categorical structures. In method it is the exegesis of taxonomy and taxic systems.

To begin with, then, the classification of types of systems – philosophical, religious, theological – requires explanation.

A philosophical system forms its learning inductively and syllogistically by appeal to the neutral evidence of the rules shown by the observation of the order of universally accessible nature and society.

A religious system frames its propositions deductively and exegetically by appeal to the privileged evidence of a corpus of writing deemed revealed by God.

A theological system imposes upon a religious one systematic modes of thought of philosophy, so in its message regularizing and ordering in a cogent and intellectually rigorous way the materials received from a religious system. The movement from the religious to the theological will involve the systematization and harmonization of the religious categories, their re-formation into a single tight and cogent statement. It is an initiative as radical, in its way, as the passage from the philosophical to religious formation is in its way. For the modes of thought, media of expression, and, as a matter of fact, categorical structure and system are reworked in the enterprise of turning a merely imputed order, imputed within the single heart of the faith, into a wholly public order, subject to sustained and cogent representation and expression, each component in its place and proper sequence, beginning, middle, and end. Religious conviction differs from theological proposition as do bricks and mortar from a building.

Religious and the theological systems of course work over the same issues in ways that are common to themselves and that also distinguish them jointly from philosophical ones. But the rigorous task of forming of religious attitudes and convictions a cogent composition, a system and not merely a structure of beliefs, imposes on systems of the theological sort disciplines of mind and perception, modes of thought and media of expression, quite different from those that characterize the work of making a religious system. The connection is of course intimate, for a theological system succeeding and reshaping a religious one appeals to the same sources of truth in setting forth (often identical) answers to (ordinarily) the same urgent questions. But the theological type of system is different from the religious type in fundamental ways as well, for while there can be a religious system without theological order, there can be no theological system without a religious core. So much for the distinctions among types of systems.

In the transformation of the Judaic system from philosophical to religious in its basic character, the very raw materials, the categories themselves, undergo transformation. When a philosophical becomes a religious system, the categorical change yields not the reframing or re-formation or re-presentation. What happens is rather the fundamental revaluation of categories, which I call "counterpart categories." Transvaluation and transformation – these comprise the history of religion, so far as history records connections, comparisons, and contrasts, between one thing and something else.

How do I know that these categorical transformations and reconsiderations have taken place in the systems in transition? The answer requires us to read literary evidence as testament to systemic formation. The evidence for systems of world construction, such as those with which we deal in the history of Judaism, derives from the correct description and analysis of the surviving writings of the formative age. These provide our evidence of how system builders chose to express their ideas (rhetoric), conceived that their ideas expressed cogent thought and formed intelligible statements to be shared by others (logic of cogent discourse), and formed the categories through which the facts attained sense and constituted orderly and systematic accounts of the world (topical, propositional program). All three together – the mode of discourse, the media of thought and expression, the message brought to representation through the particular rhetoric and logic at hand – prove accessible when we ask the documentary heritage of the system builders to point us toward the system expressed therein in detail. Now let me define the documentary evidence of Judaism, beginning with the Mishnah.

The evidence is canonical, because the canon recapitulates the system that animates the mentality of the framers of canonical writings and the authorities that adopted those writings for a single canonical composite. That canon in the case of the Judaism under study consisted of the Hebrew Scriptures of ancient Israel ("the Old Testament"), called in this Judaism the Written Torah, and a set of writings later on accorded the status of Torah as well and assigned origin at Sinai through a process of oral formulation and oral transmission, hence, the Oral Torah. The first of those writings comprising the Oral Torah was the Mishnah, ca. 200; this document carried in its wake two sustained amplifications and extensions called talmuds, the one produced in the Land of Israel, hence the Talmud of the Land of Israel, ca. 400, the other in Babylonia, in the Iranian Empire, hence the Talmud of Babylonia, ca. 600.

The other half of the Torah, the written part, served analogously and received a variety of sustained amplifications, called Midrash compilations. These were in three sets. The first, ca. 200-400, addressed the books of Exodus, Leviticus, Numbers, and Deuteronomy, in Mekhilta Attributed to R. Ishmael for Exodus, Sifra, for Leviticus, one Sifré to

Numbers, another Sifré to Deuteronomy.[7] The second, ca. 400-500, took up the books of Genesis and Leviticus, in Genesis Rabbah and Leviticus Rabbah, and the latter begat Pesiqta deRab Kahana in its model. The third, ca. 500-600, addressed a lectionary cycle of the synagogue, dealing with the books of Lamentations (read on the ninth of Ab), Esther (read on Purim), Ruth (read on Pentecost), and Song of Songs (read on Passover), in Lamentations Rabbah, Esther Rabbah I (the first two chapters only), Ruth Rabbah, and Song of Songs Rabbah. The first of the three groups presents marks of transition and mediation from one system to the next; the second, Genesis Rabbah and Leviticus Rabbah, together with Pesiqta deRab Kahana, form a single circle with the Talmud of the Land of Israel, and the third, the final Rabbah compilations, belong together with the Talmud of Babylonia.

The documentary evidence set forth a system of a very particular kind. I have already defined a system as a cogent account of the social order. From beginning to end, the Judaic systems defined as their problem the construction of a social world. Each, in succession, framed its categories for intelligible thought by appeal to the issues of the world framed by a particular ethnos, the social entity (the most neutral language I can find), which was called (an) "Israel," and every Judaic system would take as its task the definition of the social world of an Israel: the way of life or (broadly speaking) ethics, the worldview or ethos, and the account of the social entity or the "Israel" that realized in its shared and corporate being the ethics (again, broadly construed), and explained that ethnos by appeal to the ethos. So, as a matter of definition, a Judaic system is a system that derives its generative categories from the (theoretical) requirements of framing a social order: who are "we," what do we do together, and why are we the corporate body that we are, thus, ethnos, ethics, ethos. And that brings us back to the first of the great Judaic systems that in the end formed Judaism, the system to which the authorship of the Mishnah refer in framing their writing.

The Mishnah set forth in the form of a law code an account of the world ("worldview"), a pattern for everyday and material activities and relationships ("way of life"), and a definition of the social entity ("nation," "people," "us" as against "outsiders," "Israel") that realized

---

[7]In a separate work, *The Canonical History of Ideas. The Place of the So-called Tannaite Midrashim, Mekhilta Attributed to R. Ishmael, Sifra, Sifré to Numbers, and Sifré to Deuteronomy* (Atlanta, 1990: Scholars Press for South Florida Studies in the History of Judaism), I position the so-called Tannaitic Midrashim in relationship to the two systems, the Mishnah's and the Yerushalmi's. The results are somewhat ambiguous but suggestive.

that way of life and explained it by appeal to that worldview. Successor documents, closed two centuries later, addressed the Mishnah's system and recast its categories into a connected, but also quite revised, one. These documents attached themselves to the Mishnah, on the one side, and the Hebrew Scriptures, on the other, within the nascent theory that the one stood for the Oral, the other, the Written, revelation, or Torah, of God to Moses at Mount Sinai. The Talmud of the Land of Israel (hereinafter: the Yerushalmi, or Talmud of Jerusalem), formed around thirty-nine of the Mishnah's sixty-two tractates, and Genesis Rabbah and Leviticus Rabbah (joined by Pesiqta deRab Kahana), formed around the first and third books of Moses, respectively, along with some other documents, attest to a system that both extended and recast the categorical structure of the system for which the Mishnah stands, and also framed new categories within the same large-scale structure, involving way of life, worldview, and social entity, taken up in the Mishnah's system. The transformation of the one to the other stands for the movement from a philosophical to a religious mode of thinking. For the system to which the Mishnah as a document attests is essentially philosophical in its rhetorical, logical, and topical program; the successor system, fundamentally religious in these same principal and indicative traits of medium of intellect and mentality.

This system of the Mishnah designed the social order by an account of the principal components, a philosophy, an economics, and a politics, corresponding to worldview, way of life, and social entity. The philosophy explained how to think and identified the agenda for sustained thought and learning; the economics set forth a theory of rational action in the face of scarcity and in the increase and disposition of wealth; the politics laid out an account of precisely how power, encompassing legitimate violence, embodied in institutions and their staff, was to realize in everyday social transactions the social entity, "Israel." These categories in the successor documents, the Talmud of the Land of Israel for the Mishnah, the Midrash compilations Genesis Rabbah and Leviticus Rabbah together with Pesiqta deRab Kahana for Scripture, underwent revision, and, alongside, these same documents set forth their own categories for those served, initially, by philosophy, politics, and economics.

These general observations explain the task I propose, which is to characterize the basic traits of intellect of the system represented by the Mishnah and to compare and contrast that system with the one adumbrated by the Talmud of the Land of Israel, Genesis Rabbah, and Leviticus Rabbah with Pesiqta deRab Kahana. Our question, specifically, is simple: How shall we classify the Mishnah in its context? When we compare and contrast the Mishnah in its classification as to rhetoric and logic with the successor documents, do we find those later writings like the Mishnah or unlike it?   If like, then of course we classify those documents as we have classified the Mishnah. But if unlike, then how – as a matter of hypothesis – may we classify the system represented by the successor writings? That is the work of comparison of religions, in this case, connected but distinct religious systems within the same religion, that seems to me to yield very interesting results indeed.

6

The Dating of Sayings in Rabbinic Literature

The problem of identifying the setting to which a saying, either anonymous or assigned to a named authority, attests finds one of three solutions. The first, which presently predominates, is to accept as fact all attributions of sayings and therefore to assume that if a document's authorship presents a saying in a given sage's name, that sage really made such a statement, which therefore tells us what he, and perhaps others, were thinking in the time and place in which he lived. A corollary to this position is that a saying that bears no attribution is "earlier than" a saying that has one. Hence what is anonymous is older than what is assigned (how much older depends on the requirement of the person who assumes that fact). These two complementary positions presuppose a literary process in which sayings circulated independently of the documents in which they (later on) are written down and took shape within the circle of the disciples of a master to whom they are attributed. That position on the literary process that yields the documents that now contain these sayings has not yet been squared with the literary traits of those same documents, and, as we shall see in the case at hand, analysis of those traits scarcely sustains the hypothesis of inerrant attribution and its corollary.

The second, held *ab initio* by no one, is to treat as fact only the final date assigned to a given document by the prevailing scholarly consensus. All materials in a given compilation attest only to the mind of the authorship responsible for the compilation: selection, arrangement, and fabrication of the materials alike. That position contradicts the traits of the documents, which time and again show that editorial work independent of the requirements of a given document has taken place, for example, composites were formed of prior compositions and only then utilized in a given document.

The third, with which I identify, is to treat as a problem to be dealt with in the context of the traits and program of a document's authorship the attributions of sayings contained within that document, neither taking at face value nor rejecting out of hand all attributions. The literary analysis required to sustain that position must show that the requirements of a document do not obscure the program of framers of compositions and even sizable composites utilized in the formation of said document.

That is the position I set forth and explain, in the setting of Sifra, in what follows. Sifra is a Midrash compilation on the book of Leviticus; most of the authorities mentioned in the document are assumed to have flourished in the second century. The upshot of my analysis leads to the conclusion that, for Sifra, whatever we have attests to what the final redactors wished us to have, which is to say, the document and everything in it tell us about the viewpoint of its ultimate redactors, to which whatever the document preserves gives expression; everything beside the point of the whole is episodic, trivial, and inconsequential.[1]

The occasion for this exposition should be specified, lest readers suppose I have invented an opponent readily dismissed out of hand. In fact, this exposition responds to the somewhat puzzling position, announced in the recent past by Professor Lawrence H. Schiffman, New York University, which is to take account of the point of closure of a document while at the same time consistently treating as fact the attributions of sayings to named authorities within that document.[2] The first and second positions enjoy the advantages of consistency, believing, respectively, everything or nothing. It is the third that requires sustained exploration in the setting of each document of the rabbinic canon.[3] And

---

[1]But we cannot make that statement of other Midrash compilations. For example, my work on Mekhilta Attributed to R. Ishmael (now in progress) yields a quite different result, and that on Sifré to Deuteronomy (cited below) is hardly so decisive as the picture of Sifra. Consequently, any generalization about the literature as a whole, or the Midrash compilations in particular, is premature. I adopt the second of the three positions just now outlined for Sifra and the third of the three for Mekhilta. A full catalogue of the results of analysis of the other Midrash compilations as I have completed that analysis is not required for the present purpose.

[2]Lawrence H. Schiffman, "Neusner's *Messiah in Context*," *Jewish Quarterly Review* 1987, 72:240-243.

[3]Schiffman characterizes my position as follows: "Neusner's refusal...to deal with the fact that much in the rabbinic collections is earlier in date than the text as a whole, denies us the opportunity to reconstruct much of the historical context of the material." It is Schiffman's certainty about the specified fact that gives me

this address to Sifra allows us to evaluate the position that Schiffman announces.

1. Dating Sayings: The Issue, the Stakes

The third of the three positions outlined above, which is mine, now requires amplification. The view that documents *may* provide us with data concerning the period prior to their ultimate redaction or closure surely requires initial assent. No one can claim that, in the setting of cumulative aggregations such as the rabbinic documents of late antiquity comprise, the ultimate authorship made everything up. Quite to the contrary, we can demonstrate that a process of formulation of materials in the case of some documents went on prior to, and quite separate from, the process of formation of materials into the compositions we now have.[4] The issue is only, which documents do provide us with data about the age prior to their closure, and how are we to identify those items, within said documents, that reliably inform us about an earlier period and those that do not. In the case of the Mishnah, I found that the traits of the document made possible a fairly elaborate system of sorting out sequences of conceptions.[5] Specifically, the disciplined attribution of

pause. In my view his sole basis for assigning "material" to an earlier period is that it bears an attribution to an authority who lived earlier than the time of redaction. If there is any other reason for thinking that a document contains sizable and sustained materials that derive from and address a period prior to its own redaction, Schiffman does not indicate it; I do think that there are other reasons besides attributions for imputing to a composition within a composite an earlier date than the composite as a whole, but the particularization of a determinate place and time hardly enjoys ample warrant. In my view reliance on attributions alone or in the main requires demonstration and can scarcely form the premise of argument.

[4]I have done so in my analyses of various Midrash compilations and in a more systematic way in my *Judaism. The Classic Statement. The Evidence of the Bavli* (Chicago, 1985: University of Chicago Press).

[5]In all fairness Schiffman acknowledges that fact, op. cit., p. 241. But he does not then draw the conclusion that the same work has to be done on all the other documents; I have in fact done it on all the documents I have translated, which now encompass nearly all of the canonical writings of late antiquity, but I have not published the results in the detail in which I did for the Mishnah, since the main lines seemed to me rather obvious. Shiffman has a fair complaint that I ought to have done so in a more explicit and detailed way. As to his view that the Tannaitic Midrash are not amoraic, he seems to me to contradict the position of Heer, cited presently. I know of no academic scholarship that today assigns to any so-called Tannaitic Midrash compilation a date of redaction prior to 200 C.E. The sole basis for maintaining that these compilations derive from the period prior to the Mishnah is the attributions of sayings to authorities assumed to have lived in that time. And that brings us back to what is at stake in the present discussion.

sayings within groups of names, for example, all of a given period, proves to correspond to the logical sequences of the unfolding of problems or even conceptions on given topics. Consequently, we find some warrant, in important parts of the document, to claim that certain principles circulated, within circles that stood in a continuous line of tradition from the earlier to the later stages in the formation of the system to which the document attests, at earlier stages, and others were precipitated by, and developed later than, those conceptions.[6]

Other documents' authorships scarcely replicate the highly disciplined program, as to the match between attributions and the unfolding of the logic of what is attributed, of the Mishnah's writers. For the Tosefta's, for example, the attributions of sayings in the Mishnah prove a point not of departure but of difficulty. Accordingly, Tosefta's authorship undertakes a sustained critique of the Mishnah's attributions, claiming that what is attributed to X belongs to Y, or that the principle assigned to X is in reality narrower or broader than, or simply different from, what the Mishnah's authorship claims. Not only so, but approximately three-fourths of the Tosefta's materials depend upon, and therefore derive from a period later than, the Mishnah. Citing the Mishnah verbatim and then commenting on the citation accounts for part, framing ideas that can be wholly and completely understood only in the setting of the Mishnah accounts for the other part, of this predominate type of materials in the Tosefta. On that basis, we cannot compose, for the Tosefta, a study of the hypothesis that attributions prove reliable or that they prove unreliable. We simply do not know. Citing a saying attributed by the Tosefta's authorship to a prior authority, however, at this time may be characterized only as an act of faith, there being no means of composing a null hypothesis by which to test those attributions.[7]

Clearly, each document in the canon presents its own traits, that is to say, the traits imposed by its ultimate redactors. All therefore require detailed analysis, one by one. The claim that attributions in a given document carry us back to the age prior to redaction of that document, on its own, bears no compelling powers of persuasion; what we cannot

---

[6]On that foundation, I conducted the detailed analysis that yielded my *History of the Mishnaic Law* (Leiden, 1974-85: E.J. Brill) in forty-three volumes. But the entire result of that work, summarized and interpreted in *Judaism: The Evidence of the Mishnah* (Atlanta, 1988: Scholars Press for Brown Judaic Studies), second edition, augmented, consists in the details of the sequences worked out, item by item.

[7]That the Tosefta constitutes a document of what is conventionally called "amoraic times," that is, the period after 200 C.E., is therefore self-evident, contrary to Schiffman's position. Here, too, I appeal to the authority of Heer's classic, if brief, treatment of the subject.

show, we do not know. Since everyone recognizes the fluidity of attributions, with a saying in one document assigned to one authority, but in another, to a different authority, and since the vagaries of manuscript evidence even of one document provide still more puzzling data, none can at this time claim certainty on the matter. Consequently, all scholarship that, on the basis of attributions of sayings, in diverse writings, to named authority, claims to tell us the state of opinion (all the more so events) on a given topic at a given time rests on somewhat dubious premises and, for the moment, will have to be set aside. While we can scarcely claim to know the history of ideas held by specific groups at particular times, we can trace the canonical history of ideas, meaning, the unfolding of conceptions in a sequence of writings, and that is what I have done in a number of recent studies. But that is a quite separate project.

The beginning of the task requires characterization of a document as a whole. When we can define the program of an authorship in compiling whatever prior materials to which it had access and which it chose to use, as well as in making up whatever it wished to fabricate, we are able to develop one criterion by which to sort out what may antedate the work of the compilers and therefore may plausibly be held to derive from a period prior to redaction. Without such a characterization, by contrast, we treat the contents of a given compilation only out of context, paying no attention to the traits of the writing that contains and preserves them. We are, moreover, unable to sort out from materials received from a prior source the items the final authorship has included, whether of its own fabrication or otherwise, for its own distinctive and paramount purposes. Without reasoned argument, none can reasonably allege that those items in a document that bear the redactors' distinctive message attest to a prior period. And such reasoned argument will surely encompass the proposition that the basic proposition, the generative problematic, of a document enjoys significant canonical antecedents. Then, if we can show that that is the fact, the entire document, not merely some items within it, must be placed in a subordinate position, derivative of the earlier writing. It follows that documentary analysis forms the necessary first step toward any consideration of the use and meaning of attributions.

To illustrate these somewhat abstract propositions, let me turn to one document on which the descriptive work is complete, reviewing some of the results of sustained analysis. Since, in his article, Schiffman refers to Tannaitic Midrash compilations, including, specifically, Sifra, claiming that it contains materials of the same provenance as the Mishnah ("Tannaitic"), let us focus upon that item. Since the same names occur in both the Mishnah and Sifra, and since Sifra contains the names of few authorities that do not occur in the Mishnah, Schiffman maintains that the Sifra attests, as much as does the Mishnah, to the state of opinion in "Tannaitic times," by which is generally meant some indeterminate period, of considerable antiquity, prior to the closure of the Mishnah. No one has called into question what seems to me the definitive statement of M.D. Heer, "Since it appears that the Sifra in the present form, like the other halakhic Midrashim, was not known to the two Talmuds, it would seem to have been compiled and arranged in Erez Israel not earlier than the end of the fourth century C.E., when the Jerusalem Talmud was completed."[8] At issue, just as Schiffman says, is the simple question: What comes prior to redaction?

If we characterize the relationship of Sifra, viewed whole, to the Mishnah, we shall see the simple fact that the fundamental program and polemic of Sifra's authorship addresses the Mishnah. Sifra could not have come into being prior to, and at the same time as, the Mishnah, simply because, as I shall now show, Sifra's authorship sets forth a program defined by the traits of the Mishnah and formulated in response to those traits.[9] While that authorship draws on available materials, the criterion for the choice of most of them finds definition in the purpose of the authorship, which we can specify. Reshaping of whatever is chosen, whether explicitly (for example, from Scripture or from the Mishnah cited verbatim) or only implicitly, requires us to appeal to the contents of the document as a whole principally as evidence for ideas held in the time of the authorship of the document. The exceptions will provide slight solace for those who hold the position that the contents of a document attest to an age prior to redaction, since the exceptions are trivial, episodic, and inconsequential.[10]

---

[8]M.D. Heer, "Sifra," *Encyclopaedia Judaica* (Jerusalem, 1971: Keter), 14:1518. Why while Heer refers to both Talmuds, still he ignores the Bavli in reaching his conclusion I cannot say, nor do I know what he means when he says that Sifra was "not known" to the Talmuds. Certainly, materials in Sifra are shared with the two Talmuds. I have shown that fact at some length, and am puzzled by Heer's allegations in this regard. A close reading of his language suggests that Heer appears to have in mind the fact that we find no references to Sifra *as a completed document*, but that fact bears a variety of implications. That, too, is simply not so, for the Bavli does refer to Sifra and assign its unattributed materials to a named authority.

[9]The same statements apply to Sifré to Deuteronomy, as I have shown in my *Sifré to Deuteronomy. An Introduction to the Rhetorical, Logical, and Topical Program* (Atlanta, 1987: Scholars Press for Brown Judaic Studies). But they apply for different reasons, and the present purpose is best served by dealing only with one document.

[10]Merely reaching into Sifra and pulling out sayings that can be shown to have circulated prior to the formation of Sifra is simply beside the point, and, as I have

2. The Case of Sifra

If, as I maintain, documents are to be read whole, not only in their discrete parts, how shall I show that that is the right way of framing our inquiry into the uses of attributions for purposes defined outside the limits of the documents that contain those attributions? The answer is to demonstrate that one document differs from another not in mere detail but in its most fundamental traits of intellect. For that purpose I turn directly to one fundamental issue, which is the question of the logic of intelligible discourse. That is the logic that tells an authorship how to frame its data into cogent propositions and form of the whole a single, intelligible statement. I shall now show that two authorships, one of the Mishnah, the other of Sifra, made quite distinct judgments as to the matter of the logic of cogent argument and intelligible discourse. There, on the face of it, we see evidence in favor of my view that the right way of reading a document, to begin with, is whole and complete, not only in this detail or that. That demonstration will then yield the simple fact that the authorship of Sifra depends, not in detail alone but in its deepest structure of thought, upon the Mishnah. Whatever that authorship presents to us, therefore, has been shaped, or reshaped, for the polemical purpose that animates the writing as a whole. Anyone who claims to discern, within the writing (fabrication) or revision of materials attributed to prior authorities what is authentic to the earlier age will have to show us how and where we are to determine the difference between what is made up and attributed to an earlier figure and what derives from that earlier figure or from the age in which the sage is supposed to have lived.[11]

---

shown in my sustained work on the subject, yields results of no sustained interest. Schiffman seeks "the opportunity to reconstruct much of the historical context of the material," and I of course concur. But I do not see where or how that reconstruction has taken place, other than through constant and faithful reliance upon the attribution of sayings to particular authorities of a given place or time. But that seems to me an unlikely source of reliable data, unless within the same premise we also assign the entire Pentateuch to Moses.

[11]I look in vain in Schiffman's own writings for where and how he has shown us how to know the difference between valid and spurious attributions. See my *Reading and Believing. Ancient Judaism and Contemporary Gullibility* (Atlanta, 1986: Scholars Press for Brown Judaic Studies), where I subject one of Schiffman's more important papers to a close reading with just this issue in mind. In Schiffman's defense, I hasten to add, his work at least evinces concern for the problem. Most scholars at present simply take for granted the facticity of attributions and proceed from that point, defining their questions within the premise that answers to those questions occur in the sources. That renders dubious most historical work now under way in this field.

The authorship of Sifra undertook a vast polemic against the logic of classification that forms the foundation of the system of the Mishnah. This they did two ways. The first, and less important, was to demonstrate that the Mishnah's rules required exegetical foundations. The second, and paramount, way was to attack the very logic by which the Mishnah's authorship developed its points. To understand the polemic of Sifra, therefore, we have to grasp the fundamental logical basis for the workings of the Mishnah. Then we shall see in its polemical context the recurrent statement of the authorship of Sifra: *Classification does not work, because there is no genus, but only species.* Therefore the Mishnah's *Listenwissenschaft*, its insistence that things are either like one another, therefore follow the same rule, or opposite to one another, therefore follow the opposite rule – these fundamental building blocks of Mishnaic thought prove deeply flawed. For if nothing is ever really like something else, then we cannot classify different things together, as the same thing. And, it follows, we also can make no lists of things that, whether in a polythetic or a monothetic framework, follow the same rule and therefore generate a generalization. Since, as we shall now see, the logic of the Mishnah begins with the premise that diverse species form a single genus, so can be subjected to comparison and contrast, that dogged insistence, time and again, upon the incomparability of species, forms a fundamental critique of the practical reason of the Mishnah. A full appreciation of matters now requires that we dwell at some length upon the system of the Mishnah.

3. The System of the Mishnah and Its Logic of Classification

To see Sifra in historical context, we have to place into relationship its view of the logic of hierarchical classification with that of the Mishnah's authorship. What we shall discover is that the Sifra frames a sustained critique of a logic its authorship identifies and repeatedly demolishes as insufficient. The Mishnah's authorship invariably invokes the philosophical logic of syllogism, the rule-making logic of lists. Like good Aristotelians, they would uncover the components of the rules by comparison and contrast, showing the rule for one thing by finding out how it compared with like things and contrasted with the unlike.[12] Then, in their view, the unknown would become known, conforming to the rule of the like thing, also to the opposite of the rule governing the unlike thing. That purpose is accomplished, in particular, though list making, which places on display the data of the like and the unlike and implicitly

---

[12]Compare G.E.R. Lloyd, *Polarity and Analogy. Two Types of Argumentation in Early Greek Thought* (Cambridge, 1966: Cambridge University Press). But the core logic of *Listenwissenschaft* extends back to Sumerian times.

(ordinarily, not explicitly) then conveys the rule. That is why, in exposing the interior logic of its authorship's intellect, the Mishnah had to be a book of lists, with the implicit order, the nomothetic traits, dictating the ordinarily unstated general and encompassing rule. And all this why? It is in order to make a single statement, endless times over, and to repeat in a mass of tangled detail precisely the same fundamental judgment. The Mishnah in its way is as blatantly repetitious in its fundamental statement as is the Pentateuch. But the power of the pentateuchal authorship, denied to that of the Mishnah, lies in their capacity always to be heard, to create sound by resonance of the surfaces of things. The Pentateuch is a fundamentally popular and accessible piece of writing. By contrast, the Mishnah's writers spoke into the depths, anticipating a more acute hearing than they ever would receive. So the repetitions of Scripture reinforce the message, while the endlessly repeated paradigm of the Mishnah sits too deep in the structure of the system to gain hearing from the ear that lacks acuity or to attain visibility to the untutored eye. So much for the logic. What of the systemic message? Given the subtlety of intellect of the Mishnah's authorship, we cannot find surprising that the message speaks not only in what is said, but in what is omitted.

To account for the logic at hand, we have to turn to the circumstance addressed by the authorship, and this leads us to the necessity of characterizing the message that the document as a whole sets forth. And when we listen to the silences of the system of the Mishnah, as much as to its points of stress, we hear a single message. It is a message of a system that answered a single encompassing question, and the question formed a stunning counterpart to that of the sixth and fifth centuries B.C.E. The pentateuchal system of Ezra, ca. 450 B.C.E., addressed one reading of the events of the sixth century, highlighted by the destruction of the Jerusalem Temple in 586 B.C.E. At stake was how Israel as defined by that system related to its land, represented by its Temple, and the message may be simply stated: What appears to be the given is in fact a gift, subject to stipulations. The precipitating event for the Mishnaic system was the destruction of the Jerusalem Temple in A.D. 70, but at stake now was a quite fresh issue. It was, specifically, this: What, in the aftermath of the destruction of the holy place and holy Cult, remained of the sanctity of the holy caste, the priesthood, the Holy Land, and, above all, the holy people and its holy way of life? The answer was that sanctity persists, indelibly, in Israel, the people, in its way of life, in its land, in its priesthood, in its food, in its mode of sustaining life, in its manner of procreating and so sustaining the nation. The Mishnah's system therefore focused upon the holiness of the life of Israel, the people, a holiness that had formerly centered on the Temple. The logically consequent question was, what is the meaning of sanctity, and how shall Israel attain, or give evidence of, sanctification. The answer to the question derived from the original creation, the end of the Temple directing attention to the beginning of the natural world that the Temple had embodied (and would again). For the meaning of sanctity the framers therefore turned to that first act of sanctification, the one in creation. It came about when, all things in array, in place, each with its proper name, God blessed and sanctified the seventh day on the eve of the first Sabbath. Creation was made ready for the blessing and the sanctification when all things were very good, that is to say, in their rightful order, called by their rightful name. An orderly nature was a sanctified and blessed nature, so dictated Scripture in the name of the Supernatural. So to receive the blessing and to be made holy, all things in nature and society were to be set in right array. Given the condition of Israel, the people, in its land, in the aftermath of the catastrophe war against Rome led by Bar Kokhba in 132-135, putting things in order was no easy task. But that is why, after all, the question pressed, the answer proving inexorable and obvious. The condition of society corresponded to the critical question that obsessed the system builders.[13]

Once we discern that message, we shall also understand the logic necessary for its construction and inner structure. For the inner structure set forth by a logic of classification alone could sustain the system of ordering all things in proper place and under the proper rule. The like belongs with the like and conforms to the rule governing the like, the unlike goes over to the opposite and conforms to the opposite rule. When we make lists of the like, we also know the rule governing all the items on those lists, respectively. We know that and one other thing, namely, the opposite rule, governing all items sufficiently like to belong on those lists, but sufficiently unlike to be placed on other lists. That rigorously philosophical logic of analysis, comparison, and contrast

---

[13]That is not to suggest no other questions could have precipitated system making, either in the sixth century B.C. or in the second A.D. I cannot think of a less likely proposition. We recognize, after all, that the Pentateuchal Judaism formed the answer to the question selected by the Temple priesthood that sponsored the making of the Torah and that, institutionally, then formed its political class. Along these same lines, the Mishnaic Judaism emerged in a coalition of interests of priesthood, householders, and scribes. We do not know what other Judaisms came into being, nor can we identify the urgent questions and self-evidently valid answers represented by the worldview, way of life, and social entity invented by those other Judaic systems. All I mean to underline is the congruence between the social world and the systemic construction, not that the system formed the only, or the best possible, statement not only to that social world, but also *of* that social condition. That forms a distinct proposition, and one I reject as, if plausible, unproven.

served because it was the only logic that could serve a system that proposed to make the statement concerning order and right array that the Mishnah's authorship wished to set forth. To the urgent question, what of the holiness of Israel after the destruction of the Temple in A.D. 70, therefore, the system of the Mishnah provided the self-evidently valid answer and gave that answer in ineluctable and compelling logical form. That sanctification, as a matter of fact, from the viewpoint of the system now endured and transcended the physical destruction of the building and the cessation of sacrifices. For Israel the people was holy, enduring as the medium and the instrument of God's sanctification. The system then instructed Israel so to act as to express the holiness that inhered in the people. This Israel would accomplish by the right ordering, in accord with a single encompassing principle, of all details of the common life of the village and the home, matching the Temple and the cult.

The diverse topical program of the Mishnah, time and again making the same points on the centrality of order, works itself out in a single logic of cogent discourse, one which seeks the rule that governs diverse cases. And, as we now see, that logic states within its interior structure the fundamental point of the document as a whole. The correspondence of logic to system here, as in the Pentateuch viewed overall, hardly presents surprises. Seeing how the logic does its work within the document therefore need not detain us for very long. Let us take up one pericope of the Mishnah, chosen more or less at random,[14] and determine the logic that joins fact to fact, sentence to sentence, in a cogent proposition, that is, in our terms, a paragraph that makes a statement. To see how this intellect does its work we turn to Mishnah-tractate Sanhedrin, Chapter Two, which shows the subtle way in which list making yields a powerfully argued philosophical theorem.

The abstract allows us explicitly to identify the *and* and the *equal* of Mishnaic discourse, showing us through the making of connections and the drawing of conclusions the propositional and essentially philosophical mind that animates the Mishnah. In the following passage, drawn from Mishnah-tractate Sanhedrin Chapter Two, the authorship wishes to say that Israel has two heads, one of state, the other of cult, the king and the high priest, respectively, and that these two offices are nearly wholly congruent with one another, with a few differences based on the particular traits of each. Broadly speaking, therefore, our exercise

---

[14]I claim that we can produce the same result throughout the Mishnah, so anyone may test this proposal. Pericopes in all Mishnah tractates other than Eduyyot and of course Abot conform to the logic of *Listenwissenschaft*, except those put together within not a fixed logic of cogent discourse but rather a fixed rhetorical framework, e.g., "the only difference between X and Y is Z."

is one of setting forth the genus and the species. The genus is head of holy Israel. The species are king and high priest. Here are the traits in common and those not shared, and the exercise is fully exposed for what it is, an inquiry into the rules that govern, the points of regularity and order, in this minor matter, of political structure. My outline, imposed in boldface type, makes the point important in this setting.

Mishnah-tractate Sanhedrin Chapter Two

1. **The rules of the high priest: subject to the law, marital rites, conduct in bereavement**

2:1   A.   A high priest judges, and [others] judge him;

           B.   gives testimony, and [others] give testimony about him;

           C.   performs the rite of removing the shoe [Deut. 25:7-9], and [others] perform the rite of removing the shoe with his wife.

           D.   [Others] enter levirate marriage with his wife, but he does not enter into levirate marriage,

           E.   because he is prohibited to marry a widow.

           F.   [If] he suffers a death [in his family], he does not follow the bier.

           G.   "But when [the bearers of the bier] are not visible, he is visible; when they are visible, he is not.

           H.   "And he goes with them to the city gate," the words of R. Meir.

           I.   R. Judah says, "He never leaves the sanctuary,

           J.   "since it says, *'Nor shall he go out of the sanctuary'* (Lev. 21:12)."

           K.   And when he gives comfort to others

           L.   the accepted practice is for all the people to pass one after another, and the appointed [prefect of the priests] stands between him and the people.

           M.   And when he receives consolation from others,

           N.   all the people say to him, "Let us be your atonement."

           O.   And he says to them, "May you be blessed by Heaven."

           P.   And when they provide him with the funeral meal,

           Q.   all the people sit on the ground, while he sits on a stool.

2. **The rules of the king: not subject to the law, marital rites, conduct in bereavement**

2:2   A.   The king does not judge, and [others] do not judge him;

           B.   does not give testimony, and [others] do not give testimony about him;

           C.   does not perform the rite of removing the shoe, and others do not perform the rite of removing the shoe with his wife;

           D.   does not enter into levirate marriage, nor [do his brothers] enter levirate marriage with his wife.

           E.   R. Judah says, "If he wanted to perform the rite of removing the shoe or to enter into levirate marriage, his memory is a blessing."

           F.   They said to him, "They pay no attention to him [if he expressed the wish to do so]."

	G.	[Others] do not marry his widow.
	H.	R. Judah says, "A king may marry the widow of a king.
	I.	"For so we find in the case of David, that he married the widow of Saul,
	J.	"for it is said, '*And I gave you your master's house and your master's wives into your embrace*' (2 Sam. 12:8)."
2:3	A.	[If] [the king] suffers a death in his family, he does not leave the gate of his palace.
	B.	R. Judah says, "If he wants to go out after the bier, he goes out,
	C.	"for thus we find in the case of David, that he went out after the bier of Abner,
	D.	"since it is said, '*And King David followed the bier*' (2 Sam. 3:31)."
	E.	They said to him, "This action was only to appease the people."
	F.	And when they provide him with the funeral meal, all the people sit on the ground, while he sits on a couch.

3. Special rules pertinent to the king because of his calling

2:4	A.	[The king] calls out [the army to wage] a war fought by choice on the instructions of a court of seventy-one.
	B.	He [may exercise the right to] open a road for himself, and [others] may not stop him.
	C.	The royal road has no required measure.
	D.	All the people plunder and lay before him [what they have grabbed], and he takes the first portion.
	E.	"*He should not multiply wives to himself*" (Deut. 17:17) – only eighteen.
	F.	R. Judah says, "He may have as many as he wants, so long as they *do not entice him* [to abandon the Lord (Deut. 7:4)]."
	G.	R. Simeon says, "Even if there is only one who entices him [to abandon the Lord] – lo, this one should not marry her."
	H.	If so, why is it said, "He should not multiply wives to himself"
	I.	even though they should be like Abigail [1 Sam. 25:3]?
	J.	"*He should not multiply horses to himself*" (Deut. 17:16) – only enough for his chariot.
	K.	"*Neither shall he greatly multiply to himself silver and gold*" (Deut. 17:16) – only enough to pay his army.
	L.	"*And he writes out a scroll of the Torah for himself*" (Deut. 17:17).
	M.	When he goes to war, he takes it out with him; when he comes back, he brings it back with him; when he is in session in court, it is with him; when he is reclining, it is before him,
	N.	as it is said, "*And it shall be with him, and he shall read in it all the days of his life*" (Deut. 17:19).
2:5	A.	[Others may] not ride on his horse, sit on his throne, handle his scepter.
	B.	And [others may] not watch him while he is getting a haircut, or while he is nude, or in the bathhouse,
	C.	since it is said, "*You shall surely set him as king over you*" (Deut. 17:15) – that reverence for him will be upon you.

The Mishnah's authorship's philosophical cast of mind is amply revealed in this essay, which in concrete terms effects a taxonomy, a study of the genus, national leader, and its two species, [1] king, [2] high priest: how are they alike, how are they not alike, and what accounts for the differences. The premise is that national leaders are alike and follow the same rule, except where they differ and follow the opposite rule from one another. But that premise also is subject to the proof effected by the survey of the data consisting of concrete rules, those systemically inert facts that here come to life for the purposes of establishing a proposition. By itself, the fact that, for example, others may not ride on his horse, bears the burden of no systemic proposition. In the context of an argument constructed for nomothetic, taxonomic purposes, the same fact is active and weighty.

No natural historian can find the discourse and mode of thought at hand unfamiliar; it forms the foundation of all disposition of data in quest of meaning, of making connections, drawing conclusions. For if I had to specify a single mode of thought that established connections between one fact and another, it is in the search for points in common and therefore also points of contrast. We seek connection between fact and fact, sentence and sentence in the subtle and balanced rhetoric of the Mishnah, by comparing and contrasting two things that are like and not alike. At the logical level, too, the Mishnah falls into the category of familiar philosophical thought. Once we seek regularities, we propose rules. What is like another thing falls under its rule, and what is not like the other falls under the opposite rule. Accordingly, as to the species of the genus, so far as they are alike, they share the same rule. So far as they are not alike, each follows a rule contrary to that governing the other. So the work of analysis is what produces connection, and therefore the drawing of conclusions derives from comparison and contrast: the *and*, the *equal*. The proposition then that forms the conclusion concerns the essential likeness of the two offices, except where they are different, but the subterranean premise is that we can explain both likeness and difference by appeal to a principle of fundamental order and unity. To make these observations concrete, we turn to the case at hand. The important contrast comes at the outset. The high priest and king fall into a single genus, but speciation, based on traits particular to the king, then distinguishes the one from the other. In a treatise on government, organizing details into unifying rules, the propositions of the present passage would have been stated differently. But the mode of thought, the manner of reaching conclusions, above all,. the mind-set that sees connections in one way, rather than some other, that draws conclusions in this wise, not in that – these would have found an equally familiar place in the mind of both philosophy, of Aristotle's kind in particular, and the Jewish intellect represented by the Mishnah. That logic of list making, which brings to the surface a deeper intellectual structure formed of comparison and contrast, classification and exclusion, predominates throughout. Accordingly, a single logic serves to make a single statement, in behalf of both the authorship of the Pentateuch and the framers of the Mishnah.

4. Sifra's Critique of the Logic of the Mishnah

Now the intellectual labor of relating system to tradition and also of finding an appropriate logic of cogent discourse for the composition of a system could be accomplished in more than one way. And that brings us to the position of the authorship of Sifra. To state matters simply, what we shall now see in Sifra is a two-pronged polemic against the Mishnah, one a mere feint, the other the main attack.

[1]   The authorship of Sifra, as we already know,[15] commonly invokes the exact language of the Mishnah or the Tosefta, asks whether the position presented in that language, lacking all prooftexts drawn from Scripture, is not a matter of mere logic, and proves that it is not. That shows that what is required is law resting on scriptural proof.

[2]   The authorship of Sifra systematically demonstrates the futility of the logic of *Listenwissenschaft*, classification or taxonomy, comparison and contrast. This it does in a very simple way. It shows that species that *look* as though they form a common genus *do not in fact form* such a genus. Therefore it is not possible to compare and contrast two species to find the law common to the two of them, if they compare, or the law that differentiates one from the other, if they contrast.

A systemic statement could be woven into the cloak of tradition by its presentation as (mere) exegesis of a received text. The urgent question and self-evidently valid answer, not stated openly as a proposition for demonstration and argument, but merely repeated endlessly in the form of commentary, bore its own power of persuasion. Repeating the point

---

[15]I am unclear on how Schiffman can assign to Mishnaic times a document that quotes the Mishnah and forms a commentary on it. Any theory that the materials were formed, both for the Mishnah and for Sifra, prior to the redaction of either document, such as would account for what is in hand, surely requires articulation and demonstration. Otherwise all we have is refusal to address simple facts of a document.

gains for the message a self-evidence that argument and therefore counterargument can deny it. And that is the first of the two attacks of Sifra's authorship on the Mishnah, the feint. What about the other? While I should claim that the whole of the document is composed as a sustained demonstration of the improbability of the logic of classification, let me give one example, which suffices to make the point at hand. Here we see[16] one, among a great many, of Sifra's elegant demonstrations of the impossibility of relying upon the logic of *Listenwissenschaft,* which is *precisely* the logic of the Mishnah:

XVIII

II.1   A.   "The priest shall scoop out of it a handful":

      B.   Is the rule that a single handful suffices not only for a single tenth ephah of the offering, but a single handful also suffices for sixty tenth ephahs?

      C.   Or is the rule that a single handful serves only a single tenth ephah, while there must be sixty handfuls taken up out of sixty tenth ephahs?

      D.   Lo, I reason as follows:

      E.   The meal-offering requires the taking up of a handful, and it also requires frankincense. Just as in the case of frankincense, a single handful serves for a single tenth ephah, and a single handful serves also for sixty tenth ephahs, so in the case of the taking up of the handful, a single handful serves for one tenth ephah, and a single handful serves for sixty tenth ephahs.

      F.   Or try taking this route:

      G.   The meal-offering requires the taking up of a handful, and it also requires oil. Just as in the case of the oil, a single log of oil serves for a single tenth ephah, while sixty logs of oil are required for sixty tenth ephahs, so in the case of a handful, the taking up of a handful serves a single tenth ephah, while for sixty tenth ephahs, there must be sixty taking ups of handfuls.

      H.   Let us then see to the correct analogy:

      I.   We should establish an analogy from something which is wholly offered up on the altar fire to something that is wholly offered up on the altar fire, but oil should not then enter the picture, since it is not wholly burned up on the altar fire.

      J.   Or take this route:

      K.   We should establish an analogy from something in which the smaller portion is indispensable to the validity of the entire portion [for instance, if any of the required fine flour or oil is lacking, the entire meal-offering is null], but let us not propose proof from the example of frankincense, in which the lack of a smaller portion of the whole is not indispensable to the validity of the entire portion.

      L.   [Accordingly, we appeal to Scripture to settle matters, as it does when it says:] "The priest shall scoop out of it a handful":

---

[16]The translation is my own. See my *Sifra. An Analytical Translation* (Atlanta, 1988: Scholars Press for Brown Judaic Studies), I-III.

M.   It is the rule that a single handful suffices not only for a single tenth ephah of the offering, but a single handful also suffices for sixty tenth ephahs.

This elegant exercise once more proves the falsity of appealing to classification for settling a moot point, because taxonomy yields contradictory results. Scripture alone defines the correct classification of things. Appealing for correct classification to the traits of things viewed in the abstract and not in the context of the Torah's delineation of the traits of things (points in common, points of contrast) yields uncertain results; turning to Scripture for the classification of things yields true and reliable ones. That forms the sustained and vivid critique that animates Sifra and forms its re-visioning of the Torah through the insertion of the Mishnah, the Oral Torah, into the structure of thought and (consequently) the entire rhetorical framework of Scripture, the Written Torah.

5. Conclusion

Conducting a sustained and brilliant polemic against the Mishnah, the authorship of Sifra presents, in a systemic and orderly way, an amazing, subtle demonstration that there is no such thing as a genus, but only species. Then, it follows for our authorship, Scripture serves as the sole source for rules governing otherwise incomprehensible, because incomparable, species. A critical corollary is that the Mishnah not only rests upon false logic, but in failing to tie its propositions to Scripture, its authorship has set the law of the Torah upon unreliable foundations. The framers of Sifra then correct the errors of logic, on the one side, and set forth solid foundations in revelation, there alone, on the other. All of this they do while working their way through what will seem, on the surface, somewhat remote facts indeed. My hope is that the reader will find as compelling as I do the powerful, sustained, and amazingly cogent argument our authorship sets forth only in the minutia of cultic law.

The authors of Sifra, working on the book of Leviticus, have given us a mélange of materials, some of them exegetical in a narrow sense, others more broadly speculative Since all named authorities are supposed to have lived before the publication of the Mishnah in ca. 200, the work is assigned to the same period as the formation of the Mishnah. But passages in the Sifra cite verbatim both the Mishnah and the Tosefta, so the document as we have it certainly reached closure some time after ca. 200. It is an Amoraic text as much as the Tosefta and the Talmud of the Land of Israel. That fact is shown not only by the document's citing the Mishnah verbatim and pursuing an exegetical program vis-à-vis the Mishnah. There is a still more telling consideration. The polemic of the work takes account of the character of the Mishnah as a piece of writing essentially autonomous of Scripture and repeatedly claims one thing. It is that the rules of the Mishnah demand scriptural support, through exegesis. They cannot stand on their own as the result of a mere exercise in logic and reason. Accordingly, one principal purpose in the formation of the document addresses the issue of the standing of the Mishnah in relationship to Scripture (in theological terms: the Oral Torah in relationship to the Written Torah). It must follow that the document in its fundamental focus and stress derives from the period from ca. 200 to ca. 400. That is the age that also yielded the Tosefta, supplements to the Mishnah; the commentaries to Genesis and Leviticus called Genesis Rabbah and Leviticus Rabbah; the Talmud of the Land of Israel; and some of the formative layers of the Talmud of Babylonia.

Sifra has its own, strikingly polemical, purposes, for which the laws pertinent to, and even shared with, the Mishnah and the Tosefta are reshaped. Sifra proposes to present a kind of gemara, that is, an essay, worked out dialectically through questions and answers, rapidly and with great economy of expression and thought moving from point to point within discrete thematic structures. While it often enough simply cites a verse and adds a few words about its interpretation, it much more commonly then goes on to raise a series of logical questions about that primary citation and original interpretation. These questions may vary, but predominant among them, the common one is, Might one think the opposite? How do we know that the original interpretation may withstand the test of reason, the consideration of different, mostly contrary, propositions? This, I think is the definitive characteristic of gemara and justifies our calling Sifra a sort of Bavli, or Babylonian Talmud, in its own right. But I should claim that our authorship has given us a far more engaging statement than did the framers of the Bavli, because of the stunning coherence of their recurrent and methodical exercise.

One critical polemic, fundamental to Sifra's purpose, is to demonstrate the inadequacy of reason unaided by revelation. Time and again Sifra asks, Does this proposition, offered with a prooftext, really require the stated proof of revelation? Will it not stand firmly upon the basis of autonomous reason, unaided by Scripture? Sometimes Scripture will show that the opposite of the conclusion of reason is the result of exegesis. Therefore the truth is to be discovered solely through exegesis. At other times Sifra will show that reason by itself is flawed and fallible, not definitive. At important points it will seek to prove not only a given proposition, but also that that proposition is to be demonstrated solely through revelation, through exegesis of Scripture. In all it is difficult to avoid the impression that the primary purpose of the compilers of Sifra is to criticize the Mishnah and the Tosefta, documents notoriously uninterested in the exegetical foundations of their laws.

We address the result of the formation of a consensus, that is, the work not of an individual author but of an authorship, a textual community. Received in a canonical process of transmission under the auspices of a religious system, specifically, the system of the Judaism of the Dual Torah, Sifra enjoys authority and status within that canon and system. Hence it is deemed to speak for a community and to contribute to the consensus of that community. Not only so, but the most superficial trait of all tells us that Sifra itself constitutes the statement of a consensus. Sifra has no named author. Accordingly, it is represented, on the surface, as the statement of a consensus. That consensus, the anonymous authorities behind the document as we have it, I call an authorship. That authorship tells us, in the case of Sifra, what was on its mind. It therefore attests to the state of opinion in one circle of sages of the time and place; whatever facts find their way into the document from an earlier period are reshaped for the purposes of the authorship, sherds and remnants reworked essentially ab initio. Consequently, most of the attributed sayings of the document attest not to the times in which the sages to whom sayings are attributed but only to the purposes of the framers of the document itself. And those that bear facts or viewpoints held prior to the final authorship provide such scanty and episodic information as to compel only passing attention. That is the fact for Sifra. Study of other documents supposedly deriving their materials from the "Tannaitic period" will have to go forward, each in its own terms. The results, for Sifra, bear little evidence in support of Schiffman's view that, standing by themselves, attributions prove anything of consequence for historical purposes.

Let me conclude[17] by stating what I conceive to be the generative problematic of Sifra's authorship. In a simple and fundamental sense,

---

[17]I have not dealt with Schiffman's discussion of the Messiah theme because when he wrote his review he did not have access to Jacob Neusner, William S. Green, and Ernest S. Frerichs, eds., *Judaisms and Their Messiahs at the Turn of the Christian Era* (New York, 1987: Cambridge University Press). There analysis of the use, or neglect, of the Messiah theme in various Judaisms, e.g., the systems of the Essenes of Qumran, Philo, the Mishnah, as well as in diverse early Christian systems, represented for instance by Mark and Matthew, shows a simple fact. There was no single "Messiah idea of Judaism," any more than there was a single Judaism to which all documents attest (except the documents that are deemed not canonical or normative). Each Judaism made use of the Messiah theme for its own systemic purposes. Hence Schiffman's entire thesis harmonizes what are, in fact, discrete systems, and he presents a unitary picture of a single Judaism where there were, in fact, several Judaisms, each with its own assessment of the use and interest of the Messiah theme (as of all other received themes and topics).

Sifra joins the two Torahs into a single statement, accomplishing a re-presentation of the Written Torah in topic and in program and in the logic of cogent discourse, and within that rewriting of the Written Torah, a re-presentation of the Oral Torah in its paramount problematic and in many of its substantive propositions. Stated simply, the Written Torah provides the form, the Oral Torah, the content. What emerges is not merely a united, Dual Torah, but *The* Torah, stated whole and complete, in the context defined by the book of Leviticus. Here the authorship of Sifra presents, through its re-presentation, The Torah as a proper noun, all together, all at once, and, above all, complete and utterly coherent. In order to do so our authorship has constructed through its document, first, the sustained critique of the Mishnah's *Listenwissenschaft*, then, the defense of the Mishnah's propositions on the foundation of scriptural principles of taxonomy, hierarchical classification in particular. Characteristic of Sifra in rhetoric, logic, and topic is the disquisition on the logic of the Mishnah and the program of the Mishnah. Sifra's authorship demonstrates that *Listenwissenschaft* is a self-evidently valid mode of demonstrating the truth of propositions. But *the* source of the correct classification of things is Scripture and only Scripture. Without Scripture's intervention into the taxonomy of the world, we should have no knowledge at all of which things fall into which classifications and therefore are governed by which rules. Scripture provides reliable taxa and dictates the indicative characteristics of those taxa. Scripture *alone* can set forth the proper names of things: classifications and their hierarchical order. What all this has to do with ideas held in the first or second centuries remains to be demonstrated by those who maintain that Sifra addresses any age prior to that of its authorship, who were evidently situated, at the earliest, in the fifth century.

In the present context, if we ask ourselves to identify a single line of Sifra that has been preserved entirely on its own, without the requirements of Sifra's program and argument in mind, we shall find it difficult to find one. Nearly every line in that compilation serves a well-defined polemical purpose. Since that trait characterizes not only the attributed, but the unattributed statements in the document, any claim that the latter are "earlier" than the former becomes incomprehensible; the whole forms a single literary unity. Do we then have to maintain that the entire document was made up only at the end? I think not. A

Schiffman's discussion of the problem rests upon G. Scholem, *The Messianic Idea in Judaism* (New York, 1971: Schocken), cf. Schiffman, op. cit., p. 242. In his "Messiah in Judaism: Rethinking the Question," in *Judaisms and Their Messiahs*, pp. 1-14, however, William Scott Green has refuted the basic premises on which Scholem and Klausner, upon whose work Schiffman relies, depend.

reading of the document will identify not only prior sources, which clearly are cited verbatim – Mishnah and Tosefta throughout! – but also completed compositions, formed into larger composites, then used in the service of the prevailing documentary program. If these observations prove plausible for so unitary and cogent a document as Sifra, all the more so will they characterize the literary history of, therefore the rules of historical evidence that govern in, the Talmuds of the Land of Israel and of Babylonia, not to mention other Midrash compilations.

7

Thematic or Sytemic Description: The Case of Mishnah's Division of Women

When we take up the study of an area defined by a common theme, rather than by a discipline or method, we first of all confront the problem of defining that which is to be studied. For a theme encompasses so wide a range of data that further definition, within the limits of the stated theme, becomes necessary. If, for example, our general topic is Jewish studies, black studies, Russian studies, American studies, or women's studies, our urgent task is to describe that part of the corpus of data relevant to Jews, blacks, Russians, Americans, or women; and we shall undertake to examine it. The second problem is locating useful issues worth investigating within the stated frame of data, that is, to interpret what we choose to describe. Description and interpretation, of course, form a dialectical system. For data which have been selected for description contain within themselves a core of issues or propositions (if only the self-validating, *self-evidently* interesting character of the data themselves) which define the task of interpretation. And when we attempt to interpret, to make sense of, the data, we find ourselves drawing upon disciplines and methods which themselves constitute results attained in the work of forming an intelligible picture of quite other data. Again to be more concrete: If we interpret through their own stated perspectives those data pertinent to Jews, blacks, Russians, Americans, or women, which have been chosen for description and interpretation, we learn nothing we did not know in selecting the data. But once we want to find out something the data do not contain and openly tell us, we step outside the frame of the area chosen for study. Then we draw upon those disciplinary considerations, those rigorous methods, which we reject when, to begin with, we choose to work in a

121

thematic area rather than in accord with a stated discipline. The tension between defining our work through theme or topic, on the one side, and defining what we do through the requirements of a given discipline, on the other, is especially fructifying and engaging when we perceive the choices to be made.

My contribution to the exemplification of that proposition consists in the presentation of a particular case and its heuristic alternatives, namely, the problem of making sense of the treatment of women in a specific ancient Jewish document, the Mishnah. In so doing, I shall try to show the methodological choices to be made and to explain and spell out the ones I make in interpreting the way in which women are treated within the limits of that ancient document and its system. The problem is in two parts. We have first of all to account for the way in which the data are selected and laid forth, that is, the principle of selection and, it follows, the mode by which data are put forth as description. We must, second, apply that principle of selection and show how, in interpreting the data which have been laid forth, that principle leads to results of sense and worth, that is, how it yields meaning. The particular relevance of this exercise to the field of women's studies is in showing how that field, through its distinctive thematic and theoretical concerns, contributes to the interpretation of data totally unrelated to the topics and interests of the field itself. I shall suggest specifically that, from the way in which the ancient document before us treats women, we are able to make some sense of the way in which that same document selects and treats its other principal themes and topics. This I believe to be an important result.

The document to which reference is made is Mishnah, a six-part code of rules formed toward the end of the second century A.D. by a small number of Jewish sages and put forth as the constitution of Judaism under the sponsorship of Judah the Patriarch, the head of the Jewish community of Palestine at the end of that century. The reason the document is important is that Mishnah forms the definitive foundation for the Babylonian and Palestinian Talmuds. It therefore joins the Hebrew Bible as the document upon which the Judaism of the past nineteen hundred years is constructed. What makes the document urgent in this context is that, of the six principal divisions of which Mishnah is composed, one is devoted to women. While other ancient Jewish texts contain vast numbers of allusions to women, it is only Mishnah which treats that topic as constitutive, fundamental to the whole. Here women appear not merely tangentially and in other contexts but as a distinct focus of discourse. To underline this point, I list the other five divisions: (1) agricultural rules, (2) laws governing appointed seasons, for example, Sabbaths and festivals, (3) the system of civil and criminal law (corresponding to what we today should regard as "the legal system"), (4) laws for the conduct of the cult and the Temple, and (5) laws on the preservation of cultic purity both in the Temple and under domestic circumstances, with special reference to the table and bed. In fact, as we see, Mishnah's six divisions are meant to define the whole range and realm of reality. Beyond these frontiers, to Mishnah's sages' way of thinking, is nothing worthy of attention. To them the map is the territory. So when we observe that, to the framers of Mishnah, women form one of the six constitutive and definitive parts of reality, we realize that, in the circumstance of Mishnah, when we make sense of how women are treated, we find ourselves at the hermeneutical center of a much larger worldview.

Now the principal problem facing us is how to treat the data about women presented by Mishnah: how to describe and how to interpret them. In my view, there are two possibilities. First, we may lay out the Mishnah's data on women in discrete fashion and bring these data into relationship, for example, for comparative purposes, with other discrete facts about women drawn from diverse Jewish and gentile sources. That is, we may work thematically. Second, we may view Mishnah's data on women as a system within a larger system. The choice I shall both propose and put into effect is the latter: systemic description and interpretation, as against thematic description and interpretation.

I

Facts by themselves mean little. It is when they are brought into relationship with other facts to form a *context* that they begin to make those statements of meaning which the system as a whole wants to express. Merely knowing, for example, that a woman receives a marriage contract when she is betrothed and wed, and that she receives a writ of divorce when she is sent away, tells us very little. These are the sorts of things which, "common sense" tells us, women in general will have to receive in these circumstances. But what if we ask whether a principle of selection is to be discerned? Then, in seeking that principle, we ask fresh and fructifying questions. We want, for instance, to understand why it is that one given system wishes to talk, in particular, about the documentation of the transfer of women while some other system wants to speak about the prohibitions of consanguinity, the behavior of mothers in relationship to children, or the sexual activities of women when they are at diverse points in relationship to men. Then, I think, we begin to find something worth knowing. For what leads us into the center of a worldview, of a religious worldview in the case of an ancient Israelite document such as this one, is the capacity to discern and explain the principles of selection or inclusion, on the one side, and of disinterest or exclusion, on the other. Why this topic and not some other? These seem to me the questions of the most fundamental, and therefore most revealing, character. For the answers to them lay out before our eyes the principles of selection and permit us to understand, by contrasting one set of principles with some other, the taxonomy of systems, both within a given cultural framework and across frontiers of space and time.

I have now to explain the methodological choice before us in describing and explaining the Mishnaic system of women. There are, as I see it, two approaches to the description and explanation of data, thematic and systemic. Thematic description takes a given topic and assembles data relevant to that topic from various contexts. The criterion of relevance is topical. Perforce one must ignore the boundaries of contexts, since material on the stated theme derives from many of them. The purposes of description, then, are accomplished by the thematic method when the pertinent data have been assembled into a construction which permits thematic questions to be framed and answered. The focus of interest is in the relationship of data drawn from one context to data drawn from some other. But this does not effect comparison. In the present instance one approach is to consider the theme of women in general and to bring into relationship data of all sorts and relevant to all matters of the present corpus of rules. The questions to be addressed to these bodies of facts, then, will emerge from the theme common to all of them, women: their status, role, activities, and similar subjects. A further, thematic inquiry would be into the legal facts of our seven tractates, for example, marriage and divorce law – here, there, and everywhere.

Systemic description, by contrast, aims at making sense of facts by reference to the context in which they occur and only then, if then, asking about the relationship of one fully articulated system, in its context, to some other, in its setting. Once a context has been defined and its perimeters carefully delineated and justified, the work of description involves placing into that context all data, without regard to theme, drawn out of that context. That is to say, we have to make sense of the parts in the context of the whole, and of the whole (that is, facts about many themes and topics) by reference to the parts. The principal intellectual challenge is to find out how rules about one matter may express a viewpoint, a detail of a harmonious and comprehensive and cogent worldview, shared and expressed in some other, indeed in many other, rules and details about other matters. But then the principal point of concern is not the data pertinent to a given theme but the systemic interrelationships of data on many themes.

Comparison, when it comes, is not among materials drawn from diverse contexts and relevant to a single theme, for example, woman, or, more concretely, the character of divorce documents and rules. Comparison is between one system and some other system. The appropriate task, in a taxonomy of systems compared to one another, will be to uncover the principles of selection, on the one side, and the relationships between those principles of selection and the encompassing ecological framework (using the word ecology in a social and historical sense) among the several systems under study, on the other.

External to its context, no fact bears on its own exegesis. But it is the context – and that alone – which supplies the exegesis. I do not conceive that within a given theme or topic is to be located a logic so compelling as to supply for thematic description and analysis the cogency and internal structure which context does for systemic description and analysis. I cannot imagine what it is that the theme of "women" or of "the writ of divorce" tells me, so that, out of context, I may bring together, in the work of hermeneutics, diverse facts about that theme. There is no structure but in context. But context, too, is not structure. For mere definition of context also is insufficient for the work of interpretation. The meaning of what we find is to be perceived within the system located and constructed in context. Context is not a priori, but merely prior to the work of interpretation.

Having said so much about context, I clearly intend to justify the approach of systemic, as against thematic, description and interpretation. It follows, therefore, that the definition of what makes a system systemic becomes a critical problem. While diverse, subtle definitions of the drawing of lines of context may be attempted, I am inclined for the present purpose to choose the simplest. The boundaries of a system are drawn by the coincidence of the lines of a particular literary document with the lines of a particular, clearly defined social group. Obviously, I have drawn my definition from the document which, to begin with, I perceive as a system composed of systems: namely, Mishnah. That document is whole – by definition. It is complete since it knows its own subdivisions but, internal evidence indicates, depends upon no others for exegesis, let alone for application. It clearly proposes to describe a society and a social canopy for a worldview. We obviously do not know whether any of the law, at the time it was made up, was practical and applied.[1] That is why knowledge of a clearly defined social group,

---

[1]Of Mishnah's six divisions at least two, on the Temple and cult and on cultic uncleanness, in no way could be relevant to the authorities who made up the document. For after A.D. 70 there was no Temple. But many other tractates are equally remote from everyday reality, e.g., the one which describes a court and

whose conceptions are contained within the document, is essential. The *Sitz im Leben* of Mishnah is the circle of authorities who made up Mishnah, the disciples and masters of the later first and second generation in what appears to be an intellectual continuum of nearly two centuries, but certainly a century and a half.

The systemic limits I have proposed are therefore literary and social. They are literary, so that we may be sure we have all the relevant data and no irrelevant ones. They are social, so that we may confidently claim to describe not merely a collection of facts but something addressed to a particular world by a particular group from its inner-facing perspective. This definition, of course, is narrow, as dictated by the circumstances and facts with which we must contend.

Systemic constructions need not be defined within the limits of documents. But then the lines and boundaries must be vividly drawn in some other way, for instance, by social walls so high as to be perceptible even long after the fact or by institutional boundaries crossed only through conversion or apostasy, depending on the direction of movement. But whether the facts derive from a book or from social realities related in many books and other sources of information (for instance, gravestones, broken pots, mosaic floors, and surviving walls of churches, temples, or synagogues), there must be a social referent. The facts must speak for someone and to someone, or we do not have a system, only a fantasy.

Mishnah speaks for the disciples and masters of the document. It addresses a world not fully realized, but not wholly imaginary. Its worldview forms a judgment on how things are and also a design for a society expressive of the way things are meant by God to be. When, in time to come, there is a taxonomy of systems, this one will find its place on the list of those which hover somewhere between ideal and reality, within the division of systems made by intellectuals but meant for others, and in the subset of systems of man's (and only man's) power of sanctification of this life. But it is too soon to speak of taxonomies. As we shall see, in its own context, whether defined synchronically or delineated diachronically, Mishnah's system appears to be the sole extant systemic construction on its chosen theme. It is, alas, unique in that very taxonomic context which should prohibit our finding anything unique.

The stress on the hermeneutical priority of systemic description and analysis over thematic description and analysis, the description of how facts fit into their own context rather than relate to thematically relevant

---

government structure, Sanhedrin, which was in no way realized by the rabbis; and there are others as well. That is why the social parameters of the system are defined by the people who made it up, not by the world in which they lived.

facts drawn out of some other context, surely does not begin here. For one example, Mary Boyce says precisely the same thing in connection with Zoroaster's eschatology:

> Zoroaster's eschatological teachings, with the individual judgment, the resurrection of the body, the Last Judgment, and life everlasting, became profoundly familiar, through borrowings, to Jews, Christians, and Muslims, and have exerted enormous influence on the lives and thoughts of men in many lands. *Yet it was in the framework of his own faith that they attained their fullest logical coherence....* (Neusner, *Mishnaic Law of Purities*, 1977, XXII:13)

At this point in the analysis of the Mishnah's whole system, we cannot make a similar statement of what it is that defines that systemic conviction, expressed equally in all the parts, which reveals the full, logical coherence of the whole and the meaning of these parts. Obviously, the fundamental message of the division of Women is that actions, including documents, having to do with the transfer of women both invoke the sacred and are subject to the oversight of heaven. In a system which throughout its parts expresses the conception that man[2] is capable of effecting sanctification through his will and his work, it is no wonder that, as we shall see, what is written on a piece of paper is read in heaven as it is on earth. Heaven responds to man's deeds on earth. Heaven shares that realm of the heart, governing will, intention, purpose, and plan, which is definitive of the weight and meaning of deeds.

II

Having explained why in my view the appropriate mode of description is systemic and not thematic, I have now to describe what I believe to be the principal intellectual components of the Mishnaic system of women, viewed both over all and with special reference to the seven Mishnaic tractates, defined by theme, which form Mishnah's division of Women and therefore constitute the system at hand. We begin with some generalizations and proceed to a brief account of the tractates themselves; and we shall end, later on, with a theory of the system's meaning.

The Mishnaic system of women defines the position of women in the social economy of Israel's supernatural and natural reality. That position acquires definition wholly in relationship to men, who impart form to the

---

[2]In this system, it is man, not woman, who takes the active and definitive role. Whether in the theory of the document women also have the power to effect sanctification, I cannot say. It does not matter. As we shall see at some length, Mishnah's system of women permits us to speak of *man*, not woman, in the present context.

Israelite social economy. It is effected through both supernatural and natural, this-worldly action. What man and woman do on earth provokes a response in heaven, and the correspondences are perfect. So the position of women is defined and secured both in heaven and here on earth, and that position is always and invariably relative to men. The principal interest for Mishnah is the point at which a woman becomes, and ceases to be, *holy* to a particular man, that is, enters and leaves the marital union. These transfers of women are the dangerous and disorderly points in the relationship of woman to man, therefore, as I said, to society as well. Five of the seven tractates of this division are devoted to the formation and dissolution of the marital bond. Of them, three treat what is done here on earth by man, that is, formation of a marital bond through betrothal and marriage contract and dissolution through divorce and its consequences: Qiddushin,[3] Ketubot,[4] and Gittin.[5] One of them is devoted to what is done here on earth by woman: Sotah.[6] And Yebamot,[7] greatest of the seven in size and in formal and substantive brilliance, deals with the corresponding heavenly intervention into the formation and end of a marriage: the effect of death upon the marital bond and the dissolution, through death, of that bond. The other two tractates, Nedarim[8] and Nazir,[9] draw into one the two realms of reality, heaven and earth, as they work out the effects of vows taken by women and subject to the confirmation or abrogation of the father or husband. These vows make a deep impact upon the marital life of the woman who has taken such a vow. So, in all, the division and its system delineate the natural and supernatural character of the woman's role in the social economy framed by man: the beginning, end, and middle of that relationship.

The Mishnaic system of women thus focuses upon the two crucial stages in the transfer of women and of property from one domain to another: the leaving of the father's house and of the husband's at its dissolution through divorce or through the husband's death. There is yet a third point of interest, though it is much less important than these first two stages: the duration of the marriage. Finally, included within the

---

[3]Betrothals.
[4]Marriage contracts and the settlement thereof; the transfer of property in connection with the transfer of a woman from the father's to the husband's domain.
[5]Writs of divorce.
[6]The wife suspected of adultery and the rite of drinking the bitter water described in Num. 5.
[7]Levirate marriages, in accord with the rule of Deut. 25:10-15.
[8]Vows.
[9]The vow of the Nazirite, as in Num. 6.

division and at a few points relevant to women in particular are rules of vows in general and of the special vow to be a Nazir, the former included because, in the scriptural treatment of the theme, the rights of the father or husband to annul the vows of a daughter or wife form the central problematic, and the latter included for no very clear reason except that it is a species of which the vow is the genus.

To the message and the purpose of the Mishnaic system of women, woman is essential and central. But she is not critical. She sets the stage for the processes of the sacred. It is she who can be made sacred to man. It is she who ceases to stand within a man's sacred circle. But God, through supernature, and man, through the documentary expression of his will and intention, possess the active power of sanctification. Like the Holy Land of Mishnah's division of Agriculture, the Holy Temple of the division of Sacrifices, and the potentially holy realm of the clean of the division of Purities, women for the division of Women define a principal component of the Mishnah's orderly conception of reality. Women form a chief component of the six-part realm of the sacred. It is, as I said, their position in the social economy of the Israelite reality, natural and supernatural, which is the subject of the division and its tractates. But the whole – this six-part realm – is always important in *relationship* to man on earth and God in heaven. Sanctification is effected through process and through relationship. The center of logical tension is critical relationship. The problematic of the subject is generated *at* the critical points of the relationship. The relationship, that is, *the process,* is what makes holy or marks as profane. God and man shape and affect that process. Earth, woman, cult, and the cultlike realm of the clean – these foci of the sacred form that inert matter made holy or marked as profane by the will and deed of God and of man, who is like God. This, I conceive, is the problematic so phrased as to elicit the desired response in our division. *The system shapes the problematic which defines how the topic will be explored and made consequential.* Mishnah's is a system of sanctification through the word of God and through that which corresponds to God's word on earth, which is the will of man. If, as I have said, the division yields no propositions of encompassing and fundamental importance but merely legal facts about documents and relationships signified through documents, it still says a great deal both as a system and also in behalf of Mishnah's system as a whole.

Let us now consider the seven tractates and rapidly survey their principal topics.

Yebamot   The levirate connection is null in a case of consanguinity; *halisah* (Deut. 25:10ff. – the rite of removing the shoe) but no levirate marriage; a normal levirate connection, worked out through *halisah* or consummation of the marriage; marriage into the priesthood and the right to eat heave-offering; severing the marital bond; marital ties subject to doubt; the rite of *halisah;* the right of refusal; infirm marital bonds; the deaf-mute, the minor male; severing the marital bond through death of the husband; the woman's testimony; identifying a corpse.

Ketubot   The material rights of the parties to the marital union; the wife, the father, the husband; conflicting claims; fines paid to the father in the case of rape or seduction; the father's material rights; the husband's material rights; rules for the duration of the marriage; the wife's duties to the husband; the husband's marital rights and duties; the dowry; property rights of the wife while she is married; settlement of the marriage contract in the event of the husband's death; multiple claims on an estate; the support of the widow.

Nedarim   The language of vows: euphemisms; language of no effect or of limited effect; the binding effects of vows, not to derive benefit in general, not to eat some specific kind of food in particular, and not to use certain objects; temporal application of vows; the absolution of vows; grounds for absolution; annulling the vows of a daughter and of a wife; the husband's power to annul the wife's vows; vows of a woman who is not subject to abrogation.

Nazir   Becoming a Nazir with special reference to the vow: the language of the vow, stipulations, the duration of the vow; annulling the Nazirite vow; the offerings required of the Nazir; designation and disposition; prohibitions on the Nazir; the grape, contracting corpse uncleanness, cutting the hair.

Sotah   Invoking the ordeal of the bitter water, narrative of the ordeal and its conduct; rules of the ordeal: exemptions and applicability, testimony; rites conducted in Hebrew: the anointed for battle and the draft exemptions, the rite of the heifer and the neglected corpse.

Gittin   Delivering a writ of divorce; preparing a writ of divorce; two irrelevant constructions: (1) confirming the prevailing supposition; (2) fifteen rulings made for the good order of society; the law of agency in writs of divorce; receiving the writ, appointing an agent to prepare and deliver a writ of divorce; stipulations in writs of divorce; invalid and impaired writs of divorce; improper delivery, improper preparation, improper stipulations, improper witnesses; grounds for divorce.

Qiddushin   Rules of acquisition of a woman in betrothal; procedures of betrothal; agency, the token of betrothal, stipulations; impaired betrothals, stipulations; doubts in matters of betrothal; appropriate candidates for betrothal; castes and outcastes; the status of the offspring of impaired marriages; castes and marriage among castes; miscellanies and homilies.

We see in this detailed account of the division's repertoire of themes that we have an encompassing account of the formation, duration, and dissolution of marriages. The topic is worked out in a fairly systematic and orderly way. The Mishnaic system of women clearly does not pretend to deal with every topic pertinent to women. Indeed, it is what we do not find, as much as what we do, which permits us to claim we have a system. For when we can point to exclusions, we realize decisions have been made, within the potentialities of the *theme* of women, on what belongs and what does not belong to a distinctive *system* of women.

III

Efforts at thematic description and interpretation are inadequate not merely because they rest upon false epistemological foundations, wrenching out of context and depriving of all specific meaning the facts of the themes subject to description and interpretation. They are inadequate because the result produces exercises in confusion, triteness, and banality. Thematic approach to the data of our seven tractates, among a vast profusion of facts about "women in ancient Judaism," illustrates this proposition. To begin with, it is to be said that the topic of "woman" (or "woman in Judaism") is a snare and delusion. "The position of women" reduces even the great Evans-Pritchard to a series of banalities and trite remarks (in *The Position of Women in Primitive Societies and Other Essays in Social Anthropology*, 1965). Lacking all purpose and definition, scholars in the fields of Old Testament (Bird in Rosemary R. Reuther, *Religion and Sexism: Images of Woman in the Jewish and Christian Traditions*, 1974:41-88), Talmud (Hauptman in Reuther, 1974:184-212), and countless other fields are forced to substitute lists and catalogues for questions and insights. They have nothing to say. Lest I be thought to exaggerate, let us see how the descriptive and interpretive work is done by a scholar who has given us a sustained, complete picture of work defined along thematic lines, indeed, a whole book on *Women in Judaism*.

Leonard Swidler (*Women in Judaism: The Status of Women in Formative Judaism*, 1976:n.1) provides a stunningly apt illustration of the helplessness of thematic description in the face of the diverse data required by its program. In the end he can only set up two categories for interpretation, and they produce no interpretation at all. These are first, positive, and second, negative, sayings. He culls innumerable, diverse rabbinic sayings in favor of women and diverse sayings against them. He then concludes:

> On the basis of the evidence of both the positive and negative rabbinic statements about women thus far analyzed...it would be correct to conclude that quantitatively and qualitatively the negative attitude vastly outweighs the positive. It can be said, therefore, that the attitude of the ancient rabbis toward women was a continuation of the negative attitude toward women that evolved from the return from the Exile through the later Wisdom, apocryphal, and pseudepigraphical literature. In fact, it was in a way an intensification of it, in that the rabbis, through their great influence on the masses of Judaism, projected it most forcefully into the everyday life of the observant Jew.... (1976:82)

It follows that, for Swidler, masses of material have been suitably pigeonholed and utilized by his judgment; some are favorable, some unfavorable; and, in the balance, the overall effect is negative. What we learn from this judgment, how we better understand the data he has assembled, and the means by which we may interpret in a richer and fuller way than before the larger constructions out of which the data are drawn are questions he does not answer. He cannot. There is yet one question I do not see answered. If it is so that "the negative attitude vastly outweighs the positive," then what do we learn which we want to know? That is, if we exclude acutely contemporary aspirations for reform, then – so what? It does not appear to a fair number of scholars that their task includes the making of such judgments in this context.

IV

In this setting of the analysis of women in ancient Judaism, I point now to Isaksson (Abel Isaksson, *Marriage and Ministry in the New Temple: A Study with Special Reference to Mt. 19:1-22 and 1 Cor. 11:3-16*, 1965). For, while he does not show that there was an Essenic system of women (indeed, he shows there was none), he does make the effort to relate unsystematized *facts* about women in the Essene writings to the larger integrated system of the Essenes. His main point is that the details of the Essene writings take on meaning only within their own system (much as Boyce says of Zoroaster's teachings about eschatology) and cannot be properly interpreted when they stand apart from that system. I quote his summary and conclusions at great length in order to show how he both makes the point and demonstrates the correct methodology important for our study:

> In spite of their literal interpretation of the Pentateuch, the Qumran people came to maintain a view of marriage and a practice of marriage which differed greatly from the O.T. view and the view expressed in the rabbinical literature. This fact has proved to be entirely due to the basically eschatological ideology of the Qumran community. They considered themselves to be engaged in a war in the eschatological period against the children of darkness. They therefore live in accordance with the laws relating to the holy war, even as regards marriage. The young man has a right to take a wife and live with her for a period of five years. After this period, the laws relating to the holy war stipulate that he is to refrain entirely from sexual cohabitation with his wife. Should his wife die during this five-year period, the man has nevertheless done his duty in propagating his race. He may not take another wife. Anyone who does so shows that he is not capable of living in accordance with the laws of the holy war but is addicted to fornication. The husband does not need to divorce his wife when he reaches the age of 25 but it is likely that such divorces occurred, sometimes perhaps on the plea that the husband wished to avoid all suspicion that he had sexual intercourse with his wife even after the age of 25, when under the laws of the holy war he was no longer allowed to have it. The man who had reached the age of 25 was to live in sexual abstinence, in order to be able to do his part in the holy war against the children of darkness.
>
> The men of Qumran were not monks governed by ascetic rules and refraining from marriage in order to combat the lust of the flesh or from aversion to women. They were soldiers mustered and sanctified to fight in the eschatological war against the children of darkness. The laws of this war allowed them to be married for a period in their youth and to live with their wives and beget children. But these laws also required them to live for the greater part of their lives in sexual abstinence. Every detail in the Qumran community's view of marriage and every detail in which its marriage *halakah* differs from those of other contemporary Jewish groups has proved to have originated in the basically eschatological ideology which dominated the life of the whole sect. This also means that the Qumran community's view of marriage must not be interpreted as an isolated detail in its ethical system. *Its moral principles on the subject of marriage are indissolubly linked with its eschatology.* (1965:64-65)

Isaksson properly italicizes his concluding sentence. It would be difficult to improve upon his approach. We now very rapidly review other candidates, in the period in which Mishnah's system comes into being, for comparison, whether of minor details or of whole systems. The work will not detail us for very long.

V

Because we do not have literary evidence of systems such as Mishnah's does not mean that in ancient Judaism there were no systems encompassing women and in which, as in Mishnah, the topic of women filled an important place. But the absence of literary evidence does mean that we are not able to effect a comparison between Mishnah's system of women and some other system of the same time and place. So far as I am able to see, neither the Israelite nor the Greco-Roman world produced a document on women analogous to Mishnah's. Of the Israelite world we may be certain: among extant materials there is no system involving women as a principal component although all constructions we do have in hand include facts about, and references to, women – a very different thing. Obviously, the treatment of women, the role accorded to them in society, the place enjoyed by them in the imaginative and religious life of the diverse groups of late antiquity – all of these aspects of life required, and certainly received, attention. But how the facts about these matters fit into the larger context of which they were a part, and how these larger contexts may be described and so made available for comparison and systemic analysis I do not know. When, therefore, we state, as we must, that Mishnah is the only system of women known to us in late antiquity, the appropriate qualifications have been made. Let us now survey other Israelite writings of approximately the same time as Mishnah comes into being.

The Zadokite Document (CD) presents laws but "not a comprehensive handbook of *halakhah* [law]." Rather we have "a series of *halakhic* statements, roughly arranged by subjects" (Rabin, *The Zadokite Documents. I. The Admonition. II. The Laws* 1958:x). It follows that we cannot ask for the traits of CD's system as a whole, since we do not have access to the whole. We do have complete pericopae devoted to the oath, the order of the judges, purification with water, the Sabbath, the camp overseer, the meeting of all camps, preparing the requirements of the community, a woman's oath, and freewill gifts. The rule of the woman's oath (XVI, 10-13) simply observes that since the husband can annul the oath of the wife, he should not annul it unless he knows whether it ought to be carried out or annulled. If it is such as to lead to transgression of the covenant, let him annul it and not carry it out. Likewise is the rule for her father (Rabin, 1958:76). It goes without saying that, so far as the presuppositions of Mishnah tractate on vows, Nedarim, go, a vow contrary to what is written in the Torah is null to begin with and therefore will not require the husband's abrogation. An oath contrary to what is written in the Torah also is not binding. This hardly constitutes an ample "doctrine," let alone a system, of women or corpus of women's law. It is further forbidden to have sexual relations in Jerusalem (XII, 43), for reasons having to do with the theory of the character of the city, along the lines of Lev. 15:18 (Rabin, 1958:58-59).

The relevant evidence in the Temple Scroll is summarized by Professor Baruch A. Levine as follows:

> 1) Col. 65:7-66:12 of the *Scroll* present a version of Deut. 2:13-23:1. There are lacunae in the *Scroll,* which can be reliably restored since, in other respects, the *Scroll's* version is faithful to the biblical original. The only variations are dialectical and orthographic.
>
> 2) Col. 66:12-17 take up the cue of Deut. 23:1, which is a statement on incest, prohibiting marriage with the wife of one's father, and link to what preceded a version of the incest code of Lev. 18 (cf. Lev. 20). The *Scroll,* as preserved, breaks off before this code is completed. Originally, it undoubtedly took up a part of the missing last column, col. 67. The listed incestuous unions are as follows: a) the wife of one's brother, including a half-brother, either by one's father or mother, b) one's sister, including one's half-sister, either by one's father or mother, c) the sister of one's father or the sister of one's mother (aunts), and d) one's niece, the daughter of one's brother or one's sister.
>
> The significant addition here is, of course, the prohibition of marriage with nieces, not mentioned in Leviticus or elsewhere in Scripture (cf. *Zadokite Document* Vf.).
>
> 3) Col. 57:15-19 of the *Scroll* introduce into the code of conduct for Israelite kings two provisions, deriving from Deut. 17:17: a) the king must be monogamous, and b) the king is not only forbidden to marry gentile women, but must marry a woman from his father's household, or family (cf. *Zadokite Document* IV:20f. and Ezek. 36:16).
>
> The prohibition of marriage with nieces, and the question of monogamy are discussed in: Baruch A. Levine, "The *Temple Scroll:* Aspects of Its Historical Provenance and Literary Character," *BASOR,* no. 232 (1979).
>
> 4) Col. 53:14-54:5 contain the *Scroll's* version of Num. 30:3f. on the matter of vows (*nedarim*) and the respective roles of father and husband regarding vows pronounced by women. Except for the conversion of 3rd person references to God into 1st person references ("to Me," instead of "to the Lord,") the *Scroll's* version is essentially faithful to the biblical original.
>
> 5) Col. 63:10-15 of the *Scroll* present a version of the law governing marriage with captive women, Deut. 21:10f. The statements regarding marriage are biblical, but the *Scroll* adds a stricture, which actually concerns purity, more than marriage, itself. The *Scroll* forbids the captive wife from partaking of *selamim* offerings or what it calls *tohorah* "pure, sanctified food" for seven years.[10]

---

[10]Personal letter, September 10, 1978.

On the basis of this evidence it is not possible to maintain that the Temple Scroll presents anything like a system of women. Apart from a couple of scriptural rules, the Temple Scroll and Mishnah's systemic construction have nothing in common. Two of the points at which the theme of women is important to the Temple Scroll and on which the author has something to say other than to cite Scripture – Levine's Nos. 2, 5 – are not treated at all by Mishnah's division of Women. The third – Levine's No. 2 – is shared, both in theme and detail, in Yebamot. For Yebamot, however, the list of incestuous unions forms a part of the factual substructure of the tractate. It scarcely forms a focus of inquiry or defines a critical problematic. So there is one point of intersection at the factual level, and none at that of generative conceptions, between Mishnah's division of Women and the Temple Scroll's allusions to women. Of greater consequence, the latter document in no way treats the theme of women systematically – for example, within the program of Scripture's available allusions – nor does the theme play a major role in the Temple Scroll's system. What Mishnah and the Temple Scroll share is simply Scripture or, more accurately, a couple of facts supplied to both by Scripture.

If our problem were the position of women in general, then germane to our account would be the prominence assigned to women in all four Gospels. The women of Jesus' day and country seem to have had great liberty of movement and action (Donaldson, *Woman. Her Position and Influence in Ancient Greece and Rome and among the Early Christians,* 1907:149). But there is no doctrine of women in the Gospels, nor can we find in the occasional remarks in Paul's letters even a remote equivalent to the Mishnaic system of women.

The Gospels' picture of women as a prominent and independent group in society is confirmed by the trove of legal documents belonging to a Jewish woman of the early second century. Among the Cave of Letters of the Bar Kokhba finds is the marriage contract of a woman, among other legal documents pertaining to her affairs (Yadin, *Bar Kokhba. The Rediscovery of the Legendary Hero of the Second Jewish Revolt against Rome,* 1971:222-253). The account of the affairs of this woman, Babata, leaves no doubt of her legal capacities. She received all the properties of her husband during his own lifetime and took possession of them when he died. She remarried and inherited another large property. She undertook and effected numerous important litigations and in general supervised what was hers. Any picture of the Israelite woman of the second century as chattel and a dumb animal hardly accords with the actualities revealed in the legal documents of Babata.

It is hardly necessary to observe that we have not accomplished a synchronic comparison between Mishnah's system of women and some other Israelite system(s) of women of approximately the same time and place. The reason is that we have not located an equivalent, nor partially equivalent, integrated and whole system of women other than Mishnah's. We have diverse rules on topics relevant to women. On their basis no progress toward the interpretation of Mishnah's system is possible.

VI

Mishnah's system may be brought into relationship with more than the systems of its own time and place, on one side, and of its distinct cultural continuum, on the other. It also may be usefully juxtaposed to systems of women worked out in other societies, in other times, and in other parts of the world. For there surely is a common continuum of humankind, a context of humanity, which will yield its contrasts and comparisons. But, to my knowledge, the work cannot yet be done. It is too soon. For while we may formulate a fruitful and well-constructed question, we do not, so far as I now, have a suitable formulation of data out of which to answer such a question. For example, if we ask, What is it we learn about the traits of Israelite society, as envisaged by Mishnah, from Mishnah's system of women? we are unable to provide an answer. The reason is that, to my knowledge, we have no comparative studies of diverse possibilities of how women may be treated, the position which may be accorded to them or which they, for their own part, may define for themselves. Without taxonomies, we consequently do not know what sorts of societies will opt for which type of system among several possibilities and, still more interesting, what we learn about such societies from their choices in regard to women.

To spell this out: Mishnah's system of women deals with the transfer of women and of property associated with that transfer. It would be interesting to know the sorts of systems by which other societies (or the philosophers of other societies) arrange the same transaction. It would, further, be worth knowing what we learn about a society which does things in one way instead of some other. What do we learn about the world envisaged by Mishnah from the choices made by Mishnah in the matter of the transfer of women? Or, to state matters more accurately, what *else* do we learn? The answer to this type of question seems to me to lie in the future.

Still, anthropologists have not left us wholly without observations of a fructifying character. For example, R. Rosaldo observes:

A woman's status will be lowest in those societies where there is a firm differentiation between domestic and public spheres of activity and where women are isolated from one another and placed under a single man's authority, in the home (*Woman, Culture, and Society*, 1974:36).

It would appear at first glance that the present system accords to the woman a low status indeed for it conforms in its basic social and familial datum to Rosaldo's definition. Women not only are assigned tasks limited to the home, but they also are given few tasks in common and, outside of the home, are perceived merely to gossip in the moonlight.

But this is somewhat misleading. We observe, for one thing, that even while married, women may become property owners of substance, if their fathers leave them land. True, the husband enjoys the usufruct so long as the marriage continues. But the woman is ultimate owner. That means the husband has every material reason to want to preserve those conditions which will secure and perpetuate the marriage. Moreover, Mishnah makes provision for a husband's relinquishing his rights over his wife's property, even as a condition of marriage. This means that the world outside the linguistic frame of Mishnah looked much different from that inside, as the case of Babata suggests. Of greater importance than practical affairs, Mishnah within its theoretical frame does accord the woman rights of property. It does secure the marriage, through the marriage contract and its settlement upon the occasion of divorce or death of the husband, so that in no way is the wife utterly and completely dependent upon the husband. That does not mean the woman enjoys a position, in her realm, equivalent to that of the man, in his. But it does mean that a woman's status in this system is not utterly lacking a measure of autonomy, dignity, and control of her own affairs. The measure, to be sure, is not overflowing.

Mishnah is produced within, and can only imagine, a patriarchal society. Its legislation on women to begin with expresses the values of that society. This is self-evident in that the critical points of the system – beginning, end of marriage – define what is important about woman. What requires close attention and regulation is important because the relationship of woman to man constitutes the criterion of significance. Women's relationships to other women never come under discussion, except as a realm from which a woman may not be wholly cut off at her husband's whim. But if there were activities used by women "as a basis for female solidarity and worth," Mishnah does not legislate about them. Since it is what Mishnah deems important that Mishnah chooses for its careful scrutiny, the point is obvious. Mishnah does not imagine that men live apart from women or that women exist outside of relationship with, and therefore control of, men. Mishnah is a man's document and imagines a man's world. Women have rights, protected by man and heaven alike. But these rights pertain, specifically, to the relationship of women to men (and heaven), and specified among them is none of consequence outside of male society.

VII

The critical issue of the meaning of Mishnah's system of women brings us to the center of Mishnah's meaning, which the system of women, like all other Mishnaic systems, expresses in language particular to its topic. What Mishnah wishes to state it states systemically, as a whole. The parts and the details take on meaning only as part of that whole. At this point, therefore, while we may make some observations about what a subset of the Mishnaic system appears to wish to say, the full expression of that message must wait the completion of work on the whole.[11] For only when we understand why Mishnah chooses the six topics it chooses, and not some other set of six – or five, or nine or sixty-three – topics shall we make sense of what Mishnah says about, and through, each of those topics. To that inquiry, women mean no more, and no less, than albatrosses, rocks, trees, or study of Torah, on which we have neither tractates nor divisions, or torts, purities, or agricultural-offerings to priests, on which we have both.

The first and most important point is that Mishnah's meaning is defined not only by, but also in behalf of, Mishnah's authorities. All we have in hand is a statement of how they imagine things should be. As I said, whole divisions (for instance, Holy Things and Purities) dwell upon matters which, at the moment at which the systems came into being and were worked out, simply did not exist. Others speak of matters which, at the time of discourse, lay wholly outside the practical power and authority of the participants to the discussion, for example, the organization of a government spelled out in Sanhedrin. Still others take for granted that only a small number of people will keep the law properly, as in the case of the larger part of Agricultural Rules. So Mishnah speaks for its authorities and tells us what is on their minds, that alone. Only in later times would the Israelite world come to approximate, and even to conform to, Mishnah's vision of reality. But the meaning of which we presently speak is in the minds of a handful of men.

From these men's perspective, second, women are abnormal; men are normal.[12] I am inclined to think that the reason they choose to work

---

[11]I lay out three of Mishnah's six divisions, with stress on the history and structure of the law (1974-77: I-XXII; 1978-80: I-VI; 1980f: I-V).

[12]The notion of the woman as anomalous, which I first read in Beauvoir, *The Second Sex* (1953) will now come to the fore as the hermeneutical fulcrum for the interpretation of the Mishnah's system of Women and, as I shall argue, of Mishnah's system as a whole. It is a commonplace in women's studies, but an exceptionally fresh and fructifying idea for the study of ancient Judaism. I underline this fact to indicate why I think women's studies as an academic field

out a division on women flows from that fact. And, when we recall that the only other systems of women worthy of the name come to us under priestly auspices, in the priestly code (Lev. 1-15) and in the Holiness Code (Lev. 17ff.), we can hardly be surprised at the selection of women, for the men before us create Mishnah as a scribal-priestly document. Women in the priestly perspective of the holy life are excluded from the centers of holiness. They cannot enter the sensitive domain of the cult, cannot perform the cultic service, and cannot participate even in the cultic liturgy. Likewise, in time to come, when Rabbinic Judaism comes to full expression so that study of Torah comes to be seen as a cultic act, the rabbi as equivalent to the priest, and the community of Israel assembled for study of Torah as equivalent to the holy Temple, it would be perfectly "natural" to continue the exclusion of women. Rabbinism is a Judaic system in which people who are neither priests nor scribes take up the method of the priests and the message of the scribes. To all of this, women form an anomaly and a threat, just as the priests concluded in Ezra's time when they produced Leviticus. That is why, as in other matters of anomaly or threat, Mishnah must devote a rather considerable measure of attention to forming a system of women – a system of law to regulate the irregular.

We shall now dwell on this matter of woman as anomaly because, as I have now indicated, I am inclined to see in it the core and key to the worldview laid out for us in the division of Women. I shall now try to show that, as I claimed at the outset, the treatment and selection of women constitute the exegetical fulcrum for the Mishnaic system as a whole. To repeat my main proposition: When we make sense of Mishnah's choice of the theme, women, and what it wishes to say about that theme, we shall find ourselves at the heart of the Mishnaic system of reality building.

To begin with, if we are going to be able to make sense of Mishnah's choices, its inclusions and exclusions in its discourse on women, it must, I think, be because of the basic conception of women. They are abnormal and excluded, something out of the ordinary. That is why they form a focus on sanctification: restoration of the extraordinary to the ordinary and the normal.

Let me spell this out. Mishnah cannot declare a dead creeping thing clean. Mishnah cannot make women into men. It can provide for the purification of what is made unclean. It can provide for a world in which it is normal for woman to be subject to man – father or husband – and a system which regularizes the transfer of women from the hand of the

---

have the potential to make rich contributions to the unfolding of other areas of study.

father to that of the husband. The regulation of the transfer of women is Mishnah's way of effecting the sanctification of what, for the moment, disturbs and disorders the orderly world. The work of sanctification *becomes* necessary in particular at the point of danger and disorder. An order of women must be devoted, therefore, to just these things, so as to preserve the normal modes of creation ("how these things really are") so that maleness, that is, normality, may encompass all, even and especially at the critical point of transfer.

In this sense the process outlined in the division of Purities for the restoration of normality, meaning cleanness, to what is abnormal, meaning uncleanness, is suggestive. What Mishnah proposes is to restore the equilibrium disturbed by the encounter with the disruptive, disorganizing, and abnormal sources of uncleanness specified in the priestly writings. So the division of Purities centers attention on the point of abnormality and its restoration to normality: sources of uncleanness, foci of uncleanness, modes of purification.[13] Now, when we reflect on the view of women contained in Mishnah, we observe a parallel interest in the point of abnormality and the restoration to normality of women: the moment at which a woman changes hands. So Rosaldo states:

> The fact that men, in contrast to women, can be said to be associated with culture reflects another aspect of cultural definitions of the female. Recent studies of symbolic culture have suggested that whatever violates a society's sense of order will be seen as threatening, nasty, disorderly, or wrong....The idea of "order" depends, logically, on "disorder" as its opposite....Now I would suggest that women in many societies will be seen as something "anomalous." Insofar as men, in their institutionalized relations of kinships, politics, and so on, define the public order, women are their opposite. Where men are classified in terms of ranked, institutional positions, women are simply women and their activities, interests, and differences receive only idiosyncratic note. Where male activities are justified and rationalized by a fine societal classification, by a system of norms acknowledging their different pursuits, women are classified together, and their particular goals are ignored. From the point of view of the larger social system, they are seen as deviants or manipulators; because systems of social classification rarely make room for their interests, they are not publicly understood. But women defy the ideal of the male order. They may be defined as virgins, yet be necessary to the group's regeneration. They may be excluded from authority, yet exercise all sorts of informal power. Their status may be derived from their male relations, yet they outlive their husbands and fathers. And insofar as the presence of women does introduce such contradictions, women will be seen as anomalous and defined as dangerous, dirty, and polluting, as something to be set apart. (1974:31-32)

---

[13]This fact is spelled out at great length in my *Purities*, XXII (1977).

Rosaldo further states: "Women in conventional roles are not threatening. A woman who is a wife and a mother is benign" (1974). Now, as we have observed, it is the point at which a woman is perceived as threatening – when she has the capacity to become a wife and a mother but is not yet in a position of realizing it, or when she ceases to be a wife – that her status requires the regulation, ordering, and protection of Mishnah's elaborate and reverent intellectual attention.

About woman as wife Mishnah has little to say; about woman as mother, I cannot think of ten relevant lines in Mishnah's division of Women[!]. For these are not the topics to which Mishnah will devote itself. The three systemically anomalous tractates from this perspective are not so far out of line. Sotah, of course, attends to the wife who is not a good wife. Nedarim, bearing Nazir in its wake, treats those moments specified by Scripture as especially important in the daughter's relationship to the father or the wife's to the husband. These are moments at which the father or the husband may intervene in the relationship of daughter or wife to God. In the present context, that relationship is unruly and dangerous, exactly like the relationship of daughter leaving father or of wife leaving husband, that is, at the critical moment of betrothal and consummation of the marriage, with attendant property settlement; or divorce or husband's death, at the critical moment of the dissolution of the marriage, with attendant property settlement.

Mishnah's system addresses and means to create an ordered and well-regulated world. Mishnah states that which is the order and regulation for such a world. The division of Purities spells out the balance and wholeness of the system of cleanness, defining what is a source of uncleanness, a focus affected by uncleanness, and a mode of effecting cleanness or restoring the balance and the wholeness of the system in stasis. It is the most complete statement of that wholeness and regulation which are at every point besought and realized. The division of Holy Things addresses a different sort of message, speaking, as the division of Purities does not, to a real world. But it is the message which is unreal, for in A.D. 200 there is no cult. Holy Things provides a map for a world which is both no more and not yet, for a Temple which was and will be. The stasis attained therein, it must follow, is to portray how things truly are, at a moment at which they are not that way at all. By contrast to Purities, which conceives of a sequence of states in a reality out there and tells the regulations for each of those states, Holy Things speaks of how things are in mind, at a moment at which mind is all there is. When we come to the division of Women, therefore, we find ourselves confronted by a familiar problem, expressed through (merely) unfamiliar facts. The familiar problem is an anomalous fact. An anomaly is for this system a situation requiring human interventions so that affairs may be brought into stasis, that is, made to conform with the heavenly projections of the created world. That quest for stasis, order, and regulation, which constitute wholeness and completeness, in the division of Women takes up yet another circumstance of uncertainty. This it confronts at its most uncertain. The system subjects the anomaly of woman to the capacity for ordering and regulating, which is the gift and skill of priests and scribes.

The anomaly of woman therefore is addressed at its most anomalous, that is, disorderly and dangerous, moment, the point at which women move from one setting and status to another. The very essence of the anomaly, woman's sexuality, is scarcely mentioned. But it always is just beneath the surface. For what defines the woman's status – what is rarely made explicit in the division of Women – is not whether or not she may have sexual relations, but with whom she may have them and with what consequence. It is assumed that, from long before the advent of puberty, a girl may be married and in any event is a candidate for sexuality. From puberty onward she will be married. But what is selected for intense and continuing concern is with whom she may legitimately do so, and with what economic and social effect. There is no sexual deed without public consequence; and only rarely will a sexual deed not yield economic results, in the aspect of the transfer of property from one hand to another. So, as I said, what is anomalous is the woman's sexuality, which is treated in a way wholly different from man's. And the goal and purpose of Mishnah's division of Women are to bring under control and force into stasis all of the wild and unruly potentialities of sexuality, with their dreadful threat of uncontrolled shifts in personal status and material possession alike.

Mishnah invokes heaven's interest in this most critical moment for individual and society alike. Its conception is that what is rightly done on earth is confirmed in heaven. A married woman who has sexual relations with any man but her husband has not merely committed a crime on earth. She has sinned against heaven. It follows that when a married woman receives a writ of divorce and so is free to enter into relationships with any man of her choosing, the perceptions of that woman are affected in heaven just as much as are man's perceptions of her on earth. What was beforehand a crime and a sin afterward is holy, not subject to punishment at all. The woman may contract a new marriage on earth which heaven, for its part, will oversee and sanctify. What is stated in these simple propositions is that those crucial and critical turnings at which a woman changes hands produce concern and response in heaven above as much as on earth below. And the reason, as I suggested at the beginning, is that heaven is invoked specifically at those times, and in those circumstances, in which Mishnah confronts a situation of anomaly or disorder and proposes to effect suitable regulation and besought order.

To conclude: It is to a situation which is so fraught with danger as to threaten the order and regularity of the stable, sacred society in its perfection and at its point of stasis that Mishnah will devote its principal cognitive and legislative efforts. For that situation, Mishnah will invoke heaven and express its most vivid concern for sanctification. What breaks established routine or what is broken out of established routine is what is subject to the fully articulated and extensive reflections of a whole division of Mishnah, or, in Hebrew, a *seder*, an order, of the whole. Mishnah, as usual, provides its own most reliable exegesis in calling each one of its six principal divisions a *seder*, an order. The anomaly of woman is worked out – that is, held in stasis – by assigning her to man's domain. It follows that the stasis is disturbed at the point when she changes hands. Then Mishnah's instincts for regulating and thereby restoring the balance and order of the world are aroused. So from the recognition of the anomalous character of women, we find ourselves moving toward the most profound and fundamental affirmations of Mishnah about the works of sanctification: the foci and the means. Women are sanctified through the deeds of men. So, too, are earth and time, the fruit of the herd and of the field, the bed,[14] chair, table, and hearth – but, in the nature of things, women most of all.

---

[14] I do not make reference to the menstrual taboo because Mishnah's Division of Women does not deal with it. Menstrual laws are a subdivision, or tractate, of the system of Purities.

Part Three

ONGOING DISPUTES

8

Publishing Too Much

Samuel Tobias Lachs, *Humanism in Talmud and Midrash*
(Rutherford, 1992: Fairleigh Dickinson University Press).

Publishing too much takes place when a scholar publishes a book that lacks a fresh idea. By that definition, one can be one too many, and, by the same criterion, five hundred may be simply too few. Much depends on whether or not one has something to say. A good case in point is a book that has nothing to say.

Here Professor Samuel Tobias Lachs, Bryn Mawr College, announces as his purpose the collection and arrangement of passages "in the Talmud and midrash" that "reflect an anthropocentric, rather than a theocentric view of the world." The passages are arranged topically, "to illustrate how some of the rabbis of the talmudic era subscribed to a view of the world which starts with man rather than with God and is reflected in their observations about the human condition." No one has done so before, he says, because, he thinks, "it is the result of theological cowardice, motivated by a fear that by assembling the data in a logical order, and examining them separately, more traditional theological approaches might be compromised or rejected." But, as we shall see, Lachs announces a distinction that makes no difference at all. That is, first, because he proposes to disprove a proposition nobody holds; and second, because he ignores all of the rules of professional scholarship.

To accomplish his stated goal, Lachs begins with an introduction, in which he explains that "the early rabbis gradually wrested the Torah and the right to its interpretation from this absolute and autocratic control of the priesthood," which they replaced: "The priesthood was not the favored institution of many of the rabbis because of its clerical nature, which was antithetical to their egalitarian view of society." The prophets, too, were succeeded by these same rabbis "as the moral conscience of the people." Lachs explains, "The prophetic movement came to an end once the people had direct access to the Torah." That brings Lachs to "the transmission of tradition from the prophets directly to the men of the Great Synagogue." So the rabbis assumed "three traditional roles...from their biblical predecessors." After this exercise in pseudo-history – not a sentence in his account stands on the critical foundations of scholarship as it is practiced today! – he reaches his topic.

"Theocentrism" is contrasted with "a strong anthropocentric orientation." The legacy of priest and prophet is "theocentric," but the sage's legacy – that of the Old Testament Wisdom literature is what he means – is "anthropocentric." Theocentrism dominated because "man stands in awe of authority"; "the Torah describes its own divine character and provenance, [so] the theocentric outlook would naturally prevail"; and "religion by its very nature is conservative. Sacred texts deemed divine in origin are said not to change....The theocentrist almost always tends to be a strict constructionist of the Law...." What is bothering him, therefore, is not theology at all, but attitudes toward the law and tradition; his "theocentrists" really are conservative, and his "humanists," not so; so the fight is between Orthodox and Conservative Judaism in eastern Pennsylvania as Lachs wishes to frame matters.

His Conservative Judaism enters when he maintains, "There were those who would not be resigned to intellectual inertia nor intimidated by the thought of change....It is precisely because of their commitment to free inquiry and this ordering of priorities that illustrates their choice of the anthropocentric over the theocentric view of the world. They deeply respected tradition, but would not permit it to immobilize them either in thought or in action. Because they questioned it and subjected it to rational inquiry they represented a healthy challenge to the comfortable stability of the exponents of an authoritative, revealed tradition." Lachs proceeds to persuade himself that he has correctly characterized Rabbinic Judaism in maintaining that it is, in his categories, "anthropocentric," and not "theocentric." It follows that his categories are wildly out of kilter, since his discussion concerns not theology but the politics of traditional Judaism in the USA. That is not to suggest he ever comes to the point. His anthology merely meanders through these categories: man and society; God; Torah; and divine revelation and human authorship. Each of the chapters consists of strung-together allusions to various passages, none of them cited or analyzed, so readers are left to believe, or disbelieve, Lachs's paraphrase and allegations as to the sense and meaning of the passages.

Lachs's polemic is that of a Conservative rabbi against Orthodox Judaism, since it is difficult to identify anyone else who to begin with might take seriously what has provoked his "research." Precisely what it means to "start with man" rather than "with God" he really does not spell out with any clarity; he seems to know that everyone agrees on the sense and importance of what he is trying to prove, and to grasp what is at stake. That, of course, is plausible only in the circle of true believers in the method and proposition at hand. Since Reform Judaism rarely constructs theological arguments on the strength of the Rabbinic documents alone, and since Orthodox Judaism in its various formulations and versions forms the butt of Lachs's polemic, Conservative Judaism – meaning, a handful of Orthodox rabbis serving Reform congregations – remains as the beneficiary.

Lachs claims that where our sages of blessed memory show respect for rigorous argument and reason, they are among his "humanists." But then the whole of Rabbinic Judaism conforms to his prescription, since, after all, there is no more rational or elegantly and rigorously argued piece of writing in world literature than the Talmud of Babylonia. That is a monument to the conviction of our sages of blessed memory that the human mind is in the model, "in our image, after our likeness," of the mind of God, made manifest through the Torah. So, as they say, *iqqar haser min hassefer*, the book forgets its main point! The stated proposition is pure gibberish. "Our sages of blessed memory" believed in a supernatural God, whom they encountered in the Torah. Everybody knows that. What it means, then, to distinguish "starting with God" from "starting with man" is not at all obvious, except to Lachs.

But it is not the substance of matters that marks the book as an exercise in confused babble. What is wrong with this book is that it contains not a single well-argued, clearly formulated, and rigorously demonstrated proposition. A person may be guilty of "publishing too much" by publishing a single book, if it lacks a fresh and important idea. And this kind of neo-primitivism – a Cro-Magnon hunting and gathering, a puerile collecting and arranging – can scarcely claim to propose any ideas at all. I am inclined to think that Lachs is obscure on that matter because he is just babbling. In fact, he has set up for himself some sort of straw man, whom it is easy to knock down. The chapters that form the shank of the book are filled with a kind of stream-of-consciousness free association. I could cite hundreds of paragraphs to illustrate the pointlessness of the run-on babble, but none would convey the flavor of the whole.

Lachs knows nothing of a vast literature of history and theology devoted to each of the topics of his chapters. That fact is proven in a very simple way. Examine his footnotes. Nearly all of them consist of brief allusions to sources; in any fifty footnotes, he cites scarcely a single monographic work, one that has covered the same sources, the same problems, the same issues. Reinventing the wheel, Lachs deliberately obscures the fact that he is not the first to take up the themes at hand. Then, too, readers are unlikely to know that his book represents a huge step backward, into an age in which "scholarship" on Judaism consisted of collecting this and that and passing one's opinion. Studies on such and such an idea "in Talmud and Midrash," lacking historical precision, documentary concreteness, and philosophical clarity, no longer are published in English, since the scholarly world no longer tolerates this kind of amateurism. Standards have risen; expectations are higher; making things up as you go along and publishing the result no longer suffices. This is not a work of scholarship, it is an act of contempt for scholarship.

It also is not a work of argument for a broad audience, since the writing is obscure and allusive, not clear and focused. I cannot imagine a nonspecialist audience for a sentence such as this (among thousands): "As the rabbis rejected Greco-Roman gnosticism and its dualistic theology so, too, they rejected and opposed the Christian concept of an antagonistic dichotomy in man." As a matter of fact, without a Ph.D. in the history of religion, readers are unlikely to know what he is talking about. And they also are not apt to realize that his characterization of "the rabbis" is challenged in study after study, beginning after all with Scholem, or that his portrait of "Christian concept" is one that will amaze, for its ignorance, a vast number of historians of Christian thought, who can cite chapter and verse of Church Fathers' writings to contradict his monolithic description of what was a highly complex and variegated set of Christian systems. Not many people any more imagine a single "Christianity" to match a single "the rabbis...."

This is, as I said, just a case of publishing a book even though the author has nothing to say in the book: hunting and gathering, collecting and arranging – and then a whole lot of free association and fabrication. Lachs has published only two books but provides a fine example of publishing too much, since his *Rabbinic Commentary on the New Testament* (1987) exhibits the same intellectual incompetence. There he collects and arranges passages he thinks relevant to various Gospels' passages and then passes his opinion on this and that; there, too, he cites only a tiny fraction of the existing literature of the same sort; there, too, he thinks hunting and gathering, collecting and arranging, is learning. And most of the reviews of that worthless exercise said exactly that.

I assume lots of Conservative synagogues will want this party platform for their libraries, even though their members are unlikely to read it. But apart from that trivial audience, the book will quickly find its way into the bowels of research libraries, which buy everything automatically, and there languish, as it should. It neither informs, nor challenges, nor makes an important argument, nor argues an intelligible thesis: it is a book that did not have to be written, the sort of which our Israeli colleagues say, "Pity the trees" (cut down to make the paper to print the book).

9

The Intellectual Fiasco of Richard Kalmin Revisited

Richard Kalmin, *The Redaction of the Babylonian Talmud: Amoraic or Saboraic?* (Cincinnati, 1989: Hebrew Union College).

In a recent issue of Hebrew Studies, Professor Richard Kalmin of Jewish Theological Seminary of America replies to my review of his book in an earlier issue of the same journal. It is worth reconsidering both the book and my criticism of it, in the context of his reply, to which I also respond here.

In his book, Kalmin addresses the question of the final stages in the redaction of the Talmud of Babylonia. He seeks knowledge of "who the redactors were, at what time period(s) they lived, and how they reworked their sources." Kalmin proposes to answer these questions in a way that will prove unfamiliar, even recondite, obscure, and eccentric, to scholars who work on the history of documents that lack clear evidence of authorship, text tradition, and the like. For ordinarily when people ask about the history of a document, they want to know where and when it is first attested by some external writing, for example, when we find the first references to, and citations of, the document under study. Furthermore, the manuscript tradition will be asked to lead us to the earlier representation of the writing at hand. Finally, traits of the document overall will be assessed as a first step in finding out whether the writing is a composite or unitary, and, if unitary, for whom the document speaks.

Kalmin rejects these universally accepted procedures. A description of his program will explain why I find the work so alien to contemporary humanistic learning. The very layout of the work is daunting. The very opening pages validate my judgment that the man is simply talking to himself.   For he begins not with a preface but with a chart of "characteristics of Talmud rabbis."   This involves "group A Amoraim (ca. 390-501) [1] strong tendency to make prescriptive and interpretative or explanatory statements; [2] independent; no tendency to appear in connection with a small number of sages; [3] multi-dimensional; active as both students and teachers; [4] their statements are integrative into the core of the sugya; [5] their statements do not refer to or respond to discussions by the Stam."   This kind of thing goes on for Group B Amoraim or Group 2 Amoraim and then Group 1 Amoraim, then Group 3 Amoraim; then the Stam (anonymous sections of the Talmud); then the Saboraim (post-Amoraic). His date for this last group is from 501. There follow three charts: theory of Saboraic redaction; theory of continuous redaction; then theory of Stammaitic redaction. All of this is given without a single definition, without the slightest interest in explaining the source of the characterizations, part of which I cited, without any introduction to what is at stake or at issue. I find puzzling just what Kalmin proposed to accomplish in these rather daunting charts.

His introduction then surveys regnant opinion on the redaction of the Babylonian Talmud. Kalmin's main interest is in Halivni's "theory of stammaitic redaction," though in his behalf it must be said that he has read the work of others as well. Kalmin sets up his problem as follows: There are three basic theories on the redaction of the Bavli. Certain features, he claims, should characterize the document, if one or another of those theories pertains.

Thus he says, "According to the theory of Saboraic redaction, we would not expect to discern evidence of a unique editorial role on the part of the late Amoraim. According to this theory the distinctive features we encounter among the final generations of Amoraim should be in line with discernible Amoraic trends. We should observe a smooth transition from the generation of Rav Ashi's teachers to the generation of Rav Ashi and from that point to the generation of Rav Ashi's students and beyond." I am not at all clear on why Kalmin is so certain that these are the characteristics that "should" emerge, and it seems to me somewhat facile on his part so to define matters as to prove his point a priori. Kalmin claims to show that "the attributed material that survives from the late Amoraic period conforms to clearly definable patterns, and that these patterns are the continuation and development of patterns exhibited by previous Amoraic generations." It goes without saying that every line of his study then rests upon the premise that all attributions are sound and reliable; without that premise, nothing can be done along the lines he has taken in this book. Only if the attributions are valid can he know which saying or composite or composition is of "the late Amoraic period," and which is not. But the fabricated argument, resting on an unsubstantiated "should be" thus and so, is true to the one important stream of Talmudic exegesis, the pilpulistic, which manufactures questions and then makes up answers to them. Not a few of the reviewers of the books by David Halivni, on which Kalmin says he bases his entire work, have dismissed as pilpulistic the same kind of argumentation.

Rather than tax the reader's patience with a précis of further stages in Kalmin's argument, let me give the center of matters in his own words, provided on the book flap (the most clearly expounded propositions in the entire book, alas): "Kalmin notes that in each case where a late Amora appears to respond to statements by the stam, it is possible, and usually preferable in the light of certain incongruities in the sugya as it presently stands, to detach the Amoraic statement from its connection to the stam and restore its original connection to an earlier Amoraic or Tannaitic source. The simplest explanation for this phenomenon...is that late Amoraim do not respond to the earlier stam discussions because there were no earlier stamot. Composition of the stam...did not begin until after the conclusion of the Amoraic period." All of this, I maintain, is simply a fabrication, which emerges when one has made up one's own definitions, invented one's own questions, and produced answers in accord with one's own program. Readers by this point will expect, in any event, a rather compendious treatment of texts, so that they may share in the inquiry that the author undertakes. Otherwise, how are we to know what it means to "detach the Amoraic statement from its connection to the stam" or to know why that is required at all? A survey of the remainder of the book produces the following: who lived during the final Amoraic generations? Rav Ashi and Ravina are the end of horaah, the theory of Hanokh Albeck; Mar bar Rav Ashi and his literary contribution, the theory of Avinoam Cohen; characteristics of the final generations of Amoraim; the final generations of Amoraim, transition or continuity? the relationship between the final generations of Amoraim and the stam and its impact on the question of redaction. That concludes the book: ninety-four pages, six chapters in all. There follow thirteen appendices. Only the first allows us to peer over Kalmin's shoulder as he reads a text: the analysis of sugyot. He treats all of five! He gives the Hebrew-Aramaic original, untranslated, and then, without telling us how he reads the passage, he proceeds to make observations about it.

So while Kalmin asks the right question, as he says, "who the redactors were, at what time period(s) they lived, and how they reworked their sources," he has not set forth a method that can answer that question, and, it must follow, as a matter of fact he has not even pretended to answer that question, nor has he answered any other. The book has no conclusion; it just trails off into a thicket of appendices. That is why his work is to be characterized as not merely obscure but obscurantist. Kalmin has contributed nothing to public discourse on the subject he has chosen. He has pursued a very private program of his own, and the result is a book that is unreadable and utterly idiosyncratic.

If this is the kind of solipsistic scholarship that the critical, scientific school at the Jewish Theological Seminary of America and Hebrew Union College-Jewish Institute of Religion aims at creating, then the rest of us will have to take our leave with no sense of having missed important and consequential learning. The yeshiva world will ignore this book because Kalmin concludes (again his book flap) "that the Talmud does not present us with an accurate picture of the rabbinic movement in Babylonia and that significant pieces are missing from the Talmud's account of the activity of most Amoraim." That conclusion will hardly win a warm welcome in the yeshiva world, which has slight patience, any more, for smart-aleck debunking.

But the academic world will ignore this book, too. The reason is not because it is poorly argued and clumsily written and disorganized and incoherent, though it is, and not because the strategy of exposition utterly fails, though it does. It is that the results, if correct, are trivial and in no way help us to answer the important questions that Kalmin claims to address. If we want to know something about the redaction of the Babylonian Talmud, we shall have to describe the Babylonian Talmud and its paramount traits of rhetoric and logic and determine whether it is a compilation or a well-crafted composition, working our way from the outside to the inside. In starting from the smallest whole units of thought, the individual sentences, Kalmin has replicated an error of several generations' standing, and the utterly useless result, comprising made-up words that only the author and his six best friends use anyhow is yet one more charge exacted by the rather aimless and self-referential (not to say self-serving) program of academic isolates in rabbinical seminaries. This is what emerges when scholars talk entirely to themselves and listen to no one else. The difference between Kalmin's version of "the redaction of the Babylonian Talmud" and an academic reading of the same problem is the difference between Nintendo baseball and the kind you play on a real baseball diamond.

So, I maintain, Professor Kalmin has written a confused, disorganized, trivial, ignorant book. Now, in defending it from my criticism in *Hebrew Studies*, he now states, "My research...builds on the theories of modern Talmudic scholars (Hyman Klein, Avraham Weiss, David Halivni, Shamma Friedman, and others). I offer no apology for accepting this scholarship, just as Neusner offers no apology for ignoring it." This is a blatant lie and a statement that is either malicious or ignorant; I prefer the latter. I have not ignored the work of any of those named but have devoted long seminar studies, an entire issue of a journal, and a whole book, to Avraham Weiss, Shamma Friedman, and David Halivni, respectively.

I call to Professor Kalmin's attention the seminar essays on Avraham Weiss in *The Formation of the Babylonian Talmud. Studies on the Achievements of Late Nineteenth- and Twentieth-Century Historical and Literary-Critical Research* (Leiden, 1970: E.J. Brill); and *The Modern Study of the Mishnah* (Leiden, 1973: E.J. Brill); the seminar essays on Shamma Friedman in *Law as Literature*, which I edited in a special issue of *Semeia*; and my own numerous essays on Halivni in those same books, most recently a whole book *Sources and Traditions. Types of Composition in the Talmud of Babylonia* (Atlanta, 1992: Scholars Press for South Florida Studies in the History of Judaism). Halivni has not replied to any of the essays I have devoted to his method and why I think he is wrong beginning to end; he has not even acknowledged receiving the essays or books devoted to him. That is his way, and Kalmin, his student, accuses me of his teacher's flaw. For my part, I do not ignore the views of people working on the same problems; I read them, reflect on them, respond to them, carefully criticize the work of those with whom I differ, stating my reasons for differing. I regret that Kalmin can only caricature his critic.

He says, "Discovery of these distinct patterns contradicts Neusner's claim that the Talmud speaks with one voice, and supports the view of most scholars that the Talmud is comprised of diverse sources." But while I do indeed maintain the Bavli speaks with one voice – that is to say, I do see the Bavli as a cogent, coherent doctrine, possessed of integrity and following rules of logic and form beginning to end – I have devoted several monographs to the proposition that the Talmud is comprised of diverse sources. I was even so generous as to send a couple of these books to Kalmin, but he did not have the manners to acknowledge receiving them. That is how he "ignores" – by priding himself on his ignorance.

It is, of course, a familiar gambit of an aggrieved author to accuse the reviewer of not having read the book, but, alas, I really did plough through pages and pages of Kalmin's slovenly, turgid prose and his murky, messy presentation of his *hiddushim*, beginning to end, including his so-called "*analyses of sugyot*." Anyone who does the same will reach the same judgment that I did concerning his incapacity to set forth a clear statement of proposition, evidence, and argument. His sweeping accusation that I ignore "redaction criticism, source criticism, and philology" is just puerile name-calling. He will find sustained redaction criticism and systematic source criticism, if not his kind of redaction and source criticism, in the monographs listed above, as the very titles themselves suggest.

Kalmin confuses the parts with the whole; the Bavli's framers did draw on available materials, and there are quite formal criteria that allow us to identify what is ready-made and what they made up themselves. No one disagrees about that. But Kalmin is so pleased with himself for having identified what he thinks are bits and pieces of the parts that he loses sight of the whole. He has his rather convoluted and I think useless exegesis of these bits and pieces of his, a kind of pseudo-critical exegesis with which to replace the received exegesis of the ages – to whose benefit, I cannot say.

But in order to advance his, and his teachers' exposition of their exegetical ingenuity, which I find nothing more than sterile, tenth-rate pilpul, without the power to illuminate the Bavli in any important way, he denies what faithful Jews know as fact. That is that the Bavli really forms a whole, not just a mass of bits and pieces, and, indeed, the longer one immerses oneself in the whole, the more profoundly one is changed, in both intellect and character. All this "redaction criticism, source criticism, and philology" to which Kalmin assigns such importance is valuable so far as it helps us better understand the Bavli itself, in its own character and terms. The challenge of the Bavli, which I have now translated beginning to end, is to understand the whole: its power, its glory, its hegemony over the intellect of Israel, the Jewish people. Kalmin and those whom he values have made no material contribution to that understanding. I am inclined to think that if Kalmin would translate the entire Bavli, he would come away from the work as impressed as I am by the document's amazing cogency and coherence – and perhaps even himself affected by the document's power of lucid argument and thought. His knowledge of the Bavli, as his book shows, is shallow, episodic, and anecdotal, not complete and fundamental as it must be to appreciate what the Bavli really achieves.

That is why we really do disagree on a matter of enormous weight. Kalmin uses boorish language ("Neusner is completely wrong" indeed), but his viewpoint should not be dismissed but should be identified as a plausible position and subjected to criticism. I indeed see the Bavli as a single, organic whole, as have scholars for fifteen hundred years. The power of the Bavli lies in its integrity, in its capacity to produce a compelling and cogent argument in behalf of its propositions. He sees it as "stratified or multi-layered, polyphonic rather than monophonic." I think he is confused, and the chaos he hears from the Bavli is in his own mind, not in that protean and magnificent work of sustained and powerful thought. Truly it has been said of Kalmin and his colleagues, *iqqar haser min hassefer:* he can explain everything about the Bavli except what it is and why it works. But the Bavli has shaped the mind of Judaism from the seventh century to the twenty-first.

Readers of Kalmin's account of the Bavli will wonder why; but readers of my account of the document will find the reason why, so far as I am able to discover it. But mine is not a lonely or personal quest, to the contrary. Every generation faces the task of finding for itself the reason for the Bavli's astonishing power to shape and form Judaism. I regret that Kalmin and his colleagues neglect that task; they prefer to explain why the Bavli is trivial and why we have to rip it to pieces in order to understand what nearly everybody else grasps by reading the document whole and with integrity. But that neglect is their own loss, no one elses.

Alas, there are other losers; their students, Conservative rabbis of the recent past, come out of their class room with remarkably little interest in, or appreciation for, the Talmud and other Rabbinic literature, which they ignore. JTSA is producing an entire generation of *am haratzim*, who really look at the Bavli as a source of quotations and wise sayings, but not as a mind-shaping, life-changing encounter. That is why, while I do not blame Kalmin for his mediocre book, I do blame him for his intellectually shoddy work in teaching a whole generation of Conservative rabbis to whom the Talmud says absolutely nothing.

10

Does Religious Dialogue Belong Only to Religious Liberals? An "Orthodox, Fundamentalist, Judaic" Reply to Lillian Sigal

Responding to an earlier article of mine, Mrs. Lillian Sigal (*Journal of Ecumenical Studies* 18:4, Fall 1991, pp. 626-630), covers a long list of topics, each with its own subdivisions. She describes herself as "a liberal Jew," but it does not strike me as a very liberal attitude to call me names, as she does when she dismisses me as "a fundamentalist." In the "liberal" context of which she speaks, "Orthodox fundamentalist Judaism" is not meant as a compliment. It is language meant to discredit and dismiss, just as would be someone's calling her a mere secularist, aiming at religious dialogue for solely worldly purposes, lacking all transcendent dimension; that would represent a dismissal equivalent to her name-calling, which, I am sure, upon reflection, she surely must regret.

Indeed, her allegation that "Orthodox fundamentalist Judaism" and its Christian counterparts obviously cannot communicate strikes me as a denial of that very requirement of mutual respect that she alleges she wishes to undertake. That is often the way with religious liberals, implacably intolerant of those unlike themselves; liberalism shades over into its own fundamentalist intolerance. I take it she wishes to conduct her interfaith dialogue with people with whom she agrees. But we cannot define the other, but have the task only of trying to find bridges of comprehension to that other. Inventing her dialogue partner, Mrs. Sigal favors theological labor-saving devices, but these do not serve authentic religious interchange.

Still, for me it is a new but on the whole rather nice experience to be labeled "Orthodox" and "fundamentalist." Mrs. Sigal assumes she is calling me nasty names and discrediting my position thereby. But I take her insult as a high compliment indeed. Considering the spiritual grandeur of the Judaic religious tradition for which Orthodox Judaism authentically stands in our world, and given the religious sacrifices undertaken by all those whom she would label "fundamentalists," the Judaic and the Christian and the Muslim – the utter commitment of the faithful to God and God's will and word – I take pride in finding my place among Mrs. Sigal's "fundamentalists." They are, after all, this world's authentic believers, and I pray God will find my faith as authentic and sincere as Mrs. Sigal alleges that she does.

However, rather than ramble along with her and pick a fight about this and that in no cogent way, let me identify what I take to be the main points of disagreement and clarify how I see the issues. If I had to say where we differ, it is in my repeated interest in knowledge of God and deeper understanding of God's self-manifestation in the Torah, an interest which, in her response, Mrs. Sigal manages to express only marginally, if at all.

1. The Purpose of Dialogue

Mrs. Sigal wants dialogue to yield "learning." But learning information, or growing "in the perception and understanding of reality," hardly requires the intervention of religious beliefs. In the academy we study about religion, and students learn a great deal about other religions; at no point do personal beliefs enter, since our task is description, analysis, and interpretation in a this-worldly context. Mrs. Sigal confuses education with theological negotiation. Religious dialogue must concern religion, not information; its goal must be a better understanding of God and what God wants of humanity. Mrs. Sigal seems to have in mind what is of mere social utility: improved intergroup relations. But Christians cannot be asked to repudiate Christianity, nor Jews Judaism, merely to overcome hatred of the other.

2. The Correct Attitude of Dialogue

Mrs. Sigal describes herself as a liberal Jew, which clarifies her difficulty in grasping that, in their classical formulations, Christianity is not Judaism, nor Judaism Christianity. These formulations, in each case, speak about God and what God demands of humanity and how humanity knows God. If God is incarnate in Jesus Christ, as nearly all Christianities maintain, then God's (prior) self-manifestation in the Torah has been superseded. If God is made manifest wholly and exhaustively in the Torah, as nearly all Judaic religious systems have maintained and now maintain, then Christian faith has to stand before the judgment of the Torah. And there, by the revealed truth of the Torah, it is found wanting.

No one familiar with the Christian and Judaic theological literature for the past two thousand years will find these statements egregious. But anyone who respects the faith of Christianity and Judaism – most Christians believing in Jesus Christ God incarnate, and most practicing Jews belieiving that God gives the Torah to Israel at Sinai day by day – will find Mrs. Sigal's liberalism irrelevant. Hers is a religious dialogue of Methodists more like Judaists than Roman Catholics or Orthodox Christians, and of Judaists more like Unitarians than like Orthodox Jews. But that dialogue ignores the generality of the faithful of both Judaism and Christianity, as a mere nose count will tell. I repeat: If for dialogue Christians must abandon the Christ of faith for the Jesus of history, or Jews the profound conviction that God is made manifest in the Torah, then dialogue must be weighed in the balance against holy faith, whether ours, whether theirs. It is not going to outweigh faith.

3. The Jewishness of Jesus

From the perspective of Christian faith, whether Roman Catholic or Orthodox or Reformation-Protestant or Mormon or Bible-believing and Evangelical, Jesus was and is Jesus Christ, son of God, God incarnate. To the overwhelming majority of Christians in the world, the advent of Jesus Christ represents a radical turning in the human condition. True, Jesus Christ was, and is, born of a Jewish mother. For that, Christianity acknowledges its heritage out of Israel, which it knows as the Old Testament, given its full meaning by the New. In these formulations of Christian language, which accurately represent the state of Christian theology for the vast majority of Christians, there is no room for discourse on the Jewishness of Jesus, because, once more, it is simply irrelevant. "The Jewishness of Jesus" simply begs the question: why Christianity? But all Christianities begin with answers to that question.

To me as a faithful and practicing Judaist and Jew, none of these statements of Christianity present offense; religions have the right to say what they believe, and, in our own time, Christianity has taken great steps away from the legacy of racism and hatred of others, especially of us Jews, that in former times made the cross a symbol of fear and an object of loathing to outsiders. And, for our part, we have made the effort to collaborate in the secular work of building, here in our own country and overseas, bridges of respect and mutual esteem between the faith communities.

But none of these efforts can, or should, obscure the profound differences between Judaic and Christian (not to mention Islamic) religions. All of us make statements of faith we hold to be truthful, and these statements contradict one another, so not all of them can (or should) be true. If, as Christians maintain, Jesus Christ is God incarnate, then the Torah has come to fulfillment in their Christ, and if, as we maintain, the Torah is God's sole and final self-manifestation, so that, through the Torah, we know God, then Jesus and Muhammed and others claiming to tell us about who God is and what God wants of us have no claim upon us.

I speak about God, but I look in vain in Mrs. Sigal's response for a trace of interest in what is at stake in Judaism, which is to live a holy life in the here and now and pray and work for the coming of the Messiah and salvation at the end of days. She talks about religion, but I want to talk about God. And if in interfaith dialogue God is not the issue, then there is nothing to discuss other than politics and sociology (including Mrs. Sigal's rather churlish and dogmatic feminism with a scowling face). And I speak about the Torah, a word I cannot find in this response of Mrs. Sigal's.

4. The Historical Jesus and the Christ of Faith

The historical Jesus is an invention of scholars in their studies. All Christians other than those with Ph.D.'s know only the Jesus Christ of the Gospels. If, therefore, there is to be religious dialogue with Christianity, it can be only with the Jesus Christ in whom Christians find salvation, and, along these same lines, if there is to be religious dialogue with Judaism, it must concern the Torah and how we are to receive it and live by it.

But let us, for the moment, contemplate this "historical Jesus," and ask ourselves whether, as a matter of fact, Mrs. Sigal expresses toward authentic Christian faith in Jesus Christ (which is what Christianity is all about) that attitude of respect that she rightly demands for Judaism.

Mrs. Sigal is naive if she honestly believes that scholarship can recover this "historical Jesus" in such a way that we have someone to discuss (or with whom to conduct dialogue) who ever lived and breathed, in the way in which, for faithful Christians, Jesus Christ lives in the Gospels. For I have never heard of a book on "the historical Moses," and while philosophers study the thought of Sophocles and Plato, few bother to tell us what the historical Sophocles really said, as distinct from what Plato says he said. Muslims know the historical Muhammed from the Quran, not asking professors in their Islamic universities to tell us what Muhammed really said, sayings selected from the many more that the Quran says he said.

But when people speak of "the historical Jesus," they express the view that (using the language of Christianity) the record of Jesus Christ in the Gospels is not a factual, historical account at all. They draw a distinction between the Christ of faith and the Jesus of history, so properly conducted, secular, objective, historical study can provide reliable facts, but the Gospels as the Christian faithful read them do not. While the quest for the historical Jesus forms a brief chapter in Christian theology of our own times, it matters because it has defined how the Gospels will be read in the secular academy and many Christian seminaries. Annual meetings where scholars debate and vote (using black, gray, pink, and red balls for what he certainly didn't say, probably didn't say, may have said, and certainly said) are routine; the Holy Spirit is pretty busy nowadays.

In taking this position, Mrs. Sigal places herself in opposition to nearly the whole of Christian faith, excluding only that handful of Protestant liberals whom she finds to quote. The bulk of Catholic Christianity – Roman, Orthodox, and Anglican – as well as Evangelical and Reformation churches alike, and all Bible-believing Christianity, stand against her. In other words, this "historical Jesus" of hers who lived and died solely a Jew, within the Torah, has no standing in religious dialogue for the vast, vast majority of believing Christians. So we find that the Judaic side has invented for itself its own suitable dialogue partner.

Where have we learned to make this distinction, and why, and to whom, does it matter? The Gospels themselves present points of disharmony, but Christians for centuries satisfied themselves with harmonies of the Gospels. The stories of the miracles have challenged faith, but Christians took it as a mark of grace that they believed. The same data that have impressed scholars in the past two centuries made no profound impression on believers for eighteen prior ones. At the beginning of the kind of historical study that promised to distinguish fact from fiction, myth or legend from authentic event, Protestant theologians, mainly in Germany, undertook to write lives of Jesus that did not simply paraphrase the Gospels but stood in judgment of them. An attitude of systematic skepticism brought to the Gospels considerations that prior generations scarcely conceived. These considerations engaged theological professors in universities in Europe and in some U.S. divinity schools and university religious studies departments in particular, with the result that a different reading of the Gospels replaced the received and still paramount one. What is at stake is the statement of one academic proponent of the historical Jesus as against the Christ of faith: "The church has to catch up with the academy." But that statement amounts to a claim on authority and authenticity that no church can concede to the academy.

The point is a simple one. Mrs. Sigal's conception of "the historical Jesus" takes for granted two facts, first, (once more using the language of

Christian faith) the Jesus Christ of the Gospels, the incarnate God who taught, did wonders, died on the cross, rose from the dead, and sits on the right hand of God, is not the Jesus (no longer: Christ) who actually lived, and, second, historians know how to tell the difference. The Gospels' Jesus simply cannot pass the test of history; the Gospels tell us more than the truth that survives the application of this historical method. Accordingly, for the purposes of dialogue, she wishes to undertake to identify the facts of history contained within the detritus of the story that the Gospels present.

5. Confusing Theology with History, Truth with Fact

If I were a Christian, I should find obnoxious the insistence that the Gospels really are wrong, but liberal theologians claiming to teach us objective facts of history can replace those Gospels. This rigorous, unbelieving historical quest actually takes up theological questions – surely no question bears more profound theological implications for Christians than what the person they believe is the incarnate God really, actually, truly said and did here on earth! But then historical method, which knows nothing of the supernatural and looks upon miracles with unreserved supefaction, is then required to answer them. The premises of this historical question (did it really happen, did he really say it?) rule out nearly the whole of Christian faith. For these are the perfectly routine, historical premises that govern the work as they would any other:

[1]   any statement we may wish to make about Jesus is just another fact of history, like the fact that George Washington crossed the Delaware on Christmas Eve, 1775;

[2]   facts of that kind form the entire historical truth about Jesus;

[3]   facts about Jesus bear the same weight and consequence as facts about George Washington (which is why points one and two are true); he is the same as any other man we investigate through ordinary, secular sources.

But statements (historical or otherwise) about the founders of religions present a truth of a different kind. Such statements are not only more important, bearing weightier implications. They also appeal to sources of a character distinct from the sources that record what George Washington did on a certain day in 1775. The sources are classified as revelation, not mere information; they claim, and those who value them believe, that they originate in God's revelation or inspiration. Asking the Gospels to give historical, not gospel truth confuses theological truth with historical fact, diminishing it to the modest measurements of this world, treating Jesus as precisely the opposite of what Christianity has always known him to be, which is, unique.

When we speak of "the historical Jesus," therefore, we turn out to dissect a sacred subject with a scalpel of secular research, and in the profound confusion of categories of truth the patient dies on the operating table; the surgeons have forgotten why they made their cut and in their confusion have removed the heart and forgotten to put it back. The statement, one and one are two, or, the Constitutional Convention met in 1787, is simply not of the same order as the statement "Moses received the Torah at Sinai" or "Jesus Christ is son of God."

What historical evidence can tell us whether or not someone really rose from the dead, or what God said to the prophet on Sinai? I cannot define a historical method congruent to the work of telling us how to sort out claims that God's son was born to a virgin girl. And how can historians, used to telling us the causes of the Civil War (whether in 1642-1651 Britain or 1861-1865 America) really speak of miracles, men rising from the dead, and other matters of broad belief among some, utter incredulity among others? Historians working with miracle stories turn out what is either paraphrastic of the faith, or indifferent to it, or merely silly. Theological truth about what is unique and matters of fact about what conforms to the rules of nature speak in different ways about altogether different issues; derive from different sources of information and verification; yield each its implications for its own realm of reality, the one eternity, the other the here and now of commonplace fact.

In a word, in allegations such as she makes, which speak in terms of secular methods of recovering this-worldly facts about a figure held by the believers to be sacred, and which address figures held to be unique as though they conformed to the commonplace rules of this world we have nothing other than theology masquerading as "critical history." If I were a Christian believer, I would ask why the crown of science has now to be placed upon the head of a Jesus reduced to this-worldly dimensions. And if I were a Christian, I would say, it is just one more crown of thorns. In my own view, as a rabbi, I may say simply, to the issues that they purport to treat, allegations such as these that she sets before us are simply, monumentally irrelevant.

For, if faithful Christians today find surprising the distinction between the Jesus of history and the Christ of faith, they continue an ancient tradition of faith, for no one before modern times knew that the one was and is not the same as the other. No Christianity before modern times, and only some in modern times, has ever produced this kind of writing, though all of them have studied the life and teachings of Jesus. But the theological context defined by "the Church," meaning, whichever Christianity pursued the study, formed the framework of learning.

Christology was never confused with quite secular biography until the nineteenth century. Distinguishing between the Jesus of history and the Christ of faith would have earlier produced utter incomprehension.

Instead of interpreting one saying in light of another and the whole in light of tradition or creed or theological premise, Gospels scholarship proposed to distinguish, by various criteria, between things Jesus really said and things that the Church, responding to its own concerns, attributed to him later on. This intense historical study is grounded in these premises, all of them inimical to historic Christianity:

[1]   not only is it the fact that Church tradition is null, only Scripture matters; but, more to the point, the faith of the Church is null, and only the declarations of historians carry weight;

[2]   historical facts by themselves bear theological consequence;

[3]   historical facts must undergo a rigorous test of skepticism, the donation of the Enlightenment (how could a whale swallow Jonah, and what else did he have for lunch that day); and

[4]   historical facts cannot comprise supernatural events, the gift of nineteenth-century German historical learning ("exactly how things were" by definition cannot include rising from the dead).

At the outset of the scholar's venture these rules dictate the result, since by definition they exclude most of what Christians by faith know to be truth: the miracles, the resurrection, the givenness of the Gospels' truth, the (admittedly Catholic) conception that the Bible is the gift of the Church, alongside that other gift, tradition. Before work gets under way, nothing is left of what makes Jesus into Christ, unique, wholly man wholly God, God incarnate, and all the other things that define Christ for Christianity, and Christianity for the world beyond.

Within such premises, the character as fundamentally secular and incredulous life of "the historical Jesus" is dictated before work commences. But then the quest begs the question: On that basis should Christians concern themselves with this particular Jesus at all (who, for both Meier and Crossan would have voted for left-wing Democrats)? And to whom does the life of a marginal Jew or a Mediterranean Jewish peasant matter very much anyhow (or a Galilean rabbi, or a homosexual magician, or any and all of the other historical Jesuses that people have produced)?

Not only so, but these premises set a standard of secular historicity that religious writings setting forth a religious faith, speaking in terms of uniqueness and the supernatural, such as the Gospels, cannot, and should not, attempt to meet. For, after all, all the givens dismiss what to the Evangelists is critical: here is a unique man, who said and did what no one else ever said or did; these things happened in the way the Church has preserved them (also) in the Gospels, tradition being a valid source; these things really did happen as the narrative says (would the Gospels lie?); and Jesus Christ assuredly performed miracles in his lifetime and rose from the dead (ours is the story of God among us). No corroborating evidence you object? But by definition there can be none; by faith we are saved.

Joseph Cardinal Ratzinger, in a variety of important and authoritative papers, has shown that historical, secular method itself dictates the character of its results. Ratzinger states very compellingly, "With such presuppositions, the figure of Jesus is predetermined." That simple sentence raises a challenge to all those, Protestant, Orthodox, and Catholic (and even Jewish) scholars, theologians manqués to a man, who deem the search for "the historical Jesus" to form a truly secular, this-worldly historical quest.

Ratzinger makes the point that for Christian faithful, at issue in the historical Jesus *is* the Christ of faith. If the question is theological truth, can the answer claim the status of secular fact? No historical work explains itself so disingenuously as work on the historical Jesus. Beginning, middle, and end the issue is theological. But how should theological truth about supernatural reality and historical fact concerning this world's activities and events ever meet? For religious faith speaks in the present tense about eternity – how things are and must be always – while historical facts tell us merely about what was once upon a time.

6. Is Dialogue Possible between Judaism and Christianity?

Mrs. Sigal sets a condition for dialogue: "Dialogue should be carried on between both academic and nonacademic Christians and Jews in light of objective scholarship that illuminates the Judaic background to Christianity." But that very statement begs the question. Christianity has always maintained that the advent of Jesus Christ (once again to use Christian language) marked a total change in the human condition. But if Jesus was just another Galilean wonder-worker, as Geza Vermes makes him out to be, or a marginal Jew, as John Meier's magisterial account alleges, or a Mediterranean Jewish peasant, as John Dominic Crossan says, or a homosexual magician and charlatan, as the disgraceful, anti-Christian caricature that Morton Smith in his loathing of Christianity dreamed up (and made up, evidence and all!), then why Christianity?

In the end, any account of Christianity satisfactory to Christians has to explain the advent of not a reform of a preexisting, unitary Judaism (which Mrs. Sigal implicitly conceives) but an utter and total break with the past. And for that explanation, facts of history are monumentally irrelevant. For the issues concern the Kingdom of God, the eschatological forgiveness of sin, salvation, atonement, resurrection, life eternal – and to those issues, the alleged facts of the life of a wonder-worker, marginal Jew, peasant, or homosexual magician are monumentally irrelevant.

My case is both negative and positive. In *Telling Tales: Making Sense of Christian and Judaic Nonsense. The Urgency and Basis for Judeo-Christian Dialogue,* I argue that there has never been a Judeo-Christian dialogue, neither side having wanted it, but there can be one. The article to which Mrs. Sigal responds summarizes my account of how I conceive such a dialogue can commence – for the first time. I do think that authentically religious dialogue can take place when each side addresses the faith of the other in the terms of the other.

Can Judaism talk with Christianity in such a way that Christianity finds itself treated with respect and its Founder with reverence – by a believing, practicing Jew? I have given an example of what I think people who themselves are religious in their respective traditions may offer for one another's religious edification. This is set forth in my *A Rabbi Talks with Jesus. An Intermillennial, Interfaith Exchange* (Doubleday). I compose an argument I would have with Matthew's Jesus on the day he gave the Sermon on the Mount. I debate with Jesus, on the common ground of the Torah, which Matthew's Jesus says he has come not to destroy but to fulfill, the very issues of salvation and God's kingdom that form the centerpiece of both the Torah and the Gospel under study. The work is one of faith meeting faith, and Christian readers of the book were meant by me to emerge from it more profoundly Christian, just as out of the writing of it, I found still more compelling the Torah's statement in God's word to Moses.

There Mrs. Sigal will find out that practicing and faithful Jews, who do not describe themselves as liberal but accept as compliments the epithets she tosses about, can undertake the tasks of religious interchange, and can do so in a manner found honorable and authentic by Catholics, Protestants, and Orthodox Jews. My dialogue partners, and they are many, all believe in God made known to humanity in specific acts – the Torah or Christ, respectively. True, toleration is irrelevant to us "fundamentalists," and certainly, we speak to people we believe are as wrong about God as the Torah (or for the other side, Christ) is right. If I did not think my Christian or Muslim counterpart did not pray to the one and the same God to whom I say my prayers, I should not take seriously their religious commitment or find it worthy of a sustained and rigorous examination – and, in the context of the Torah, refutation. Accordingly, that religious affirmation so fiercely held by all parties to the debate also renders our task more difficult, but it adds formidable weight to the work, since, after all, the stakes become transcendent.

11

The Bizarre "Judaism" of E.P. Sanders

The requirement of the theology of Christianity accounts for intense interest in the historical description of another religion altogether, namely, Judaism. Specifically, (to use Christian language) because the founder of Christianity, Jesus Christ, was born in Israel and called King of the Jews, to define Christianity, a fundamental theological task, we have also to define Judaism. But the circumstance in which this (allegedly) historical, descriptive work is undertaken yields results incommensurate to the issue. For to define Judaism in a way useful to the explanation of Christianity, we have also to answer the question: why Christianity, not Judaism? If we cannot come up with an account of what is compelling in the new religion, we also cannot complete our task of definition. That simple fact explains why, for centuries, Christian pictures of Judaism have presented a repulsive corpse.

In the present century, different, more comely Judaisms have emerged. Through allegedly historical facts Judaism is portrayed with all the grace of Christianity. Along these same lines, Jesus is represented no longer as a singular, unique figure, but as a rabbi, a Pharisee, a Galilean wonder-worker, as a Mediterranean present, as a marginal Jew, as a reforming rabbi (or even a Reform rabbi) – as anything but what Christianity to begin with affirms: Jesus Christ, God incarnate. Consequently, these accounts of both Judaism and Jesus the Jew beg the question: if this is Judaism, then why Christianity? And once we recognize that remarkable lacuna – simply stated, we have everything but the main thing – we realize that in theology, salvation is not of the Jews. Nor is theology's task accomplished through historical research. Jerusalem may relate to Athens, but has no bond with Tübingen or Göttingen. Historical facts have no bearing on theological truth, not because theology requires us to believe what is not true, but because

173

theology makes statements that rest on facts of an other-than-historical order.

An apt illustration of the peculiar results of the conventional confusion of history and theology is given just now by Professor E.P. Sanders, Duke University, in his *Judaism. Practice and Belief 63 B.C.E. - 66 C.E.* (London, 1992: SCM Press and Philadelphia, 1992: Trinity Press International).[1] There Sanders answers every question but the important one: if this was Judaism, then how come Christianity? He introduces his account of Judaism, as "the book I always wanted to write," and he certainly has done a far superior job to his predecessors; the work on the day of its publication replaces J. Jeremias's *Jerusalem in the Time of Jesus*, and in many ways excels other synthetic accounts known to me.

But Sanders's insistence on answering the Christian theological question – what is Christianity – by providing an account of one, single, comprehensive Judaism, underscores the profound misconstruction that emerges from the confusion of history and theology. So far as I know, Sanders must be the first scholar in recent times to imagine that all sources produced by Jews, anywhere, any time, by any sort of person or group, equally tell us about one and the same Judaism. Schürer was far more critical nearly a century ago. The other major "Judaisms" – Bousset-Gressman's or Moore's, for instance – select a body of evidence and work on that, not assuming that everything everywhere tells us about one thing, somewhere: Judaism. True, to account for a single Christianity, Christian theologians have also to define a single Judaism, and that explains why Sanders has fabricated a single "Judaism" out of a mass of mutually contradictory sources. But others did the work with greater acumen and discernment, and, when we examine Sanders's results closely, we see that there is less than meets the eye.

Sanders really thinks that any and every source, whoever wrote it, without regard to its time or place or venue, tells us about one and the same Judaism. The only way to see everything all together and all at once, as Sanders wishes to do, is to rise high above the evidence, so high that we no longer see the lines of rivers, the height of mountains, the undulations of plains – any of the details of the earth's true configuration. This conflation of all sources yields his fabricated Judaism. It is a "Judaism" that flourished everywhere but nowhere – Alexandria, Jerusalem, Galilee, Babylonia (to judge from the sources we mixed together); a Judaism that we find all the time but in no one period, represented equally by the historical Moses and the rabbinic one, the

---

[1] I deal with other problems in Sanders's picture of "Judaism" in my *What We Cannot Show, We Do Not Know: The New Testament and Rabbinic Literature* (Philadelphia, 1993: Trinity Press International).

pseudepigraph of the third century B.C. and the first century A.D., the Dead Sea Scrolls of the second and first centuries B.C., and, where Sanders has decided, the Mishnah of the early third century A.D.

Sanders does not identify "the synagogue" where this Judaism offered up its prayers, the community that was shaped by its rules, the functioning social order that saw the world within its vision. And of course, that failure of specificity attests to the good sense of the Jews of antiquity, who could not have affirmed everything and its opposite: the sacrifices of the Temple are valid (as many sources maintain) and also invalid (as the Dead Sea Scrolls hold); study of the Torah is critical (as the rabbinic sources adduced ad lib by Sanders) and eschatological visions prevail (as many of the pseudeipgraphic writers conceive). Philo's cool, philosophical mind and the heated imagination of visionaries form for Sanders a single Judaism, but no single corpus of evidence, deriving from a particular place, time, circumstance, and community, concurs for "Judaism." To refer to a single issue, baptism could have been for the eschatological forgiveness of sins, as John the Baptist and Jesus maintained; or it could have been for the achievement of cultic purity in an eternal rhythm of nature and cult, as the Pharisees and the Mishnah held; but not both.

Sanders sees unities where others have seen differences. The result of his Judaic equivalent of a "harmony of the Gospels" is more often than not a dreary progress through pointless information. If it seems to me his entire book begs the question it asks – if this is Judaism, then why Christianity – Sanders's relentlessly informative discourse for its part persistently left open the question, so what? I found myself wondering why Sanders thought the information he set forth important, how he imagined it mattered, what difference in the understanding of *Judaism. Practice & Belief*, one fact or another might make in his mind. If we know that his conflationary Judaism prevailed everywhere, then what else do we know about the Judaisms to which each source in turn attests (as well)? He elaborately tells us why he thinks various documents tell, or do not tell, what really happened; he never explains why he maintains these same documents and artifacts of archaeology, commonly so profoundly at variance with one another, all concur on a single Judaism or attest to a single Judaism.

Now that capricious conflation of all the sources Sanders thinks fit together and the silent omission of all the sources he rejects is something Moore, Schechter, and even Urbach never did. Urbach cited Philo but not the Dead Sea Scrolls, having decided that the one was *kosher*, the other *treif*. Sanders has decided there are no intellectual counterparts to dietary laws at all: he swallows it all and chews it up and spits out a homogenized "Judaism" lacking all specific flavor. Nor can I point to any other scholar of ancient Judaism working today who cites everything from everywhere to tell us about one and the same Judaism. The contrast between the intellectually rigorous thinking of James Dunn on defining "Judaism" in his *Partings of the Ways* and the conceptually slovenly work of Sanders on the same problem – adding up all the sources and not so much finding as inventing through mushy prose what he conceives to be the common denominator – tells the story. Sanders's *Judaism* is a mulligan stew, a four-day-old, overcooked *tcholent* – for us plain Americans, Wonder Bread, full of air and not very tasty.

This fabrication of a single Judaism is supposed to tell us something that pertains equally to all: the Judaism that forms the basis for all the sources, the common denominator among them all. If we know a book or an artifact is "Jewish" (an ethnic term, Judaic being the religious category), then we are supposed automatically to know various other facts about said book or artifact. But the upshot is either too general to mean much (monotheism) or too abstract to form an intelligible statement. Let me be specific. How Philo would have understood the Dead Sea Scrolls, the authors of apocalyptic writings, those of the Mishnah passages Sanders admits to his account of Judaism from 63 B.C. to A.D. 66, we are never told. Each of these distinctive documents gets to speak whenever Sanders wants it to; none is ever brought into relationship – comparison and contrast – with any other. The homogenization of Philo, the Mishnah, the Dead Sea Scrolls, Ben Sira, apocryphal and pseudepigraphic writings, the results of archaeology, and on and on and on turns out to yield generalizations about a religion that none of those responsible for the evidence at hand would have recognized: lifeless, dull, hopelessly abstract, lacking all social relevance. After a while, readers come to realize, it hardly matters, the results reaching so stratospheric a level of generalization that all precise vision of real people practicing a vivid religion is lost.

These remarks will appear extravagant until we take up a concrete example of the result of Sanders's huge labor of homogenization. To understand what goes into Sanders's picture of Judaism, let me now provide a reasonable sample (pp. 103-104), representative of the whole, the opening paragraphs of his discussion, Chapter Seven, entitled "Sacrifices":

> The Bible does not offer a single, clearly presented list of sacrifices. The legal books (Exodus, Leviticus, Numbers and Deuteronomy), we know now, incorporate various sources from different periods, and priestly practice evidently varied from time to time. There are three principal sources of information about sacrifices in the first century: Josephus, Philo and the Mishnah. On most points they agree among themselves and with Leviticus and Numbers; consequently the main

outline of sacrifices is not in dispute. Josephus, in my judgment, is the best source. He knew what the common practice of the priesthood of his day was: he had learned it in school, as a boy he had watched and assisted, and as an adult he had worked in the temple. It is important for evaluating his evidence to note that his description of the sacrifices sometimes disagrees with Leviticus or goes beyond it. This is not an instance in which he is simply summarizing what is written in the Bible: he is almost certainly depending on what he had learned as a priest.

Though the Mishnah is often right with regard to pre-70 temple practice, many of the discussions are from the second century: the rabbis continued to debate rules of sacrifice long after living memory of how it had been done had vanished. Consequently, in reading the Mishnah one is sometimes reading second-century theory. Occasionally this can be seen clearly. For example, there is a debate about whether or not the priest who sacrificed an animal could keep its hide if for any reason the animal was made invalid (for example, by touching something impure) after it was sacrificed but before it was flayed. The Mishnah on this topic opens with an anonymous opinion, according to which the priest did not get the hide. R. Hanina the Prefect of the Priests disagreed: "Never have I seen a hide taken out to the place of burning"; that is, the priests always kept the hides. R. Akiba (early second century) accepted this and was of the view that the priests could keep the hides of invalid sacrifices. "The Sages," however, ruled the other way (*Zevahim* 12.4). R. Hanina the Prefect of the Priests apparently worked in the temple before 70, but survived its destruction and became part of the rabbinic movement. Akiba died c. 135; "the Sages" of this passage are probably his contemporaries or possibly the rabbis of the next generation. Here we see that second-century rabbis were quite willing to vote against actual practice in discussing the behavior of the priests and the rules they followed. The problem with using the Mishnah is that there is very seldom this sort of reference to pre-70 practice that allows us to make critical distinctions: not only are we often reading second-century discussions, we may be learning only second-century theory.

Philo had visited the temple, and some of his statements about it (for example the guards) seem to be based on personal knowledge. But his discussion of the sacrifices is "bookish," and at some important points it reveals that he is passing on information derived from the Greek translation of the Hebrew Bible (the Septuagint), not from observation. The following description basically follows the Hebrew Bible and Josephus, but it sometimes incorporates details from other sources.

One may make the following distinctions among sacrifices:

With regard to what was offered: meal, wine, birds (doves or pigeons) and quadrupeds (sheep, goats and cattle).

With regard to who provided the sacrifice: the community or an individual.

With regard to the purpose of the sacrifice: worship of and communion with God, glorification of him, thanksgiving, purification, atonement for sin, and feasting.

With regard to the disposition of the sacrifice: it was either burned or eaten. The priests got most of the food that sacrifices provided, though one of the categories of sacrifice provided food for the person who brought it and his family and friends. The Passover lambs were also eaten by the worshippers.

Sacrifices were conceived as meals, or, better, banquets. The full and ideal sacrificial offering consisted of meat, cereal, oil and wine (Num. 14:1-10, Ant. 3.233f.; the menu was sometimes reduced: see below).

I ask readers to stipulate that I could have cited numerous other, sizable instances of the same sort of discourse.

Now let us ask ourselves, what, exactly, does Sanders wish to tell his readers about the sacrifices in this account of *Judaism. Practice & Belief*? He starts in the middle of things. He assumes we know what he means by "sacrifices," why they are important, what they meant, so all we require is details. He will deal with Josephus, Philo, the Mishnah, and Leviticus and Numbers. Does he then tell us the distinctive viewpoint of each? Not at all. All he wants us to know is the facts common to them all. Hence his problem is not one of description, analysis, and interpretation of documents, but a conflation of the information contained in each that he deems usable. Since that is his principal concern, he discusses "sacrifice" by telling us why the Mishnah's information is useless, except when it is usable. But Sanders never suggests to his readers what the Mishnah's discussion of sacrifice wishes to find out, or how its ideas on the subject may prove religiously engaging. It is just a rule book, so it has no ideas on the subject so Sanders; that is not my view. Philo is then set forth. Here, too, we are told why he tells us nothing, but not what he tells us. Then there follows the facts, the indented "with regard to" paragraphs.

Sanders did not have to tell us all about how Leviticus, Numbers, Philo, and Josephus and the Mishnah concur, then about how we may ignore or must cite the several documents respectively, if his sole intent was to tell us the facts of the "with regard to..." paragraphs. And how he knows that "sacrifices were conceived...," who conceived them in this way, and what sense the words made, "worship of and communion with God, glorification of him, thanksgiving, purification, atonement for sin, and feasting," and to whom they made sense, and how other Judaisms, besides the Judaism portrayed by Philo, Josephus, the Mishnah, and so on and so forth, viewed sacrifices, or the Temple as it was – none of this is set forth. The conflation has its own purpose, which the following outline of the remainder of the chapter reveals: community sacrifices; individual sacrifices ("Neither Josephus, Philo, nor other first-century Jews thought that burnt-offerings provided God with food..."), a family at the Temple, an example; the daily temple routine. In this mass of information on a subject, one question is lost: what it all meant. Sanders really does suppose that he is telling us how things were, what people did, and, in his stress on common denominator Judaism, he finds it entirely reasonable to bypass all questions of analysis and interpretation and so forgets to tell us what it all meant. His language, "worship of and communion with God, glorification of him, thanksgiving, purification, atonement for sin, and feasting" – that Protestant formulation begs every question and answers none.

But this common denominator Judaism yields little that is more than simply banal, for "common theology," for example, the statement that "the history of Israel in general, and of our period in particular, shows that Jews believed that the one God of the universe had given them his law and that they were to obey it" (p. 240). No one, obviously, can disagree, but what applies to everyone equally, in a nation so riven with division and rich in diversity, also cannot make much of a difference. That is to say, knowing that they all were monotheists or valued the Hebrew Scriptures (but which passages he does not identify, how he read them he does not say) does not tell us more than we knew about the religion of those diverse people than before. Sanders knows what people thought, because anything any Jew wrote tells us what "Jews" or most Jews or people in general thought. What makes Sanders's representation bizarre is that he proceeds to cite as evidence of what "Jews" thought opinions of Philo and Joseph, the Dead Sea Scrolls, Rabbinic literature, and so on and so forth. The generality of scholarship understands that the Dead Sea Scrolls represent their writers, Philo speaks for Philo, Josephus says what he thinks, and the Mishnah is whatever it is and is not whatever it is not. No one, to my knowledge, until Sanders has come to the facile judgment that anything any Jew thought has to have been in the mind of all the other Jews.

But it is only with that premise that we can understand the connections Sanders makes and the conclusions about large, general topics that he reaches. His juxtapositions are in fact beyond all understanding. Let me skim through his treatment of graven images, which captures the flavor of the whole:

> Comments by Philo and Josephus show how Jews could interpret other objects symbolically and thus make physical depictions acceptable, so that they were not seen as transgressions of one of the Ten Commandments, but as symbols of the glory of the God who gave them.

There follows a reference to War 5:214. Then Sanders proceeds:

> Josephus, as did Philo, found astral and other symbolism in many other things....

Some paragraphs later, in the same context, we have:

> The sun was personified and worshipped....The most important instance was when Josiah...instituted a reform of worship...[now with reference to 2 Kings 23:4f]. This is usually regarded as having been a decisive rejection of other deities, but elements derived from sun worship continued. Subsequently Ezekiel attacked those who turned "their backs to the Temple of the Lord..." (Ezek. 8:16). According to the Mishnah, at one point during the feast of Booths priests "turned their faces to the west," recalling that their predecessors had faced east and worshipped the sun and proclaimed that "our eyes are turned toward the Lord" (Sukkah 5:4). Despite this, the practice that Ezekiel condemned was continued by some. Josephs wrote that the Essenes "are particularly reverent towards the divinity...."

This is continued with a citation of the Qumran Temple Scroll and then the Tosefta:

> That the Essenes really offered prayer to the sun is made more probable by a passage in the Qumran Temple Scroll.
> Above we noted the floor of the synagogue at Hammath that had as its main decoration the signs of the zodiac in a circle....This synagogue floor, with its blatant pagan decoration, was built at the time when rabbinic Judaism was strong in Galilee – after the redaction and publication of the Mishnah, during the years when the material in the Tosefta and the Palestinian Talmud was being produced and edited. According to the Tosefta, Rabbi Judah, who flourished in the middle of the second century, said that "If anyone says a blessing over the sun – this is a heterodox practice" (T. Berakhot 6[7].6) In the light of the floor, it seems he was opposing contemporary practice.

And so on and on he goes, introducing in the paragraph that follows references to Christian symbols (John 1:9, 15:1); the issue of whether "one God" meant there were no other supernatural beings (yielding a citation to Paul who was a Pharisee, with reference to Phil. 3:2-6). And so he runs on, for five hundred tedious pages. This is simply chaos.

Cui bono? Sanders aims at one conclusion. He sets himself up as judge of his data and issues a final ruling that surpasses, in condescension and self-absorption, any lines I have ever read, whether philo- or anti-Semitic in origin, about Judaism and the Pharisees:

> I rather like the Pharisees. They loved detail and precision. They wanted to get everything just right. I like that. They loved God, they thought he had blessed them, and they thought that he *wanted* them to get everything just right. I do not doubt that some of them were priggish. This is a common fault of the pious, one that is amply displayed in modern criticism of the Pharisees. The Pharisees, we know, intended to be humble before God, and they thought that intention mattered more than outward show. Those are worthy ideals. The other pietists strike me as being less attractive than the Pharisees. The surviving literature depicts them as not having much of a program for all Israel, and as being too ready to cultivate hatred of others: learn *our*

secrets or God will destroy you. But probably they weren't all that bad, and we can give them credit for loving God and being honest.

Mostly, I like the ordinary people. They worked at their jobs, they believed the Bible [sic! he means, the Old Testament, of course], they carried out the small routines and celebrations of the religion; they prayed every day, thanked God for his blessings, and on the sabbath went to the synagogue, asked teachers questions, and listened respectfully. What could be better? Every now and again they took their hard-earned second tithe money to Jerusalem, devoutly performed their sacrifices, carried the meat out of the temple to share with their family and friends, brought some wine and maybe even some spirits, and feasted the night away. Then it was back to the regular grind. This may not sound like much, but in their view, they were living as God wished. The history of the time shows how firmly they believed in God, who gave them the law [he means, the Torah] and promised them deliverance.

Quite what is at stake here I cannot see; there is far less than meets the eye. Any objective person familiar with both this picture and also the Gospels is going to wonder what, in the Gospels, all the fuss is about. But that is beside the point in describing Judaism in the first century B.C. and A.D., since at issue is not history but theology. That is what I meant when I observed that asking what really happened and how things really were – the quest for the historical Jesus – forms a narrowly theological venture, in which what are called "historical facts" take the place of centuries of theological truths.

In the context of theology, not history, nothing I have said in criticism of Sanders bears consequence. Christians like Sanders aim to shape a Christianity for the future different from the one we know in the past, a future Christianity in which "Silent Night" could never be sung by Christian racist murderers, as it was sung on Christmas after Christmas by the mass murderers, Poles, Germans, Lithuanians, and other good Catholics and Protestants and Orthodox Christians, at Auschwitz. Never forget Sanders's vocation and its source: divinity students of Kittel and Jeremias served in the SS; priests and ministers worshipped Jesus Christ with, and for, the guards at Auschwitz. That fact defines the context in which Christian readers of Sanders's *Judaism. Practice & Belief 63 B.C.E. - 66 C.E.* are required to learn lessons of not history but theology. These are simple: [1] stop reviling Judaism – let it be, and [2] stop killing Jews.

Part Four

THEOLOGICAL TURNING

12

Israel:
The Future of the Jewish People?
What People?

Before we can speculate on the future of the Jewish people in the coming century, we had best pause to ask ourselves, just what do we mean by "the Jewish people"? For a moment's reflection tells us that the conception of "a people set apart," or "a people, one people," forms a construct of the theology of Judaism, on the one side, and a fabrication of the ideology of Zionism, on the other – both of them powerful artifacts of imagination. That is so because neither construct is susceptible of this-worldly, secular analysis: verification or falsification by appeal to hard facts of social reality. In fact, if we suppose that in speculating on the Jewish people, we deal with a secular fact, a given that can be documented out of the data of perceived reality, we err. The error, specifically, is that of reification, treating as a thing what is not palpable at all. What theology of Judaism means by "Israel" has nothing to do with demography, and what Zionism means by "a people, one people," pertains to politics and empowerment, not to the ordinary, workaday condition of Jews here, there, and everywhere. Theology and ideology organize data within their respective imaginative constructs, their systemic fantasies. For that purpose, tests of verification and falsification, null hypotheses and independent variables, prove monumentally irrelevant.

Nothing is so intangible as a theological entity or an ideological construct: "Israel" God's people, on the one side, or "Israel," the people, one people, on the other. If we invoke any of the ordinary criteria for a social entity of the here and now, we find that none fits the category, "Jewish people." A social entity in the here and now defines itself by commonalities, whether of territory, or of language and culture, or some other tangible, shared qualities. But of these, the Jews have none. Jews live all over the world; they do not have a single language in common (though English serves best of all), and by the criteria of economics, on the one side, or politics, on the second, or shared culture, on the third, nothing binds them together. No one is so naive as to imagine that all Jews are children of a single couple of remote antiquity, Abraham and Sarah, and no one but a convicted sentimentalist can conceive that all the Jews feel the same way (if they do not think the same thing) about any subject or experience at all. Nor can we be detained by the self-serving notion of a "community of fate," since it is the simple fact that the Jews throughout the world share the destiny of the societies and nations of which they are a part, but no common destiny at all. It follows that before we give thought to what we conceive is going to happen to "the Jewish people" in the twenty-first century, we have to define for ourselves that concerning which we propose to speculate: which Jews? what people? And, as soon as we do, we realize that discourse on the topic, "the Jewish people," itself forms an act of theology (for Judaism) or ideology (for Zionism and other formations of a secular Judaic system).

Why do I insist that "the Jewish people" is a construct of imagination, a topic of theological or ideological intellection, a chapter of other-worldly faith – but not something that, in the here and now, we can examine, concerning which, out of this-worldly data, we can project trends and make secular predictions? The reason, as I argued in my *Judaism and Its Social Metaphors. Israel in the History of Jewish Thought* (New York, 1988: Cambridge University Press), is that we do not experience but only imagine "society," because "society" viewed whole is something too abstract and remote from everyday life to afford a concrete encounter. We know individual people. But we generalize and so in our minds conceive, or imagine, that the concrete persons we encounter represent, form part of, that abstraction, society. And that is a natural course of our making sense of the world beyond the here and the now of everyday life. We move from what we know, the concrete and immediate, to what we do not know. And whatever lies beyond our experience, encompassing all modes of abstraction and all conceptions of not merely event but process, demands to be set into relationship with what we already know. Connections that we make, abstractions that we perceive only in their concrete manifestations, processes that we can imagine but not identify in the here and now – not the blow but power, not the caress but love – these form the raw material of mind. Accordingly, when we name and treat as real and concrete what are in fact abstractions and intangible processes, we impose upon ourselves the need to compare the abstract to the concrete. We therefore think in a process of analogy, contrast, comparison, and metaphor about that thing which, to begin with, we ourselves have identified and so made up in our minds.

Take a group for example. When two or more persons perceive themselves to bear traits in common and to constitute a group on account of those indicative traits, they face a range of choices in thinking about the classification and character of that social entity, that group, that they imagine they comprise. It can be immediate, but it does not have to be. A family, a village, a neighborhood, a town – these form part of felt experience; we can walk in the streets, recognize relationship with persons we know and our relationship to whom we can name, and we can trace the outer limits of the settled area. But when people identify with others they have not met and may never meet, the process of the search for appropriate metaphors to take the place of absent experience in the everyday world begins. Then metaphors for the social group present themselves. In thinking about such abstractions as social entities, people appeal to comparisons between the concrete things they know and the abstract things they seek to explain and express for themselves.

That is why, when we speak of such large abstractions as society, or people, or nation, for instance, use the word "family" to mean a social entity or aggregate of persons beyond the one in which we grow up and to which we bear blood relationships, for example, calling a friend or a political ally a "brother," we move onward from the concrete to the abstract. And the notion of "Jewish people" best illustrates that movement, the utterly abstract and general reading of diverse and incongruous concrete facts, for example, of family or a sense of locality (for Israelis) or connection to others of a common family history (for example, immigration from the same general area), genealogy, religion, or gastronomic taste (for the Golah). Jews in the Yiddish-speaking East before World War II assuredly did constitute "a people, one people," by any and every criterion, however strictly imposed: territory, language, culture, politics, genealogy, economy, class structure and marital patterns and child raising taboos, and the like. All variables pointed to a single conclusion: this really did constitute "a people, one people," and, theologically, the Jews of Eastern Europe could be credibly represented as holy Israel.

Jews in the English- (or Portuguese-, French-, Spanish-, Italian-, or German-) speaking West certainly do not exhibit a counterpart cogency. For one thing, Jews in the State of Israel form a political entity, defined by empowerment. Jews in the Golah do not. Between Jews in the State of Israel and Jews in the Golah only an evanescent sentiment presently forms some sort of common bond. But gossamer threads of sentimentality attenuate, and the future of the sentiment that Jews in the Golah and Jews in the State of Israel form "a people, one people," appears neither healthy nor hopeful. Golah Jews go to the State of Israel, look around, feel great, and then go home. Israelis are glad to see them go – and many want to join them.

So the conception of "the Jewish people" itself calls into question whether we deal with this-worldly data subject to analysis and prognosticating thought. Acts of imagination, whether theological or ideological, are just that: inventions for the moment. That metaphorical mode of thought permits us to speak about things though we cannot point in diurnal encounter to the concrete experience of those things. A principal abstraction and process therefore comprises a social entity that transcends the concrete experience and pragmatic knowledge of two or more people together. How we think about those abstractions that in the most general and indeterminate terms we may call "social entities," the result of generalization from the here and now to the out there, the outcome of a process of imagination, fantasy, and reflection, the results of that intellectual process – these lend substance to our perception, through now-real and concrete expectation, of the hitherto unknown and unfelt but merely imagined. In these processes of thought we resort to metaphor so as to treat as a thing what originates out of process or abstraction. That is how reflection and imagination in general terms about the commonalities of specific things form an exercise in metaphorical thought.

And this brings us to the matter of a religious system as a mode of the nurture of metaphors for interpreting our social experience of the concrete. The future of "the Jewish people" imagined by Judaism is secure. For Judaism as a religious system has never been more solidly grounded in both intellect and politics as it is today. We recall the difference between caress, the concrete, and love, the abstraction, or between a knock on the head and power. How we move from the immediate to the general forms the problem of reflection, and through reflection, generalization. People are used to thinking of philosophy and also of science as modes of rigorous generalization. But religion, no less than philosophy and science, also forms a principal mode of profound thought about process and abstraction. For religion gives concrete definition to what lies beyond immediate experience, as much as to what is formed of concrete encounter, mediating between immediate encounter and the abstract and generalizing theology.

For example, religion has the power of transforming cells of like-minded persons into believers, and believers into a Church or the saved or holy people or a supernatural family or (as is most common) even a social entity that is altogether *sui generis*. That is why religion as a mode of thought competes with philosophy and science. The reason is that all three – religion, philosophy, science – exercise that same power of turning into a thing we can define and identify what is, in fact, ineffable abstraction, intangible relationship, process beyond palpable perception. And that is assuredly the fact, whether religion addresses God in heaven or speaks of humanity in the home, street, and town, identifies a building as holy, defines a properly performed gesture as sanctifying, or declares two or three individuals to form a society, a holy entity, for instance, the embodiment here and now of God's people or God's own person or body. That is the context in which the future of the Jewish people is secure, for we, holy Israel, form an integral and essential element of a religious system that exhibits only robust health. The measure of that health taken by any and every kind of test – institutional and intellectual alike – yields only good results. No religion practiced in the world today shows itself more robust or more at peace with itself than Judaism in its classical forms.

Among the many supernatural works of enchantment accomplished by religion, the one studied here is the capacity of religion to transform individuals and families into a corporate body, imputing relationships other than those natural to location or family genealogy. That is the power of religion to name and treat as real the otherwise random confluence, in belief and behavior, of isolated groups of people, to persuade those families that they form part of something larger than their limited congeries, even though no one in those families has ever seen, or can ever encompass in a single vision, the entirety of that something more, that entire nation, mystical body, entity *sui generis*. In simple terms, religions speak of social entities made up of their devotees. These they turn from concrete entity in the here and now into abstractions merely represented, in the here and now, by the present exemplar. The social entity turns into a symbol for something more. So the social group (defined presently) is transformed from what the world sees to what the eye of faith perceives, becoming, in the case of a Judaism, an "Israel."

But the same health and strength characterize the notion of "a people, one people," that is set forth in the fabrication of Zionism and fully realized in the State of Israel today. There, too, we see a healthy, robust society, secure in its future, which appeals to the notion of "Israel" to explain itself. Its "Israel" to be sure is not the same "Israel" as is imagined by Judaism; it has its own systemic formation, its own sense of a worldview, way of life, account of the social entity that sees the world through a particular view and lives out its life in that way. "Israel" is a people that constitutes an empowered entity, a nation; a people that possesses, and is possessed by, its land; a nation that speaks a single language, forms a cogent society, builds a common culture, shares a common national experience, and endures a common fate. So for both

Judaism and Zionism, the Jewish people forms a useful construction, one rich in perceived validations, full of practical meaning.

And yet, it is clear, in both systems, "Israel" forms a metaphor. Why does thinking about the social entity in particular demand metaphorical thinking? It is because a social group that does not rest, for its being, upon constant and palpable interaction exists mainly in the abstract. It is as an abstraction that is (merely) exemplified in the here and now by the group near at hand, the one that does consist of individuals who do interact. When people think about that abstraction, for example, about the Church or the Israel of which they form a part (or "the nation of Islam" for that matter), they invoke a variety of concrete metaphors, for example, family. They may turn to metaphors of another sort altogether than "family," for instance, "people" or "nation." They could just as well call themselves "the wolf pack" or "the clan." But, in all, they are engaged in a transaction of a symbolic character, in which they propose to express their sense not by reference to what they can see and touch, but to what, in the things they can see and touch, corresponds to that entity – that social entity – that is under discussion.

But in answering the question as I have, I of course have resorted to a disingenuous revision of what is under discussion. For when people ask about the future of the Jewish people, they do not mean, the future of the usefulness of the construct, "Jewish people" or "Israel," but the future, in the here and now, of the social entity, "Israel," or "the Jewish people." So if we accept the conventional definition of what is subject to discussion, we have to ask about the future of "the Jewish people," as a social entity. Let us now turn to that question.

By "social entity," using the most general language I can find, I mean "social group," defined as *two or more persons that exhibit traits of a group.* What are such indicative traits? Traits that characterize a social group by contrast to random individuals emerge when the participants form a common identity, express a feeling of unity concerning common goals and shared norms. The social group involves direct interaction and communication, actions to carry out a system of values. A social group may be a family, a village, or any other entity (two or more persons) in which there is a concrete encounter among persons who perceive themselves to form such a group. It is at this point that the process of abstraction begins.

Specifically, a social group may take shape among persons who do not necessarily interact and communicate with one another, but who do share a common system of values. Then the social group forms an abstraction, rather than a concrete and palpable fact. It may derive from an intangible process, with the result that participants in the group invoke metaphors from the known social world (for example, family) to explain that unknown fact of social life that, in their minds, they now have constituted. That sort of social group differs from the one formed by a family, in which, we may assume, there is interaction; or a village or a neighborhood of like-minded persons, in which there are shared values among persons who see one another and form their sense of constituting a group on the basis of everyday activity. This more abstract social group in the context of a religious system constitutes an entity defined by common goals and shared norms, but – and this explains the metaphorical character of thought about that entity – one in which all individual members do not interact.

Such social groups may prove formal or informal, but a social group constituted by a religion at its essence is formal, for it is very carefully defined with imposed norms of faith and action. A social group may appeal to extended kinship. By definition religious systems are not made up of genealogical units, though they may identify the social group formed by the religion as a family or an extended family. When they do posit shared ancestry, they engage in a symbolic transaction – once more requiring us to investigate how the *is* becomes the *ought*, which is to say, how the everyday shades into the abstract. Along these same lines, a social group may appeal to the society formed of the encounter among individuals who never, in fact, meet. Here, too, the encounter is one in theory and in the abstract, joining in a single social group persons who imagine that they know and understand one another but who in reality do not intersect.

A further instance of the power of metaphor shows us how a group may in its own mind define its relationship with the outside world. People who share traits with others may determine that they are separate from those others and constitute a minority, as against the majority formed by those others. In its own mind, therefore, a social group may be classified as a minority group, finding definition in contrast with another, more numerous group, defined within the same larger classification. By definition a religious system will create such a minority group, in that the world beyond will be made up of many such groups, of which the one at hand is not likely to form the largest, that is, to constitute a numerical majority. The symbolic transaction commences when the group defines itself by contrast to other groups, when it conceives of itself to constitute a minority-group *type* of group. In all of these ways, it is through metaphors evoked in description of the social group that we see the working of the imagination, hence "imagining society."

Our inquiry carries us deep into symbolic transactions. It is through shared imagination or perception held in common – hence, in the metaphors by which abstractions such as "society" or "nation" reach concrete form in intellect and expectation alike – that these transactions are realized. These metaphors when broadly construed form gossamer threads, yet bond persons who in fact do not commonly meet at all. The same act of imagination imposes upon persons the consciousness – and concrete character – of community. These symbolic transactions pertinent to the group life posited by a religious system constitute the social theory of that system – the social entity to which and of which the system speaks. And since the symbolic transactions come to concrete expression in metaphors – hence "social metaphors" – we find ourselves sorting out those metaphors that serve, and those that do not, in a given religious system.

In all, we deal with people who come together from time to time – hence, temporarily – but who see themselves as forming a lasting society. They by no means constitute a population, that is, pretty much everyone in a given territory. But they see themselves as a society. They do not have large-scale, enduring political organizations or social institutions to draw them together, though, in their conception of the group, they will imagine both and call themselves a nation or a people. They are more than a crowd and far more than a mere category of society, for instance, people of a given age or occupation. But they also are much less in the concrete social facts of their existence than they conceive themselves to be. Hence comes the abstraction with which we deal under the title, "social entity of a religious system," or, in the case of a Judaism, an "Israel."

Now, if we want to ask about the future of a given population, we turn to the social metaphor that that population asks to explain who it is. For a social metaphor tells a group how to identify itself, and this is in two ways. First, the metaphor identifies the type or genus of social group at hand, the genus, and, second, it will consequently define the species of the genus, or type, at hand. These are the pertinent questions: Is the social entity a family? Then how does it compare to other families? Is it a nation? Then in what way does it differ from other nations, and in what context does the category, nation, take on its definitive sense and meaning? Or a social group may declare itself *sui generis*, not like any other social group at all, but a genus unto itself, for example, a third possibility as between two available choices.

A set and sequence of social groups living in different times and places and not continuous with one another, Jews have commonly told themselves tales of how in recorded time they had come into existence as a single social entity, "Israel," in a unitary and harmonious history. In these stories Jews appealed to a variety of social metaphors, of two basic classifications. First of all, some held that the Jews – Israel – were *sui generis*, of a type of social entity lacking all counterpart, and thus not of a type into which all other social groups could be classified. Second, others maintained that Israel formed a distinct species of a common genus, whether family or nation or people. Now what I want to know about these metaphors is simple. Under what conditions or circumstances will one metaphor take priority, and when will a different metaphor appear self-evidently compelling? Along these same lines, if a given metaphor serves, does it carry in its wake a variety of other metaphorical consequences in the way in which the group that invokes the metaphor thinks about itself and explains its collective existence? To state matters simply, if I know the operative metaphor, what else do I know about the group's thinking about itself beyond the metaphor? I should want to be able to form rules of predicting what traits a theory of a social group will carry in the wake of the generative metaphor of the group. These are the sorts of questions that form the centerpiece of interest.

Now, when we attempt to answer them, we find ourselves at an impasse. On the one side, we readily point to the social metaphors that serve Judaism and Zionism. On the other hand, what social metaphors serve Jews who are neither Judaists nor Zionists? That is to say, among the sizable numbers of Jews in the Golah who do not identify themselves as practitioners of Judaism ("Judaists") or think of themselves as temporary residents where they live, en route to Jerusalem ("Zionists" in even the most minimal definition), what metaphor tells them who they are? How do they conceive of themselves, too, as Israel? And what "Israel" encompasses them? The Judaists know "Israel" in the liturgy, meaning, the holy people, "Israel" after the flesh; the Zionists know "Israel" as the place and the state. But the mass of Jews to whom the liturgy does not speak and for whom the state of (being) Israel and the State of Israel do not coincide cannot say for sure who they are in the aspect of "Israel."

That fact calls into question whether or not the Jewish people as a secular entity may look forward to more than an ephemeral future, a half-life of a generation more. It is not because the absence of a metaphor points to the demise of imagination, the decline of intellect. True, there is no accessible and evocative metaphor that in the end can account for the "Jewishness" of the masses of secular and non-Zionist Jews in the world today. But that is not because in the workaday world of Jewry in the Golah, we can identify no resources of sentiment, intellect, and emotion, capable of endowing social facts with surpassing sensibility. The reason is other. In the end, the social entity (however classified) comes prior to the metaphor adopted for itself by that social entity. If there is no social entity, then there will be no metaphor. The question, then, of where and how, and how enduringly, Jews today form a viable social entity has to be addressed, taken up in its own terms.

In the world viewed whole, Jews who are neither Judaists nor Zionists (and Israelis) do not form a social entity of any kind. But in diverse national contexts, Jews do form ethnic groups, that is, Jewish Americans, but not American Jews. They are not an American species of the genus, Jew (ethnic), but a Jewish species of the genus, American (and so for France or Belgium or Italy or Britain or Brazil or Argentina or Mexico or Canada). The reason, of course, is obvious: French-speaking secular Jews have neither religion (Judaism) nor ideology (Zionism) in common with American-speaking secular Jews; but they have much in common with other French citizens, even while, in some (rather trivial) ways, they also differ from other French citizens.

What makes anyone think that the Jews form an ethnic group? The reason is that all over the world in diverse contexts of nations Jews do exhibit traits that indicate their social continuity and corporate cohesion in the context of their various homelands. The American demographer Calvin Goldscheider, among others, has shown that the Jews do form a distinctive social group, and that the indicators of their difference are sharply etched and well framed. Goldscheider writes: "A detailed examination of family, marriage, childbearing, social class, residence, occupation and education among Jews and non-Jews leads to the unmistakable conclusion that Jews are different. Their distinctiveness as a community is further reinforced by religious and ethnic forms of cohesiveness." But these points of differentiation always prove local and particular.

Goldscheider's point is that although difference is defined in different ways in different places, everywhere the sense of being different, of being "unique," characterizes Jews. Of course, since difference is defined differently in different places, what makes a Jew different in one place will not mark him and not be recognized as a difference somewhere else. For instance, in America people think that bagels are a Jewish bread, or that corned beef is a Jewish dish, but to outsiders, American Jews appear to be Jewish Americans – and more American than Jewish. Similarly, in Morocco and Algeria, some forms of wheat used to be prepared in a way that Moroccans and Algerians considered specific to Jews and therefore Jewish, but in America we recognize no specifically Jewish way to prepare wheat. And although in Italy there is an artichoke dish that is called "Jewish artichoke," to an American, one Italian dish seems the same as any other – when you get past the garlic. Although the specific traits vary across the world, all over the world that fact of Jewish difference persists – that alone. But that bears little consequence. We already realize that mere difference fades; intermarriage guarantees the end of Jewish difference for the family whose children intermarry.

What kind of traits mark the group off from others in one context and another? Family, stratification of Jewish society, and diverse characteristics of ethnicity all identify the Jews as a group distinctive in their larger social setting. Goldscheider states, "The distinctive features of American Jewish life imply bonds and linkages among Jews which form the multiple bases of communal continuity. These ties are structural as well as cultural; they reflect deeply embedded forms of family, educational, job and residence patterns, reinforced by religious and ethnic-communal behavior, cemented by shared lifestyles and values." That is, Jewish difference is distributed across socio-economic patterns. It appears in the form of marriage, type of family, place of residence, degree of mobility a Jew enjoys in that society.

That is, we see it in his occupation, education, economic status – his social class with its communal affiliation and identification and behavior. When we consider these phenomena, we see that Jews do exhibit qualities in common. For instance, they live together, forming Jewish neighborhoods; they work in a few specific types of occupations; they marry within the group. As a result, Americans think, for example, that psychiatry is a Jewish profession while professional football is not. By contrast, in the State of Israel, Jews are identified (as was the case in biblical times) as farmers and soldiers. None of these are inherently Jewish occupations, of course, any more than they are Norwegian. But in specific contexts they indeed indicate a person's Jewishness. And thus they justify describing the Jews as a socio-ethnic group, not merely as individuals who happen to believe the same things and so have the same religion. But that is so locally, not internationally.

If, therefore, we ask whether the points of differentiation between Jewish Americans and other Americans also distinguish Jewish Britons from other Britons, we find that they do not. For example, Jewish Americans send their children to university in a far higher proportion than do other Americans; Jewish Britons do not exhibit the same conviction that their children should get a university education; that is, the proportion of young Jewish Britons who go to university does not compare with the proportion of young Jewish Americans, but it does compare with the proportion of young non-Jewish Britons of the same social class. So points of differentiation prove, in general, serviceable only in context, but not out of the context of a particular nation. Hence secular Jews do not form a differentiable social entity that transcends national boundaries; religious and Zionist Jews do, because the same differentials and variables pertain internationally.

Now to answer the question raised at the outset: I see no Jewish future for Jews outside of the State of Israel, on the one side, or the synagogue, on the other. But then, I see no compelling reason for anyone to want to be different by reason of "being Jewish" outside of either the State of Israel or the people of Israel, that is, that "Israel" of whom, in the life of eternal Israel, we say, "The one who keeps Israel neither slumbers nor sleeps." Secular Jews at home in the Golah, estranged from the synagogue on the one side and only casually connected to the State of Israel, on the other, have already shown us their future: their children intermarry in massive numbers, and their grandchildren no longer identify themselves as Jews, but only, as the grandchildren of Jews. The Israel that now defines itself as the "Israel" of the Torah, the Israel that now has decided to call itself "the State of Israel" – these two "Israels," mutually exclusive, though they are, by contrast enjoy that future into eternity that God has promised in the Torah and through the Land and people – all *of Israel.*

13

Torah:
Demonizing the Talmud
Right Here in Tampa

Television viewers around Tampa Bay saw on the six o'clock news just now something very new to our area, which is, reports from Kennedy Boulevard in inner-city Tampa itself about a sign on the side of a building denouncing the Talmud and us Talmud Jews. I suspect that among the tens of thousands of puzzled drivers who pass that sign daily, scarcely two might actually know what the Talmud is, or why a fellow from up north in Georgia should want to come down here to denounce that book. And I doubt that, in Tampa, St. Petersburg, Clearwater, and all the other bastions of holy Israel on the Florida Suncoast, even counting the rabbis, there is even a minyan of Talmud Jews, that is, Jews who regularly devote much time to learning in that holy, life-defining document. When the local boards of rabbis asked me to speak for them and I gave them some pages to study, they said I was arrogant for expecting them to prepare some Talmud and refused to examine the passages I had sent (in English) for that purpose; so the sign's "Talmud Jews" doesn't include them.

But for those few people in town who do center their lives on the Talmud, it was old news. For, as much as the people of Israel have suffered from demonization, so, too, has the Talmud – meaning not only the Talmud of Babylonia, ca. 600, but the entirety of rabbinic literature from the Mishnah, ca. 200, to that Talmud – endured many centuries of defamation. Indeed, attacks on the Talmud swept onward to assaults upon Judaism, then further still, moving forward to outrages against the Jews. From medieval times, when Christianity informed itself about Judaism and identified the Talmud as the reason that Judaism endured, to the modern age, when Jew-hatred and anti-Semitism chose the

Talmud as its target of opportunity, the classics of Judaism, for which the word "Talmud" stands, have attracted intense interest in the world at large. Important and influential anti-Semitic writings focused on that document and claimed to reveal its allegedly vile character. Not only so, but, from the beginnings of the formation, within Judaism, of diverse, reforming movements, the powerful authority of the Talmud in the received and classical Judaism won for the document enemies within as well. They, too, saw in the Talmud, along with all of the writings identified with it, the source of vitality and power of that Judaism that they wished to change. It would be difficult to point to a book with more enemies round about than that one book.

The classics of Judaism represented by the Talmud form a literature that has sustained an ongoing campaign of defamation. But that does not mean these books have been much read or studied. It would be hard to name a book more hated than read, more cited than studied, and more casually condemned than critically appreciated than the Talmud. For the Talmud's enemies, outside and in, treated the document not as a book to be studied but as a symbol of all that stood in the way of their bringing about the final solution to their particular Jewish problem, Christianity's will to make the Jews disappear, other Judaisms' need to dispose of the authority and prestige of that Judaism for which the Talmud stands. Since the Talmud defined the one Judaism that for the long past and today as well Jews, pious or otherwise, have known and now identify as authentic and the measure of inauthenticity, the Talmud defined the favored target of those who wanted in one way or another to change the Jews by getting rid of their religion.

So popes and cardinals and archbishops in medieval times ordered the Talmud to be burned, and, at a single burning in Paris in the thirteenth century, thousands of cartloads of Talmudic manuscripts were disposed of. In early modern times Jew-haters worked out their obsession by polemics against the Talmud and its contents, Talmudic Judaism and its flaws. Jewish reformers, including Reform Judaism, sought to find a path past or around the obstacle to change formed by the Talmud, which they deemed to have corrupted the true faith, and moving instead on a path toward the prophets of the Hebrew Scriptures, held to have presented the golden age of this "Judaism" they wished to regain (or renew or invent). The one full of ritual, the other, ethics, the one small, trivial, spiritually deadening, the other great-hearted, universal, and healing the wounds of humanity, the Talmud and the prophets were contrasted to the perpetual disadvantage of the Talmud. The Christian Reformation's "only Scripture" for the Judaic Reformation became, "without the Talmud." Christianity on the left flank, Reform

Judaism on the right flank, and anti-Semitism at the center, all subjected the Talmud to a long siege.

The ancient bastion stood firm. And the siege has come to an end, except among a few crackpots. The reform of Judaism has taken place, its integrationist ideal defining for nearly all Judaisms in the West the way forward; and the integrationist Judaisms, Reform, Conservative, Reconstructionist, as well as integrationist Orthodoxy, all accord to the Talmud an honored place in the curricula of their rabbinical schools and synagogue programs as well. Large and influential Christianities, authoritative Church bodies East and West, have made their piece with the persistence of holy Israel, no longer proposing that the Torah be left, never read again, in its holy ark. Anti-Semitism of course persists, but has found for itself a variety of other targets, having lost that huge academic constituency that, in the seventeenth, eighteenth, nineteenth, and much of the twentieth centuries wished to find in the Talmud learned footnotes for their hatred of Judaism and the Jewish people. Such remnants of academic anti-Semitism as survive in odd corners of the world – from today's Uppsala University in Sweden, to Tampa to Sydney, Australia, to be sure – suffer the status of crackpots and are dismissed as relics of a discredited past. The courts will not convict them for defamation; the judges laugh at them. As the Talmud says, a corpse cannot feel the scalpel.

Much has changed in our own times, except the paradox that the Talmud remains a book more talked about than studied. And, alas, when it is studied, that is mainly in yeshivas, where the Talmud provides a pretext for a long process of theorizing, not the focus for a sustained process of analysis. Not only so, but it has become a norm in many yeshivas not to study the Talmud as we know it, but thematic compilations, this passage here, that passage there, in entire indifference to the intellectual context in which this passage here takes on meaning and consequence in its proper setting, so, too, that passage there. The upshot is, where they study the Talmud, they do not study the Talmud. And, further, now that as the focus of a friendly interest, Jews and Christians alike express an interest in the writing, they impose their own disciplines and ignore the Talmud's own discipline. Scholars of earliest Christianity for most of this century have looked in its pages for "the Jewish background" of the New Testament and its stories and teachings. Judaic apologists, for their part, find in the pages of the Talmud valued stories and sayings. Not only so, but translations of the Talmud into English receive recognition in the media of mass culture formerly reserved for revelations of the secrets of kings and or beauty queens or star athletes. True, the translations reveal more of the words than the sense, the stories and sayings taken out of context convey false impressions, and what scholars identify as the Gospels' Jewish background rarely leaves "Judaism" in so positive a light as to create problems for faithful Christians.

So if the Talmud's writers still lived among us and possessed long memories, they might wonder whether their writing has found a better fate among its friends today than it did among its enemies in former days. Still, today, outside of the world of yeshivas where the Talmud is studied as part of the Torah that God gave to Moses at Sinai and gives to Israel day by day, the document yet serves symbolic, rather than authentic, intellectual purposes. And, as a matter of fact, in yeshivas, the Talmud, too, provides a mere excuse for ventures into commentaries and codes, rather than enjoying sustained and systematic attention on its own account. It is a notorious fact that in yeshivas people read three lines of the Talmud and twenty lines of commentary, heading toward discursive and abstract analysis of this, that, and the other thing; the Talmud is no longer the focus of learning, but rather, the pretext. Few in the yeshiva world have studied all thirty-seven tractates of the Bavli cover to cover, fewer still, the thirty-nine of the Yerushalmi. "The Talmud says" stands for a citation of anything from anywhere, always out of context. And, since context finds definition in the documents, whole and complete, we may say that the work of the authors of the Bavli is honored but not understood, cited but not appreciated, and never grasped as a statement of power and conviction. So, in all, if I had written the Talmud, I should regard my work as lost and wasted, an empty media event, made to mean whatever people wanted.

But what could the writers of the Talmud have expected, having paid too high a compliment to the future. For they put together a document of such density and richness, made such formidable and unrelenting demands upon their readers' powers of comprehension and analysis, insisted upon so sustained a labor of reasoning and set the precondition of so comprehensive a grasp of a spun-out but sustained argument, that enormous intellectual effort would be required to learn what those writers had to say. Asking so much, they conveyed their high opinion of those to follow. But demanding too much, they guaranteed the awful fate of their work: every prize but the one of an intelligent hearing. Truly original, extraordinarily thoughtful intellects, they took for granted they would receive the one thing they rarely got outside of limited circles indeed: a reading cover to cover, a sustained, systematic, serious effort to grasp the whole of their message, through the parts, but all together, too. But that is precisely what they have not gotten for centuries, neither in yeshivas nor elsewhere.

Some few in every age, to be sure, could read and understand and even add to the increment of learning and thought. In times past, and even in our own day, a handful in yeshivas proved worthy of the challenge and earned the ancient compliment. But most have not, and not a few who claim to have mastered the writing showed themselves charlatans, even while they claimed to tell the rest of the world who knows and who does not. So Talmudic studies became the realm of politicians, and every self-anointed saint, every second-rater, every hanger-on, every never-was-aiming-at-the-status-of-a-has-been, competed to establish the claim of priority in mediating the mysteries of this great, unknown, long-hidden secret writing, the Talmud. However grand their error in paying a compliment to ages to come, the authors of the Talmud deserved better than they got from history.

But the nature of their writing accounts, also, for the intense reception of a document either not understood at all or quite misconstrued, that the document has gotten for itself. For one thing, I doubt the writers could have conceived or ever understood that outside of Israel, the holy people sanctified by the Torah, anyone would want, or gain, access to their writing. So they never addressed what turned out to be an enormous audience interested, for malevolent reasons to be sure, in what they had to say. I cannot find a line in the document that suggests an address to the world beyond the faithful; but before our own times, outsiders to Islam and Christianity as much as to Judaism provided only the excuse and provocation for the aggression of evangelism.

For another thing, I wonder whether they imagined an audience that would make of their writing what many generations of the faithful in fact did with the document: turn it from a statement of philosophy, theology, and jurisprudence into an occasion of intense spirituality. Men of spirituality and sanctity, they found God in intellect, met God in mind. But that is what happened to their writing in yeshivas and synagogue pulpits as well: writing of substance was turned into ritual formula. What I mean may be grasped from the fact that, in the yeshiva world today, people recite chapters of the Mishnah as an act of piety, in the way in which in the synagogue and yeshiva worlds, people recite Psalms in that same spirit. Now the contents of the Psalms invite reverential repetition; the contents of Mishnah chapters do not. Not only so, but citing, in garbled form, some half-understood, misunderstood line of the Talmud, serves to validate the credentials of rabbis in their pulpit, professors at their podium. So, among the faithful, the writing was made to serve more purposes than its writers, on the evidence of their writing, could have anticipated.

And, for a third thing, I also wonder whether they could in their worst imaginings about "the nations of the world," and even "Rome" (Christianity) and "Ishmael" (Islam), have contemplated an age in which the Israel they so loved and lovingly crafted would sustain so long and unremitting a campaign of systematic defamation as to its character and demonization as to its faith as Israel and Judaism have had to endure. I am sure that, like anybody faced with the choice, had they known Jews would die because of what they wrote, they would never have written a line. But citations from the Talmud (however malevolently twisted out of all context and meaning) in intellectual form did shape attitudes that led Germans to murder Jews. They therefore had no reason to watch their words, lest the gentiles find occasion to cavil. So, surely, the writers whose work we address could never, ever have supposed that what they wrote would be called to testify against those who would value their words and live by them. But that, too, has happened, and in our own day, too.

And yet, the fact pays its tribute to the Bavli's authors. They wrote the one document that came to stand for what made Israel Israel and Judaism Judaism. Everyone had the Hebrew Scriptures/Written Torah/Old Testament; but only Israel, the holy people, and Judaism, that is, the religion of the holy people, had the Oral Torah, which the Talmud wrote down and set forth. That is to say, the single most distinctive part of the Torah that sets forth the entirety of Israel's heritage of Sinai, the oral part, written down in the Talmud and related documents, found itself transformed from a book, with a particular viewpoint and message and purpose, to a symbol of the whole. And whether it was made to stand for the whole of the faith, and so revered, or the whole of the competing faith, and so vilified, hardly mattered. That is why the document would for centuries be revered more than read, as in the yeshiva world, why knowledge of the document would serve as an instrument of personal validation and indicator of status, rather than utilized and appreciated, and why, on the other side of the boundary, the substance of the writing would be taken to define the enemy's power and therefore would be identified for a sustained campaign of demolition.

But burning the Talmud in the Middle Ages – then treating it as itself a dangerous object – or discrediting it in modern times by arguments derived from Christian theology and pseudo-scholarship produced the opposite result. Christians burned their writings, so Jews protected and valued them all the more. Anti-Semites misrepresented them, so Jews and their Christian friends when they had them addressed the misrepresentation and discredited it. Consequently, the agenda of learning found definition not in what the document said but in what outsiders to the writing had to say about it, against it or in its behalf. The result remains one and the same: the Talmud served more as a symbol than as the authoritative source of a statement bearing intellectual weight and substance. That explains why, when pieces of a couple of tractates of Adin Steinsaltz's translation of the Talmud began to appear, his publisher Random House (alleging to reveal a document never before known, though Steinsaltz's is the fifth translation of the handful of tractates he has printed so far!) pushed sales by telling people that just to have the book in their houses would make them better Jews – whether or not they ever opened it. Somehow Steinsaltz has got the Talmud confused with a mezuzah, and the coffee table with the doorposts of the house. That reasonable numbers of people bought his book (though hardly in the huge numbers the publisher, profits secured with a huge subsidy in advance, predicted) tells us one reason to begin to ask, "So what is in it?" And that our enemies still conduct their war against us by attacking a book neither they nor we have studied once again raises a possibility with little precedent in American Jewry: it is time to open the book and find out what is there.

14

God:
How, in Judaism, Do We Know God?

Theology concerns the knowledge of God that, in accord with the view of a given religion, God affords to us. In the case of Judaism all the knowledge of God that Judaism alleges God has given to humanity is contained in the Torah, which is God's self-manifestation to Israel. That is what theology of Judaism, as distinct from philosophy of Judaism, proposes to describe and explain: the rational principles that govern knowledge in general applied to knowledge of God through the designated source in particular. In Judaism, we find God in the Torah – there alone. Let me spell out why, since creative explorations in Judaism that ignore the Torah, oral and written, today take shape.

Defining the term, "Judaism," we start with two categories, the native and (equally legitimate, but different) neutral ones. Two sentences that say the same thing show what is at stake in the distinction:

[1] In secular, descriptive terms, rigorous, sustained reflection upon revelation forms the theology of Judaism.

[2] In the native language of Judaism, we say the same thing in these words: Study of the Torah as the Talmud presents the Torah teaches us the will of God.

The native category, or name, of "Judaism" in the Judaism set forth by "our sages of blessed memory" in "the Torah, written and oral," is "the Torah." When, in ordinary speech in the West, we want to speak of the religion set forth by the Torah, we call it "Judaism." So the two terms stand for two distinct, but comparable, categories, each in its own language world: the whole, complete, authoritative, fully composed religion, with its system comprising a way of life, worldview, and theory of the social entity, Israel, is Judaism (for the secular language of the West) or is what the Torah presents (for the theological language of the faith).

How then differentiate native from secular and descriptive categories? The native category "Torah" formulates truth in a mythic framework, the Western one, "Judaism," portrays in a neutral way facts or propositions in a philosophical setting of description. The appearance of the "-ism" (or "-ity") then for secular discourse signifies order, system, generalization and abstraction; the operative verbs, "teaches," or "maintains," and the like, bear the same message of generalization and principled conviction.

The use of "Torah" by contrast appeals to a text and to revelation, and the use of "says" or "as it is said" or "as it is written" with reference to the media of Torah, the sage or Scripture, respectively, appeals for sense to the act of speech, which, in context, is the medium of authority attained through not reason and persuasion but revelation. It follows that "the Torah says" and "Judaism teaches" or "believes" really do not correspond, the native category referring to revelation, the academic one, reasoned sorting out of data.

And yet, the two distinct ways of referring to the same thing – the position of the religious system, Judaism/the Torah – do bear a single purpose. It is to state the sum of all the many cases, the rule, the conclusion, the authoritative principle. Whether the language is liturgical, "Hear O Israel, the Lord our God, the Lord is one," or "Judaism is the religion of ethical monotheism," whether it is "You shall be holy, for I the Lord your God am holy," or "Judaism is a religion of covenantal nomism," the intent and effect are the same. So, too, the generic, torah, is defined not only in the character of writings and their contents, for example, "Moses received Torah at Sinai," but in the liturgical formulas that begin and conclude the proclamation of the Torah in synagogue worship: "Blessed...who has chosen us from among all the nations by giving us the Torah...blessed...who gives the Torah," and "Blessed...who has given us the authentic Torah and thereby planted within us eternal life...blessed...who gives the Torah." Another way of saying the same dogma is: [1] Israel is elect by reason of the Torah; [2] eternal life comes to us through the Torah; [3] God gives the Torah, present tense, meaning, here and now; and here and now, we receive the Torah.

The importance of recognizing the distinction between native and academic categories is in two aspects. First, we must permit "Judaism" to speak in its own terms, that is to say, as "the Torah." But, second, we must insist that "the Torah" also speak to us in language we can grasp – albeit in its native categories, idiom, and language (though in English) –

meaning, formulate its positions or principles in terms and categories that we also may understand: describe, analyze, and interpret.

It follows that, Torah being the native category, understanding "the theology of Judaism" as that theology came to full and systematic expression in its authoritative document requires an inquiry into the nature and structure of the Torah: the media designated with the status of Torah, the persons, books, gestures, hierarchical authority in the social order, modes of thought and expression, that fall into the category, Torah, and require orderly systematization as a single, coherent statement. Indeed, that statement – the theology of Judaism comes to realization in the Torah – self-evidently forms a redundancy, since, as I just said, "theology of Judaism" in one language of thought is the same as "the Torah" in the other.

It is through the Torah that God is made manifest, and, specifically, it is through the intellection exemplifed in the Torah that we know the mind of God. That means, what defines humanity and what defines God, in rationality, is the same thing: we are consubstantial in mind. I therefore allege that, first, the category, "Torah," defines the theology of Judaism, and, second, knowledge of the Torah tells us how God thinks.

Let me now state matters in the two languages at once: [1] Judaism states its theology through [2] the language and in the propositions of the Torah. Since Judaism is classified as a religion among religions, that statement ("Judaism states its theology") addresses to begin with the matter of what we know of God and how we know it. The reason is that [2] at stake in the Torah – for the religion of the Torah that is called Judaism – is knowledge of God.

Then the entire theology of Judaism may be expressed in the language of the Torah in a formulation that accommodates both Western, academic language and the forms of speech of the Torah: it is through the Torah – God's own manifestation to Moses and holy Israel, and God's self-manifestation – that faithful Israel knows God.

Now let me state the theology of Judaism in the language of the Torah, once more joining the two categories, native and secular: The Torah is the sole medium of God's revelation; it bears the unique message of God; and the Torah also conveys the correct method for the inquiry into the medium in quest of the truthful message: all three. Through learning in the Torah – singing its melody, in its words, in its rhythms, so making its natural sounds – we know God.

These statements, setting forth as generalizations of a descriptive character the generative convictions of the Torah, that is "Judaism," are unique to Judaism. The reason is not only the "context-specific" usage, "the Torah." It is more general: no other religion can make them. That is because these authoritative statements of the Torah/Judaism exclude much else that in other religions is commonly thought to afford knowledge of God: the two most common and paramount being knowledge of God, through nature and history, for instance. In the Torah God is made known not through nature on its own, nor through history uninterpreted, but through nature set forth by the Torah as God's creation ("In the beginning God created...," "The heavens declare the glory of God"), through history as explained through the Torah as a work of God's will ("You have seen how I..."). So we recover our starting point to define the term, "theology": knowing God defines the work of the theology of Judaism, or, to phrase matters in the native category and its language once more, through the Torah Israel meets God.

We may then identify the theology of this Judaism – that is to say, the truth of the Torah – with the following formulation: "All our knowledge of divine truth...depends on God's prior self-manifestation; there is no knowledge of God unless He reveals and we reason."[1] That formulation of contemporary philosophical theology in correct, academic language accurately and completely describes the entire program of the theology of Judaism. It is hardly necessary once more to translate into the language of Judaism, but an appropriate counterpart language for the same position may be identified in the liturgical setting when the Torah is proclaimed to faithful Israel at worship: "Blessed are you, Lord, our God, who has chosen us from among all nations by giving us the Torah. Blessed are you, who gives the Torah," and, at the end, "Blessed are you, Lord, our God, who has given us the true Torah and so planted within us life eternal. Blessed are you, who gives the Torah." When we know how through the Torah Israel knows God, we know the theology of Judaism. And then, about God there is nothing more to be known.

Now this brings us to the second point, namely, how the Torah reveals God's intellect and ours as well. What, exactly, is to be known about God in the theology of Judaism, or, phrasing the question in the native category: "What does the Torah say about the Holy One, blessed be He?" Obviously its messages are many, from an account of attributes ("The Lord, the Lord is merciful and long-suffering"), to the story of immediate encounter ("You shall not see my face..." "...the thin voice of silence"), and, above all, to the detailed and insistent account of what God commands Israel and covenants himself to do in regard to Israel. That, after all, is the principal message of the Torah par excellence, which is the Pentateuch. But the Torah not only sets forth propositions – things

---

[1] Ingolf Dalferth, "The Stuff of Revelation: Austin Farrer's Doctrine of Inspired Images," in Ann Loades and Michael McLain, eds., *Hermeneutics, the Bible and Literary Criticism* (London, 1992: MacMillan), p. 71.

God is, has done, or wants of us. Our sages of blessed memory notice that the Torah also lays out sentences God has said. Since through language we reveal not only what is on and in our minds, but also the very working of our minds, through the language of the Torah we gain access to God's mind.

The Torah reveals not only what God wants of humanity through Israel, but what (humanity can know of what) God is. The being of God that is revealed in the Torah – by the nature of that medium of revelation, the Torah itself, made up of words we know and sentences we can understand and forming connections we can follow and replicate – is God's will and intellect. Within the religion of the Torah called Judaism, therefore, there is ample occasion to take up the labor of learning not only what, but how God thinks. What is at stake in that lesson is how we, too, should conduct intellection. And the upshot will be, if we think the way we should, we may enter deep into the processes of the Torah and so reach propositions in the way in which God has thought things through, too. That is why I maintain, the theology of Judaism provides an account of what it means to know God through the Torah, a sentence that, I should hold, is made up of two equivalent and redundant clauses: [1] theology of Judaism proves... and [2] know God through the Torah. What makes that theology interesting is its special sense of what knowing God through the Torah involves, requires, and affords: knowing what it means rightly to know. Three steps lead to that simple conclusion.

First, knowing God and striving to be holy like God – "Let us make Man in our image...after our likeness," "You shall be holy, for I the Lord your God am holy" – define the lessons of the Torah or "Judaism."

Second, that knowledge is both unique and also sufficient: it is only through the Torah that knowledge of God comes to humanity. The Torah comes to Israel in particular because of God's decision and choice: God gave the Torah, or, in the language of liturgy, "...who gives the Torah."

Third, knowledge of God depends not only on God's self-revelation through the Torah. It requires also humanity's – therefore, uniquely, Israel's – proper grasp of the Torah. And that requires active engagement: sagacity, wit, erudition and intelligence. Gifts of intellect form instruments of grace: elements of God's self-revelation. The reason is that by thinking about thought as much as thinking thoughts, we ask the deeper question about what we can know about God, which is, God's thoughts in God's words, which, rightly grasped, expose God's thought.

Proper inquiry after God in the Torah therefore requires sound method: right questions, proper modes of analysis, reliable use of probative evidence, compelling reasoning. These are media of revelation accessible to humanity, to which through the Torah (in its oral as much as in its written components) and its everywhere unitary rules of reasoning we gain access. For the Torah comes to Israel in the medium of language – some of it written down right away, at Sinai, some of it orally formulated and transmitted and only later on written down – and Israel knows God. Knowledge of God comes through not the silence of wordless sentiment nor inchoate encounter in unarticulated experience, nor through the thin voice of silence alone, a silence without words. Knowledge of God reaches us solely through the reflection afterward on what has been felt or thought or said by the voice of silence.

Now modes of bringing upward into the form of language knowledge of God begin with the writing down of the Torah itself, which, for Israel, records not only God's will but the actual words God used in stating that will to Moses, our rabbi. Therefore knowledge of the grammar and syntax of God's thought, learned through mastery of how to read the words themselves, which words pertain here, which there, and what conclusions to draw about God, on the one side, and what humanity embodied in Israel, on the other – that knowledge begins in the right reading of the Torah. The authentic theologians of Judaism then are our sages of blessed memory, who know how, and, also, the reason why behind the how. In Judaism, we know God by studying the Torah – there alone. But that suffices.

Index

South Florida Studies in the History of Judaism